Dr. Abdirahman Mohamed Abdi

ISLAMIC BANKING:

Steady in Shaky Times?

Printed in the United States of America

First Edition, 2013

ISBN: 0615607454
ISBN-13: 9780615607450
Library of Congress Control Number: 2012934462
CreateSpace Independent Publishing Platform
North Charleston, South Carolina
Clive Pyne Book Indexing Services, Ottawa, Canada

بسم الله الرحمن الرحيم

In the Name of Allah, the Entirely Merciful,
the Especially Merciful

Dedication

This book is dedicated to my parents Rawi Omar Mursal and Mohamed Abdi Hashi and my wonderful wife, Muna Jama Abdi.

Contents

List of Tables

List of Figures

List of Abbreviations

AAOIFI	Accounting and Auditing Organization for Islamic Financial Institutions
ACRCIFI	Arbitration and Reconciliation Center for Islamic Financial Institutions
ALM	asset-liability management
BD	Bahraini dinar
CAR	capital adequacy ratio
CBB	Central of Bank of Bahrain
CI	confidence interval
DJIM	Dow Jones Islamic Market Index
EMH	efficient market hypothesis
FI	financial institution
FIH	financial instability hypothesis
GAAP	generally accepted accounting principles
GCC	Gulf Cooperation Council
GCIBFI	General Council of Islamic Banks and Financial Institutions
HSBC	Hong Kong and Shanghai Banking Corporation
IAS	international accounting standard
IDB	Islamic Development Bank
IFSB	Islamic Financial Services Board
IICCS	Islamic interbank check-clearing system
IIFM	International Islamic Financial Market
IIRA	International Islamic Rating Agency

IMF	International Monetary Fund
IRTI	Islamic Research and Training Institute
ITFC	Islamic Trade Finance Corporation
LIBOR	London Interbank Offered Rate
LTCM	Long-Term Capital Management
MENA	Middle East and North Africa
MYR	Malaysian Riggint
OIC	Organization of Islamic Countries
PLS	profit-loss sharing

Acknowledgments

I would like to thank the late Professor Charles K. Rowley, Dr. Omar Al-Ubaydli and Dr. John Paden all of George Mason University for their valuable commentary and advice.

Special appreciation to my wife, Muna, who inspired me to undertake with good cheers the lonely task of researching and writing this book. She also was of tremendous help in finding rare books and literature about Islamic finance.

I also owe a great debt of gratitude to Saeed Mahyoub and Ben Sutton of the IMF, whose kind assistance was indispensable in obtaining the data for my empirical work on Bahrain and Malaysia. Last but not least, I am grateful to Dr. Anwar Hajjaj, Director of the American Open University, for a critical reading of chapter 7 and his innumerable comments.

Glossary of Islamic Terms

Ahadith (Hadith)	Plural of *hadith*. *Hadith* is sayings, deeds and endorsements of the Prophet (peace be upon him) narrated by his companions.
Amana	Literally means trust. Technically refers to deposits held at the bank for the purpose of safekeeping. They are guaranteed in capital value and earn no return.
Arbun	A non-refundable deposit to secure the right to cancel or proceed with a sale during a certain period of time.
Ariya	Lending for gratuitous use. Lending of an asset takes place between a lender and a borrower with the agreement that the former will not charge anything.
Bay'	Sale of a property or commodity for a price.
Bay' al-dayn	Sale of debt. According to a large majority of *fuqaha'*, debt cannot be sold except at its face value.
Bay' al-'inah	A contract that involves the sale and buyback of assets by a seller (deferred sale, then he rebuys it at a lower price)

Bay' al-mu'ajjal	The seller can sell a product on the basis of a deferred payment, in installments or in a lump sum. The price of the product is agreed upon between the buyer and the seller at the time of the sale and cannot include any charges for deferring payment.
Bay' al-salam	The buyer pays the seller the full-negotiated price of a product that the seller promises to deliver at a future date.
Bidah	Linguistically, any type of innovation or creation of something upon an unprecedented example. Technically, anything that has no basis in the *Qur'an, Sunna* or sayings of any of the companions, hence it is considered heresy.
Fatawa (Fatwa)	Plural of *fatwa*. Religious verdicts by *fuqaha'*
Fiqh	*Fiqh* refers to Islamic jurisprudence that covers all aspects of life: religious, political, social, and economic. *Fiqh* is mainly based on interpretations of the *Qur'an* and *Sunna* (sayings and deeds of the Prophet).
Fuqaha' (Faqih)	Plural of *faqih*, meaning jurist, who gives rulings on various juristic issues in the light of the *Qur'an* and the *Sunna*.

Gharar	Literally means deception, risk, uncertainty or speculation. Technically, means exposing oneself to excessive risk and danger in a business transaction as a result of uncertainty about the price, the quality and the quantity of the counter value, the date of delivery, the ability of either the buyer or the seller to fulfill his commitment, or ambiguity in the terms of the deal, thereby exposing either of the two parties too unnecessary risks.
Ghish	Literally, means deception or fraud. Technically, means trying to deceive someone by concealing vital information in a deal.
Hiyal (Hila)	Plural of *hila*. The use of legal manipulations or ruse.
Ijara	A party leases a particular product for a specific sum and a specific time period. In another words, it is a sale contract, which is not the sale of a tangible asset but rather a sale of the usufruct for a specified period of time.
Ijara wa iqtina'	A hire-purchase contract, which is similar to conventional lease-purchase agreements. In addition to the regular contract of *ijara*, another contract is added which includes a promise by the lessor/owner to sell the leased asset to the lessee at the end of the original lease agreement.

Istisna'	A manufacturer (contractor) agrees to produce (build) and to deliver a certain good (or premise) at a given price on a given date in the future. The price does not have to be paid in advance (in contrast to *bay' al-salam*). It may be paid in installments or part may be paid in advance with the balance to be paid later on, based on the preferences of the parties.
Ju'ala	A party pays another a specified amount of money as a fee for rendering a specific service in accordance to the terms of the contract stipulated between the two parties. This mode usually applies to transactions, such as consultations and professional services, fund placements, and trust services.
Kafala	*Kafala* is a pledge given to a creditor that the debtor will pay the debt, fine, or liability. A third party becomes surety for the payment of the debt if unpaid by the person originally liable.
Maqasid al-shari'a	Basic objectives of the *shari'a*. These are protection of faith, life, reason, progeny, and property.
Maysir	Means gambling, from pre-Islamic game of hazard.
Mudaraba	*Rabb-ul-mal* (capital's owner) provides the entire capital needed to finance a project while the entrepreneur offers his labor and expertise. Profits are shared between them at a certain fixed ratio, whereas financial losses are exclusively borne by *rabb-ul-mal*. The liability of the entrepreneur is limited only to his time and effort.

Mufti	A religious scholar *(faqih)* who issues edicts *(fatwas).*
Murabaha	The seller informs the buyer of his cost of acquiring or producing a specified product. The profit margin is then negotiated between them. The total cost is usually paid in installments.
Musharaka	The bank enters into an equity partnership agreement with one or more partners to jointly finance an investment project. Profits (and losses) are shared strictly in relation to the respective capital contributions.
Nass	An explicit or fixed text within the *Qur'an* or *Sunna* upon which a ruling is based. Precisely, it is a term used to distinguish between text as a human production and revelation as a divine source of *Shari'a.* Plural of *Nass* is *Nusus.*
Qarad hasan	These are zero-return loans that the *Qur'an* encourages Muslims to make to the needy, where a loan is also extended without any other compensation from the borrower. Even though, banks are allowed to charge borrowers a service fee to cover the administrative expenses of handling the loan, the fee should not be related to the loan amount or maturity.
Riba	Literally, means excess or increase, and the term covers interest and usury.
Sarf	Sale by exchange of money-for-money on the spot.
Shari'a	The Islamic law extracted from the *Qur'an* and *Sunna* (sayings and deeds of the Prophet).

Sukuk (Sakk)	Plural of *sakk*, which refers to a financial paper showing entitlement of the holder to the amount of money shown on it. The English word "cheque" has been derived from it. Technically, *sukuk* are financial instruments entitling their holders to some financial claims.
Takaful	The Arabic name for insurance based on *Shari'a* rules. Islamic insurance is a collective protection scheme. It literally means solidarity. *Takaful* reflects solidarity and is akin to mutual insurance.
Wadi'a	A contract whereby a person leaves valuables with someone for safekeeping. The keeper can charge a fee, even though in Islamic culture it is encouraged to provide this service free of charge or to recover only the costs of safekeeping without any profit.
Wakala	An agency contract, which may include in its terms a fee for the agent. The same contract can also be used to give power of attorney to someone to represent another's interests.
Waqf	Appropriation or tying up a property in perpetuity for specific purposes. No property rights can be exercised over the corpus. Only the usufruct is applied towards the objectives (usually charitable) of the *waqf*.
Zakat	Religious tax to be deducted from wealth to be paid to the needy.

Sources: Hassan and Lewis (2007), Chapra and Ahmed (2002), Iqbal and Llewellyn (2002) and Iqbal and Ahmad (2005) and author.

Introduction

An Islamic financial system is a rule-based system comprised of a set of rules and laws, collectively referred to as *Shari'a*. *Shari'a* is derived from four sources (Hallaq 1997, 1). The main source of *Shari'a* is the *Qur'an*, considered by Muslims to be divine scripture. The second most authoritative source of *Shari'a* is *hadith*—the practices, conduct, and sayings of Prophet Mohammad. If further clarity is required, jurists use reasoning and analogy and apply an accepted principle or assumption to arrive at a rule of law. The central tenet of the financial system is the prohibition of *riba*—a term literally meaning "an excess" and interpreted as "any unjustifiable increase of capital whether in loans or sales" (Greuning & Iqbal, 2008, 3). More precisely, any positive, fixed, or predetermined rate tied to the maturity and the amount of the principal (i.e., guaranteed regardless of the performance of the investment) is considered *riba* and is prohibited.

The Islamic financial system is, for the most part, similar to Western or conventional financial systems. Both types of system involve banking (commercial, savings, and investment banking) and nonbanking activities (investment funds and insurance). However, as I indicated earlier, the foundation of the Islamic financial system is the absolute prohibition of the payment or receipt of any predetermined guaranteed rate of return. Therefore, this closes the door on the concept of interest and precludes the use of and trading of debt-based instruments (in chapter 5 I explain the economic and moral rationale for the prohibition of interest). The Islamic system also strongly encourages risk-sharing by making profit-and-loss sharing its primary mode of financing business activities, promotes entrepreneurship, and discourages speculative behavior that arises from debt leveraging and securitization, particularly in real estate, stocks, and derivative instruments. Like its counterpart in the conventional financial system, Islamic banking and finance also upholds the sanctity of contracts as well as the protection and enforcement of property rights. Given the promotion of these activities and owing to the elimination of debt financing without underlying real assets or economic activities, scarce resources may be more efficiently allocated and stable under a well-developed Islamic financial system than is feasible under the conventional financial systems.

Most of the economic activities in the Islamic financial system occur in the banking sector; therefore, the book will focus on the banking sector. Most of the empirical research undertaken in Islamic banking examines issues relating to efficiency (e.g., Yudistira 2004; and Moktar, Abdullah, and Al-Habshi 2006).[1] However, relatively little empirical analysis has been done on the stability of Islamic banks in general.[2]

So, the central question I will attempt to answer in the book is whether Islamic banks are more stable than conventional banks in general and, more important, during periods of severe financial crisis. As the recent global financial crisis of 2007-09 has demonstrated, the importance and consequences of instability in the financial and banking system came as a surprise to the world in general, but came as a rude awakening to taxpayers of developed countries who footed the huge bill for the bail-outs necessary to avert global economic depression.

To answer the central question of the book, I have selected the Kingdom of Bahrain and Malaysia as my test cases. Why Bahrain and Malaysia? I used three criteria for selecting countries for empirical examination. First, conventional and Islamic banks must be running parallel. Second, only banks offering *Shari'a* compliant services or products would be considered an Islamic bank. This means the regulatory agency that issued its license must have classified the bank fully Islamic – in other words, it is not a window of a conventional bank offering Islamic products or services. Finally, the banking industry in the country should be deemed as competitive – I used the Herfindahl index as a guide whether the industry of an economy is concentrated and therefore less competitive. This means there is no single or couple of banks that dominate either the conventional or Islamic banking sectors. In the GCC, only Bahrain met this qualification using data from BankScope and the central banks[3]. In South East Asia, Malaysia also meet this criteria.

The political and economic evolution of Bahrain and Malaysia in the two decades prior to 2010 offers us an important opportunity to assess the economic effect of Islamic banking. Bahrain and Malaysia have been pioneers in the innovation and development of Islamic banking. Moreover, data availability at the bank level from the central banks and other supervisory institutions in both countries are more widely considered to be reliable, in contrast to most other countries in the world where Islamic and conventional banking run in parallel. Before summarizing the key chapters in the book, I will briefly describe the unique characteristics for each of these two countries.

Beginning in the 1980s, the Kingdom of Bahrain has been the center of innovation and marketing for Islamic financial products and instruments in the Middle East. The cosmopolitan lifestyle and freedom of its capital, Manama, appealed to both Western and Arab professional and intellectual elites, further nurturing this dynamic environment, which led to the proliferation of Islamic banking before Dubai emerged in the mid-1990s as a rival.

Bahrain has the freest economy in the Middle East; according to the 2006 Index of Economic Freedom published by the Heritage Foundation/ *Wall Street Journal* and is twenty-fifth freest overall in the world. In 2008, Bahrain was named the world's fastest-growing financial center by the City of London's Global Financial Centres Index. The country's banking and financial services sector, particularly Islamic banking, benefited from the regional oil boom. However, the political turmoil in 2011 is a sobering reminder of the importance of political stability and its ramifications on the economy and people's welfare.

Malaysia is an open economy and has experienced remarkable growth in the last three decades. In 2007, the economy of Malaysia was the twenty-ninth largest economy in the world in terms of purchasing power parity GDP and was estimated at $359.9 billion.[4] During the 1970s, Malaysia modeled itself on the original four Asian Tigers (Taiwan, South Korea, Hong Kong, and Singapore) and committed itself to transitioning from dependence on mining and agriculture to manufacturing. With Japan's assistance, heavy industry flourished and in a matter of years Malaysian exports became the country's primary growth industry.

Malaysia had a consistent economic growth of at least 7 percent in the 1980s and 1990s as well as a low rate of inflation. Foreign direct investment played an important role in the transformation of Malaysia's economic development. The country is also endowed with natural resources: agriculture (rubber and palm oil), forestry (timber), and minerals (tin, oil, and gas). Palm oil is a major generator of foreign exchange. Oil and natural gas took over from tin in the mid-1970s as the major mineral extraction sector. Oil and natural gas continued to contribute significantly to the Malaysian economy as well. The national oil company, Petronas, provides 32 percent of the federal budget in taxes, dividends, and royalties.[5] The 1997 East Asian financial crisis adversely impacted Malaysia. The ringgit depreciated substantially, and foreign direct investment fell significantly.

Interestingly, during the recent global financial crisis, many scholars and investment advisors pointed to the strong performance of Islamic investment index funds in the United States in comparison to the major U.S. equity indexes (see figure 1 at the end of this chapter) as evidence in support of the comparative advantage in terms of financial stability of Islamic finance.

Chapter 1 provides the institutional purview of the current state of Islamic finance and banking in the world with regard to asset size, geographical distribution, and the future prospects of this nascent and quickly growing asset class. Chapter 2 starts with a review of the history of financial crises in Western countries and then provides a critical evaluation of what economic theories consider to be the causes as well as the remedies.

The world is just emerging from what is considered the most severe economic and financial crisis since the Great Depression. Even though there are many views as to what the causes of the 2007 to 2009 global financial crisis are, there is a wide consensus among financial and economic experts that it was caused by speculative and aggressive use of debt leveraging, accompanied by lax supervision and an ineffective market discipline.[6] These issues as well as the roles herding, coordination failure, and bank runs play in triggering banking crises will be examined in chapter 3. According to many articles in the financial press, Islamic banks and financial institutions seem not to have been as strongly affected by the recent global financial crisis. Without supporting empirical data, it is reasonable not to accept these assertions at their face value.

Chapter 4 provides a review of the theoretical concept of financial intermediation and then explores the differing characteristics of non-Islamic and Islamic banks and more specifically how these differences are manifested with regard to asymmetric information, market risk, and principal-agent relationship.

Chapter 5 gives an in-depth explanation of the nature of Islamic finance. In particular, the concept of an interest rate is defined as understood in the conventional financial system, and then the differing view Islamic law prescribes in dealing with the concept of interest is explained. The chapter also thoroughly examines a key feature of Islamic finance—risk-sharing, as reflected in the design of financial contracts or instruments (Islamic modes of financing) and as shown in their banks' balance sheets.

In Chapter 6, the key advantages and challenges of Islamic finance are described. The notion that Islamic finance may make the financial system more stable in comparison to the conventional financial system is more fully explained and closely examined as well. Chapter 7 provides background on the origins and evolution of Islamic law and finance as well as a brief synopsis of the sources of Islamic law and the role the Four Major Islamic Schools of Thought play in interpreting whether particular transactions or financial instruments are deemed to be in compliance with the intent of the fundamental principles of Islam. The methodology and data for measuring and testing financial stability using regression and descriptive statistics is outlined in chapter 8. This chapter also addresses the advantages and shortcomings inherent in each of the methods used in measuring and testing financial stability.

Chapters 9 and 10 provide an analytical history and present the results of the regression and descriptive statistics for Bahrain and Malaysia, respectively. The analytical history reviews the impact of changes in laws, regulations, and institutions due to the introduction of Islamic banking. The regression and historical analytical review covers a period of fifteen years (1996–2010). In chapter 11, the implications of the regression and descriptive statistics results are discussed, and chapter 12 provides conclusions.

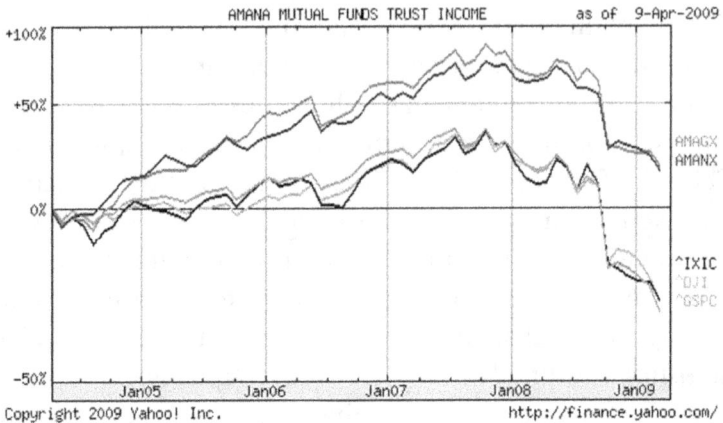

Figure 1.0 Comparison of U.S. Islamic Equity with Major U.S. Equity Indexes
Source: Finance.Yahoo.com (April 10, 2009)—Five-year period (April 2004–April 2009)

AMANX—Amana Trust Income (Islamic Index Fund, focuses mainly on drug companies, energy stocks, and mining).

AMAGX—Amana Growth Fund (Islamic Index Fund—invests in technology and health-care stocks with low debt; its biggest holding is Apple Computers).

^IXIC—NASDAQ Composite Index

^DJI—Dow Jones Industrial Average Composite

^GSPC—S&P 500 Index

Note: All investment funds were affected by the same macroeconomic risk factors; however, because Islamic funds excluded firms that do not meet *Shari'a* guidelines, such as the prohibition of interest (i.e., banks and nonbank financial firms, and companies with a debt ratio greater than 33 percent of their capitalization), they fared better in the severe debt deleveraging and credit freeze.

Endnotes

1. A major portion of the available literature contains comparisons of instruments used in Islamic banking with those of conventional commercial banking as well as issues related to regulatory challenges (e.g., Sundarajan and Errico (2002); World Bank and IMF (2005); Ainley et al. (2007); Sole (2007); Jobst (2007)).

2. The only study I was able to find addressing the financial stability of Islamic banks is Cihak and Hesse (2008), "Islamic Banks and Financial Stability: An Empirical Analysis," IMF working paper WP/08/16.

3. Based on 2010 data from BankScope: Qatar Islamic Bank and Masraf Al Rayan had market share of 46 and 31 percent respectively of the Islamic banking sector in Qatar. In Saudi Arabia, The National Commercial Bank (Al-Ahli Bank) and Al-Rajhi Bank had 55 and 36 percent respectively of the Islamic Banking sector. Dubai Islamic Bank and Abu Dhabi Islamic Bank had 34 and 29 percent respectively of the UAE Islamic banking sector. Finally, the Kuwait Finance House dominates the Islamic banking sector in Kuwait with a market share of 72 percent.

4. "Malaysia Resilient against Global Economic Slump," *The Edge*, http://www.theedgedaily.com/cms/content.jsp?=com.tms.article.Article.

5. Fortune, «Fortune Global 500—2007: Petronas,» *Fortune Magazine*.

6. Market discipline falls more heavily on smaller institutions, which in turn motivates them to merge into larger entities protected by the too-big-to-fail umbrella.

The Institutional Background

This chapter provides an overview of this fast-growing international financial market, in terms of its size and geographical distribution.

"Islamic finance, long considered in the West as more of an oddity than an opportunity, is going mainstream."[7] This observation is an indication of the evolution of attitudes toward this new investment asset class in the global capital and securities markets.

The 1970s witnessed a rise in the price of oil leading to an accumulation of oil revenues in several oil-rich Muslim countries, especially in the Middle East. These so-called "petro-dollars" are considered by many to be what gave birth to the launching of modern Islamic banking, starting with the establishment of Dubai Islamic Bank in 1975.

When it first appeared in the mid-1970s, Islamic finance was generally dismissed as an inconsequential by-product of the oil boom. In its first couple of decades, conventional financial institutions, as well as international regulators, largely ignored the Islamic banking sector. The involvement of large financial institutions started when Citibank created Citi Islamic in Bahrain in 1996. Two years later, Hong Kong and Shanghai Banking Corporation (HSBC) established Amanah Finance, a global Islamic financial services division. Since that time, ABN AMRO, BNP Paribas, Standard Chartered, UBS, Goldman Sachs, and many others have become significant players in Islamic finance.

Indeed, today, one would be hard pressed to find a large global financial institution that is not involved in one way or another in Islamic finance. The massive participation by global players has led to greater innovation, more competitiveness, and increasing acceptance of Islamic finance. Once confined to corporate and investment banking, the Islamic sector has penetrated the retail market. A significant development was the creation in the United Kingdom of the Islamic Bank of Britain, the first fully *Shari'a*-compliant bank in Europe, in 2004.

According to *The Banker's* 2010 survey,[8] financial institutions practicing Islamic-finance-compliant banking saw their assets rise by 8.8 percent from US$822 billion in 2009 to US$895 billion in 2010. The Islamic finance industry had a compound annual growth rate of 23.46 percent (2006 to 2010) (see table 1.1) and is estimated to have hit over US$1 trillion in 2011. The growth of Islamic finance is outpacing almost every other business segment of the global banking system, such as private banking, wealth management, risk management, and assets/ liabilities management.

Although many *Shari'a*-compliant institutions were not directly adversely impacted by the global financial crisis, there were indirect consequences from the global assets' downward readjustment due to financial deleveraging. As a result, the *Shari'a*-compliant industry's overall growth momentum slowed down from 2009's turbo-charged growth of almost 29 percent to single digits in 2010. Most of the decrease in the growth rate of the Islamic institutions' assets in 2010 were due to crisis in the property markets in a number of regions, reduced trade, and decline in tourism and foreign direct investments. Central banks in the region responded by focusing on improving the quality of domestic markets. Even Islamic financial institutions in areas relatively unaffected by the crisis increased their capital positions.

The Islamic finance markets still continue to suffer from two shortcomings. First, there is a widespread statistical latency due to poor reporting frequency, because institutions provide data late. Second, the numbers do not reflect off-balance-sheet activity, which has increased dramatically in recent times. Taken together, these factors adversely impact the timeliness and relevancy of financial statements and obscure which Islamic finance activities are on or off the balance sheet. These issues are currently being addressed in discussions between organizations, such as the Islamic Financial Services Board (ISFB), the Accounting and Auditing Organization for Islamic Financial Institutions (AAOIFI), the International Monetary Fund, and central banks, which are working to improve overall reporting in the future.

The geographic distribution of reported *Shari'a*-compliant assets of Islamic financial institutions in table 1.1 is an aggregate across forty-eight countries and is divided into three core geographical areas: the six Gulf Cooperation Council (GCC) states, the non-GCC states of the Middle East and North Africa (MENA), and the remaining non-MENA states across the globe, led by Malaysia.

Table 1.1

Regional and Global Reported *Shari'a* Assets in Millions of USDs.

Regional and Global Growth (USD Million)

Region	2006	2007	% Change	2008	% Change	2009	% Change	2010	% Change
GCC	127,876.6	178,129.6	39.4	262,665.4	47.5	353,237.5	34.5	372,484.2	5.4
Non-GCC MENA	136,157.6	176,822.1	29.9	248,264.0	40.4	315,090.5	26.9	339,949.8	7.3
MENA Total	**264,157.6**	**354,951.7**	**34.5**	**510,929.4**	**43.9**	**668,328.0**	**30.8**	**710,434.0**	**6.3**
Sub-Saharan Africa	3,039.3	4,708.0	54.9	6,662.1	41.5	8,369.7	25.6	10,765.1	28.6
Asia	98,709.6	119,246.5	20.9	86,360.3	-27.6	106,797.3	23.7	130,904.1	22.6
Australia/Europe/America	20,300.2	21,475.7	5.8	35,105.2	63.5	38,654.8	10.1	42,779.5	10.7
Global Total	**386,083.3**	**500,381.9**	**29.7**	**639,057.0**	**27.7**	**822,149.8**	**28.7**	**894,882.7**	**8.8**
% of MENA Total to Global Total	68.4	70.9		79.9		81.3		79.4	

Source: (The Banker, 2010)

The GCC states remained the dominant segment of Islamic finance, with US$372.5 billion or 41.5 percent of the global aggregate in 2010. Saudi Arabian institutions provide the largest share of the GCC total, accounting for 37 percent, followed by the United Arab Emirates with 23 percent of the total GCC claiming the second largest slice of the regional aggregate. Kuwait accounts for 19 percent or US$69.1 billion; Bahrain 12 percent, or US$44.8 billion; and Qatar 9 percent or US$34.7 billion.[9] Oman which is a member of the GCC had no Islamic banking and finance sector in 2010; however, the first Islamic bank was inaugurated in Muscat in 2012.

Shari'a-compliant Iranian institutions reported assets of US$314.9 billion or 35.1 percent of the global total, which represents 93 percent of the total non-GCC MENA region. Elsewhere in this region, Egypt accounted for US$7.2 billion or 2.1 percent of the regional aggregate, with Syria, Jordan, Yemen, Tunisia, Algeria, and the Palestinian Territories accounting for 4.5 percent of the region's total aggregate.

Outside the MENA region, Malaysia's US$102.6 billion *Shari'a*-compliant assets account for 11.5 percent of the global total aggregate and 55.7 percent of the non-MENA global total.

Islamic finance has moved well beyond its roots in commercial finance; Islamic markets now exist for bond-like products, insurance, real estate and infrastructure financing, and retail banking. Many market participants expect that, in time, Islamic products will replicate nearly all types of commercial financing instruments.

The highest profile segment on the international scene today is *sukuk*, asset-backed securities that are akin to bonds. First issued only in 2000, *sukuk* are emerging as the best-known form of Islamic finance outside the Middle East and Asia, and one of the most dynamic areas of the market. Issuance has soared since 2007, reaching approximately US$50 billion; however, it experienced a marked slowdown in 2008 and the first half of 2009 due to the following reasons:

- Challenging market conditions and drying up of liquidity
- Wide credit spreads and shortages of USD funding in issuing countries
- Challenging economic environment in the GCC countries, particularly in the UAE

Nevertheless, as the overall market conditions improved, the primary *sukuk* market rebounded in the second half of 2009. For 2009, total global *sukuk* issued amounted to US$24.6 billion, 60.1 percent higher than the US$15.3 billion raised in 2008[10] (see figure 1.1). The market was expected to expand significantly in 2010 because of recovery of global economic activities, and more sovereign issuers are expected, including potential debuts of Japan, Hong Kong, Thailand, Australia, Kazakhstan, and Russia.

Sovereign *sukuk* issued by Bahrain and Malaysia played an important early role in building liquidity, establishing benchmarks, and credentializing the *sukuk* market. Corporate issuance has, as of June 2007, assumed a leading role, accounting for 90 percent of the total over the past two years. Malaysia has been at the forefront of the market, but the Gulf Cooperation Council (GCC) states are increasingly gaining market share, accounting for more than 40 percent.[11]

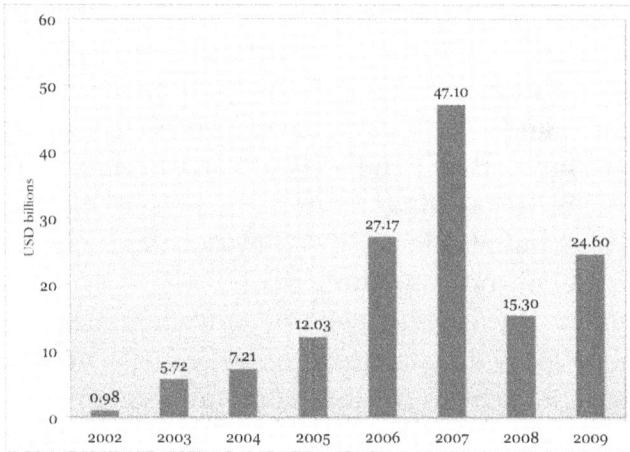

Figure 1.1 - Global *Sukuk* Issuance

At the end of 2009, MENA accounted for 39.7 percent of *sukuk* issued globally, dominated by the United Arab Emirates (37.3 percent). The remaining 60.3 percent of *sukuk* issues came from other regions, led by Malaysia (49.9 percent). Ringgit-denominated papers dominated the primary *sukuk* market with 48.5 percent of total issuances, followed closely by USD-denominated *sukuk* issuance at 35.2 percent.

The broadening appeal of Islamic finance is also evident in the move by large international banks and other private-sector financial institutions to provide Islamic finance services. This includes the establishment of exchange-traded funds that are screened to ensure their conformity with Islamic investment principles, as well as offering *takaful,* or Islamic insurance.

More and more non-Muslims are looking at Islamic banking and finance as a noninterest, noncommercial, ethical-style of investment. Swiss-based Bank Sarasin, well known for its focus on sustainable investment (solar energy, forests, and agriculture) and private banking (wealth management), has been very successful in its investments in Islamic finance and aim to serve a global industry in Islamic finance, not only in Zurich, London, and Paris, but also in the GCC by opening branches in Dubai, Qatar, and Bahrain.[12]

Finally, an Islamic banking and financial system exists to provide a variety of religiously acceptable financial services to Muslim communities. In addition to this special function, the banking and financial institutions, like all other aspects of Islamic society, are expected to contribute richly to the achievement of the major socioeconomic goals of Islam (Chapra 1985). Mr. Chapra defines the most important role of Islamic banking and financial institutions as to promote "... economic well-being with full employment and a high rate of economic growth, socioeconomic justice and an equitable distribution on income and wealth, stability in the value of money, and the mobilization and investment of savings for economic development in such a way that a just (profit-sharing) return is ensured to all parties involved" p.34.

Thus, financial systems are focused on the elimination of the payment and receipt of interest in whatever forms it takes. It is this principle—the prohibition of interest—that makes Islamic banking different from its conventional counterpart.

Table 1.2

Modern History of Islamic Banking

Pre-1950s	• Barclays Bank opens its Cairo branch in the 1890s to process the financial transactions related to the construction of the Suez Canal. Islamic scholars challenge the operations of the bank, in relation to its dealings with interest. This critique also spreads to other Arab regions and to the Indian subcontinent, where there was a sizeable Muslim community. • The majority of *Shari'a* scholars declare that interest in all its forms amounts to the prohibited element of *riba.*
1950s–60s	• Initial theoretical work in Islamic economics begins. By 1953, Islamic economists offer the first description of an interest-free bank based either on two-tier *mudaraba* or *wakala.* • Mit Ghamr Bank in Egypt and Pilgrimage Fund in Malaysia are established.
1970s	• First Islamic commercial bank, Dubai Islamic Bank, opens in 1974. • Islamic Development Bank (IDB) is established in 1975. • Accumulation of oil revenues and petro-dollars increases demand for *Shari'a*-compliant products.

The 1980s	• Economies in the Islamic Republic of Iran, Pakistan, and Sudan are Islamized, and the banking systems are converted to interest-free banking systems. • Increased demand attracts conventional intermediation institutions. • The Islamic Research and Training Institute (IRIT) is established by the Islamic Development Bank (IDB) in 1981. • Countries like Bahrain and Malaysia promote Islamic banking parallel to the conventional banking system.
The 1990s	• Attention is paid to the need for accounting standards and regulatory frameworks. The Accounting and Auditing Organization for Islamic Financial Institutions (AAOIFI) is established. • Islamic Insurance (*takaful*) is introduced. • Islamic Equity Funds are established. • Dow Jones Islamic Index and FTSE Index of *Shari'a*-compatible stocks are developed.
2000–2010	• Islamic Financial Services Board (IFSB) is established to deal with regulatory, supervisory, and corporate governance issues. • *Sukuks* (Islamic bonds) are launched. • International Islamic Rating Agency (IIRA) • Malaysia International Islamic Financial Centre (MIIFC) • International Islamic Financial Market (IIFM) • Liquidity Management Center (LMC)

Source: Iqbal and Mirakhor (2007) with minor modification by the author.

Endnotes

7. "Islamic Finance: Calling the Faithful," *The Economist* (December 7, 2006).

8. "Top 500 Islamic Financial Institutions," *The Banker* (November 2009), a publication of the *Financial Times*.

9. *The Banker* (November 2010).

10. Source: Global Sukuk Update, *Kuwait Finance House* (January 11, 2010).

11. See "Infrastructure Paves the Way to Long-Term Growth in the Gulf," *Global Economics Weekly* 07/15 (April 25, 2007).

12. "Bank Sarasin to lead in Islamic Wealth Management," AME Info (www.ameinfo.com), *Middle East Business News* Web site on November 23, 2008.

Theories of Western Financial Crises

The purpose of this chapter is *not* to explore the empirical literature of Western financial crises beyond the scope of my book, but a theoretical economic foundation of what causes economic disequilibrium and more specifically financial crises and crashes in Western countries.[13]

In order to better understand the different theories of Western financial crises, I think it would be useful to start with the main views of economic and financial instability as espoused in the classical and neoclassical approach on the one hand and in the Keynesian and New Keynesian approaches on the other hand. I will then discuss three nonmainstream theoretical economic views of what causes financial crises and the remedies each of these approaches offer. Finally, I will give my view of what I consider the strengths and weaknesses of each theoretical economic approach and express my viewpoint on which theory might have potential remedy in minimizing the adverse effects from financial crises.

A. Classical and Neoclassical Approach

In general, classical economics is that body of thought that existed prior to the publication of Keynes' *The General Theory of Employment, Interest and Money* in 1936.[14] It is associated with the idea that free markets can self-regulate. According to this view, free markets will be essentially perfect and stable. Under classical economics, it is assumed that people are rational and pursue their economic interests. There is little, if any, need for government interference. To the contrary, the only risk of major depression today, or in the future, comes from government intervention.

This system places great faith on the natural market adjustment mechanisms as a means of maintaining full employment equilibrium. In other words, full employment is the normal state of affairs. However, classical economists acknowledge that the economy could deviate from its equilibrium level of output and employment but only temporarily. Such imbalances are very short-lived.

Since the main underlying idea of the of invisible hand in Adam Smith's *Wealth of Nations* (Smith 1937 [1776]) is that markets have inherently self-optimizing and self-stabilizing qualities, which implies markets are adaptive and stable. Put differently, for markets to be efficient, stable systems, they must, when disturbed, be able to reorganize themselves in response to the disturbance and be able to find the new equilibrium state. What should not happen in an efficient market is for the effect of a small initial disturbance to become amplified without limit by forces generated by processes internal to the market.

The major weakness in the classical view is evident from the consistent recurrences of financial crises, which point to the presence of instability in the asset markets, credit markets, and the capital market system in general. Therefore, it can credibly be argued that once disturbed, asset and credit markets are prone to undergo expansions and contractions that, in principle, may have no limit and no stable equilibrium state.

The Great Depression is the best empirical evidence in support of the instability inherent under this economic theory. It may not explain, for example, why 25 percent of the U.S. labor workforce was unemployed in 1933 at the height of the Great Depression.

The New Classical View

The beginning of the 1970s triggered a resurgence in the belief that a market economy is capable of achieving stability provided government intervention in discretionary monetary and fiscal policies is prevented. This new confidence in the credibility of market economy came about in light of the "Great Stagflation" of the 1970s, which many economists attributed to the Keynesian activist policies that were pursued as well as theories that were considered fundamentally flawed.

Also during the 1970s, another group of economists provided a much more damaging critique of Keynesian economics. Their main argument against Keynes and the Keynesians was that they had failed to explore the full implication of endogenously formed expectations on the behavior of economic agents.

A key element the new classical economic theory shares with the classical theory is that markets completely and continuously clear wages and prices. Other features of the new classical theory include strong microfoundation underpinnings within a Walrasian general equilibrium framework and the assumption of rational economic agents who do not suffer from money illusions. Robert Lucas's (Lucas 1972) key insight and critical contribution to the new classical theory was to change the classical assumption that economic agents have perfect information to an assumption that agents have imperfect information.

In his seminal paper (Lucas 1972)—with the two-island model—he focused on the goods market and the supply decision of firms. His analysis examined the structure of the information available to producers. It is assumed that, while a firm knows the current price of its own goods, knowledge of the general price level for other markets is available with a time lag. When a firm notices a change in its current price, it does not know whether it reflects a change in the good's relative price or a change in the aggregate price level. If the change is due to relative price, the firm will alter the optimal amount to produce. On the other hand, a change in the aggregate price level leaves optimal production unchanged.

In the scenario described, firms are faced with what is known as a "signal extraction" problem, in that they have to distinguish between relative and absolute price changes. The analysis of the behavior of individual agents reflected what is referred to as the Lucas "surprise" supply function, which states that output deviates from its natural level only in response to deviations of actual price level from its rationally expected value, that is, in response to unexpected (surprise) price-level changes.

Prices are mostly affected by changes in the money supply. In Lucas's model (Lucas 1972), a shift in the aggregate demand occurs through changes in the money supply. This means that assuming rational expectations, unobserved changes in the money supply are likely to have real effects on output since actual prices would be different from expected prices. Conversely, with observed money supply, each supplier will attribute change in his or her product to money and will not change his or her output. Thus, observed changes in aggregate demand affect only prices.

The result that only observed aggregate demand shocks have real effects has strong implications: monetary policy can stabilize output only if policy makers have information that is not available to private agents.

Assuming the neutrality of money, the major weakness of the new classical economic view was its inability to explain empirical evidence that pointed to business cycles involving money-to-output causality given that price stickiness was ruled out. Furthermore, Fischer (1977) and Phelps and Taylor (1977) had demonstrated changes in money supply in their models were capable of producing real effects in models incorporating rational expectations provided the assumption of continuously clearing markets was abandoned.

The main weakness of this economic theory, like that of the classical economic theory, is the consistent recurrence of financial crises, which is a strong indication of the presence of instability in the asset and credit markets.

B. Keynesian and New Keynesian Approach

Under *The General Theory* (Keynes 1997 [1936]), Keynes asserted that the economy is inherently unstable and is susceptible to random shocks. More specifically, Keynes said:

> Even apart from the instability due to speculation, there is the instability due to the characteristics of human nature that a large proportion of our positive activities depend on spontaneous optimism rather than on a mathematical expectation, whether moral or hedonistic or economic. Most, probably, our decisions

to do something positive, the full consequences of which will be drawn out over many days to come, can only be taken as a result of animal spirits—of a spontaneous urge to action rather than inaction, and not as the outcome of a weighted probability average of quantitative benefits multiplied by quantitative probabilities. (p. 161)

These shocks will manifest in the form of an inward shift of the marginal efficiency function of investments due mostly to a change in investors' "animal spirits." The theoretical novelty and central proposition of Keynes's work in *The General Theory* is the principle of effective demand, together with the equilibrating role of changes in output rather than prices (Keynes 1997 [1936]). The emphasis given to quantity rather than price adjustment in *The General Theory* is in sharp contrast to the classical model.

This means that the economy can stay under full employment for a prolonged period without intervention or stabilization policy initiatives. Generally, fiscal stabilization policies are preferred to monetary policy ones because they are deemed to be more direct, predictable, and faster acting on aggregate demand. Monetary policy is particularly more likely to be ineffective in the case of a liquidity trap, which usually occurs during periods of severe economic downturn when a stimulus is most desired.

New Keynesian View
New Keynesian economics was developed primarily as a response to the theoretical weakness exposed by Lucas in the 1970s, as I stated earlier, and to provide microeconomic foundations for Keynesian economics.

Old and new Keynesianism agree on three propositions:

1. During some periods—often extended—an excess supply of labor exists at the prevailing level of real wages.
2. The aggregate level of economic activity fluctuates markedly.
3. Money matters, at least most of the time.

There are important policy implications that flow from these three propositions. Generally, government intervention would be desirable at least sometimes so as to stabilize the level of economic activity. These three propositions also separate Keynesian and new Keynesian economic theories from the classical and new classical schools, which promote the idea that the labor market and other markets essentially always clear, with wages and prices adjusting quickly to any disturbances.

However, unlike Keynesian economic theory, new Keynesian economics shares two methodological premises with new classical economics: that macroeconomics should be grounded in microeconomic principles and that understanding macroeconomic behavior requires the construction of a simple general equilibrium model. The real difference of new Keynesian and new classical economic theory arises from the fact that the latter is "based on simple models of markets that employ perfect information, perfect competition, the absence of transaction costs, and the presence of a complete set of markets"(Greenwald and Stiglitz 1993, 24).

New Keynesian economists assume rational expectations; however, unlike the new classical economists, they usually assume a variety of market failures. More specifically, they assume that nominal prices and wages are sticky "nominal rigidities." This means prices do not adjust, but quantities do adjust through the aggregate demand. One common explanation given by new Keynesians is the presence of *menu costs*, which means the small costs incurred for adjusting nominal prices (an example would be the cost of changing the menu of a restaurant, list prices of a catalog, etc.).

According to Gregory Mankiw (1985), even though these costs seem small at the individual firm level, they could have a significant welfare effect and cause fluctuations in output and employment in the short run. However, the issue of whether small frictions can cause nominal disturbances to have large effects on aggregate economic activity hinges on the incentives of individual firms to change their prices when aggregate output changes.

Empirical evidence shows that the effect of menu costs alone is not significant enough to have a large aggregate impact on economic activity (Blinder 1998; Kashap 1995). So, more research by New Keynesians led to a variety of non-Walrasian theories of the operation of the markets. It has been suggested that non-Walrasian analyses of the labor market might serve a variety of functions other than equilibrating supply and demand. For example, in early implicit contract models, wages could represent a way the firm can provide insurance to its workers. Similarly, wages in the bargaining models and efficiency wage models could serve as a means by which firms could divide rent between the workers and the firm and predict how wage affects the productivity of labor respectively (Romer 1993).

My discussion on menu costs regarding the incomplete adjustment of nominal prices and their potential impact on aggregate demand and output assumed a static state—

it considered a one-period economy where all prices are initially at the frictionless level. This case prevails where all prices must be reset before each period, which is not realistic. However, under a dynamic state, all prices and wages are not adjusted simultaneously but are staggered.

There are several possibilities under staggered price and wage adjustment, which differ on the assumptions made about how prices and wages are set. Models that capture these diverse scenarios of nominal price and wage adjustment include the Fischer model (Fischer 1977), the Taylor model (Taylor 1979; Taylor 1980), and the Caplin-Spulber model (Caplin and Spulber 1987). The Fischer and Taylor models conjecture that wages and prices are set by multiperiod contracts. In each period, the contracts governing some fraction of wages and prices expire and must be renewed. The effect from these two models is a gradual adjustment of price level to nominal disturbances that end up causing aggregate demand disturbances, which have persistent real effects.

In both the Fischer and Taylor models, the length of time that a price adjusts is in effect determined when the price is set. Thus price adjustment is time dependent. In contrast, the Caplin-Spulber model presents pricing as state dependent. Under state-dependent pricing, price changes are triggered not by the passage of time, but by developments within the economy. As a result, the fraction of prices that change in a given time interval is endogenous.

In summary, Keynesian models, whether old or new, do make clear predictions about one major issue. A central element of all Keynesian models is that nominal prices or wages do not adjust immediately. As a result, the models predict that independent monetary disturbances affect real activity. Different theories of price adjustments make different predictions about how various changes in the path of aggregate demand affect real output over time. This means stabilization policies will be more effective in managing the economy better.

C. The Hyman Minsky Approach

There is no consensus among economists and financial historians concerning the causes of financial crises. However, there are two traditional theories. The first asserts that crises result from panics, and the second asserts that crises arise from fundamental causes that are part of the business cycle. Both have a long history. There are other theories of financial crises, which were long ignored by the mainstream economic profession and academia, financial market practitioners, and monetary policy makers.

Among those ignored are the financial instability hypothesis (FIH) espoused by the economist Hyman Minsky (which is currently getting attention and gaining momentum in light of the recent global financial crisis), the Austrian theory of the business cycle, which has a clear view of what causes financial crisis as well as what the potential solution should be.

Because the global financial crisis of 2007 to 2009 has been the worst since the Great Depression, many economists and financial thinkers are questioning assumptions and theories about financial crises while others are suggesting that a paradigm shift in thinking might be in order to gain an insight into how the financial markets really work.

The major economic theories or assumptions questioned are:

    a.   the rational expectations theory,

b. that people act independently on the basis of full and relevant information,
c. the efficient market hypothesis holds, and
d. the Capital Asset Pricing Model (CAPM)

Under the Minsky theory, financial crises occur after a credit-fueled bubble in asset prices collapses. Differences within this theory relate to how these bubbles form and collapse and their effect on the financial system. Important examples in this category are the recent global financial crisis of 2007 to 2009, which was caused by a housing bubble in the United States; the Japanese real estate and stock prices bubble in the mid-1980s; the Scandinavian crises in the late 1980s; and the East Asian crisis of 1997, just to name a few. Charles Kindleberger (1978), in describing historic bubbles, noted the critical role of this factor: "Speculative manias gather speed through expansion of money and credit or perhaps, in some cases, get started because of initial expansion of money and credit." p. 44.

Banking Crises
Economists such as Milton Friedman and Anna Schwartz (Friedman and Schwartz 1963) and Charles Kindleberger (1978) argued that many banking crises are the result of unwarranted panics and that most of the banks that were forced to close in such episodes were illiquid rather than insolvent.

Others such as Mitchel (1941) claimed that financial crises occur when the depositors have reasons to believe that economic fundamentals in the near future look poor. In that case, depositors, anticipating that future loan defaults will make it impossible for the bank to repay its deposits, withdraw their money now. The depositors in this case are anticipating insolvency rather than illiquidity.

The seminal papers of Bryant (1980) and Diamond and Dybvig (1983) contributed significantly to the modeling of banks even though the economic theory of banking goes back over two hundred years. Although the objective of the papers was to provide an explanation of bank runs, an equally important contribution was to provide a microeconomic account of banking activity that was distinct from other financial institutions. The impact on the theory of banking from these papers has been the creation of four separate elements:

- a *maturity structure* of bank assets, in which less liquid assets earn higher returns;
- a theory of *liquidity preference*;
- the representation of a bank as an intermediary that provides *insurance* to depositors against liquidity shocks;
- an explanation of bank runs by depositors— In the case of Diamond and Dybvig (1983), bank runs are modeled as the result of *self-fulfilling prophecies or panics*; while under Bryant (1980), they are modeled as being the result of *fundamentals*.

Financial Instability Hypothesis (FIH)

This hypothesis of the causes of credit bubbles and financial crashes was developed by American economist Hyman Minsky (1986). This theory points to the boom and subsequent bust inherent in the business cycle and centers on the episodic nature of the manias and subsequent crises. It is used to interpret the financial crises in the

United States, Great Britain, and other market economies. Minsky highlighted the procyclical changes in the supply of credit, which increased when the economy was booming and decreased during economic slowdowns.

During the expansion phase, investors became more optimistic about the future; they revised upward profitability estimates for a wide range of investments and became more eager to borrow. At the same time, lenders' risk assessment of individual investments as well as their risk averseness declined and they became more willing to make loans, including investments that were previously deemed too risky.

When economic activity slowed, investors became less optimistic and more cautious. At the same time, lenders' loan losses increased, making them also much more cautious, which culminated in the decline of the supply of credit that led to financial fragility and the likelihood of a financial crisis.

Minsky's model is in the tradition of the classical economists, including John Stuart Mill (Mill 192 [1848]), Alfred Marshall (Marshall 1965 [1923]), Knut Wicksell (Wicksell 1936 [1898]), and Irving Fisher (Fisher 1911), who also focused on the instability in the supply of credit. Fisher, who was one of the most prominent American economists during the Great Depression era, argued that two dominant factors were responsible for each boom and depression: overindebtedness in relation to equity, gold, or income, which starts a boom, and deflation consisting of a fall in asset prices or a fall in the price level, which starts a severe recession or depression (Fisher 1933). He noted that overinvestment and overspeculation were often important, but they would have been far less serious if they were not conducted with borrowed money. That is, overindebtedness may reinforce overinvestment and overspeculation.

Minsky followed Fisher and attached great importance to the behavior of heavily indebted borrowers, particularly those who used excessive debt leverage in the expansion phase to finance the purchase of real estate, stocks, or commodities for short-term capital gains. The motive of these investors was that the anticipated rates of increase in the prices of these assets would exceed the interest rates on the funds borrowed to finance their purchases.

When the economy slowed, some of these borrowers were disappointed because the rates of increase in the prices of the assets proved smaller than the interest rates on the borrowed money, and therefore, many would sell their assets at distress levels (deleveraging at fire sale prices). Minsky argued that exogenous events would burst the credit and/or asset bubble and lead to crisis—a case in point is the subprime mortgage situation in August 2007, which triggered the recent global financial crisis.

Difference between FIH and the Mainstream Economic Theory
According to Minsky, the capitalist economy is at best "conditionally coherent" (Minksy 2008 [1986], 117). He rejected the equilibrium methodology of mainstream economics as irrelevant in analyzing a real-world capitalist economy with complex and overvalued capital assets. Instead of equilibrium, he proposed "periods of tranquility" (Minksy 2008 [1986], 197) characterized by a robust finance system and few innovations. During these periods, the financial aspects of investments are less important. However, "stability is destabilizing," as relative tranquility encourages more risk-taking and innovative behavior that increases income even as it disrupts the

conditions that generate "coherency" and "tranquility." That is, the market forces that operate when a system is stable will push it toward instability, so that even if anything like an equilibrium could be achieved, it would set off behavioral responses that would quickly move the economy away from equilibrium.

Minsky also argued that orthodox, classical, and new classical theory-based economics couldn't provide any insight into a capitalist economy like the United States. This is because instability as well as the mere existence of depression could not be explained by standard theory except through internal shocks and stubborn workers, who refuse to allow wages to respond. Thus, according to Minsky, under the classical and new classical economic theory, unemployment must be seen as retribution for obstinacy (Minksy 2008 [1986], 154). The mainstream canon dictates more laissez-faire as the solution to disequilibrium.

D. The Austrian Theory of Financial Crisis

Economists who subscribe to the Austrian School believe that Fredrick Hayek's (1967 [1935]) theory of the business cycle holds great explanatory power for what causes financial crises. Hayek's work, which builds on a theory developed by economist Ludwig von Mises (1953 [1912]), finds the root of the boom-bust cycle in the central bank. In the United States, the Federal Reserve System is responsible for setting and implementing monetary policy.

In simple terms, Austrian theory says the following: First, interest rates fall when the public saves more or the central bank artificially forces them down. Second, businesses usually respond to the lower interest rates by starting new projects. These projects tend to be those that are most interest-rate sensitive—in particular, they occur in the so-called higher-order stages of production: mining, raw materials, construction, capital equipment, etc. In other words, production processes farthest removed in time from finished consumer goods (Snowdon and Vane 2005, 474).

If the interest rate is lower because of natural causes (e.g., increased savings), the market runs smoothly. People's deferred consumption provides the material wherewithal for businesses' new investment projects to be seen through to completion. If the interest rate is lower because of artificial causes (e.g., manipulation by a central banker), these projects cannot all be completed. The necessary resources to complete them have not been saved by the public. Investors have been misled into production lines that cannot be sustained.

For Austrian economists, the housing boom is a classic example of this theory in action. Artificially low interest rates misdirected resources into home construction. This boom cannot continue because it is not sustainable since the public has not saved enough. So, according to the Austrian theory, the sooner the monetary manipulation comes to an end, the sooner the malinvestment can be shaken out and misallocated resources redirected into sustainable lines. The longer the central bank props things up, the worse the inevitable bust will be.

A homebuilder in the housing example would have been much better off if he had discovered his error sooner, because far fewer resources would have been irrevocably squandered. The same goes for the economy at large. In short, the Austrians see the central bankers as responsible for the financial crisis that will inevitably occur by making cheap credit available, which encourages excessive leverage, speculation, and indebtedness.

The prescription of Austrians to central bankers for preventing financial crises is "...do not engage in credit expansion—not even if ongoing economic growth is causing some index of output prices to fall" (Snowdon and Vane 2005, 514).

Difference with New Classical Economic Theory
Although Austrian theories do not violate rational choice axioms, there is one area in which they differ significantly from other schools of economic thought. New classical and new Keynesian economists adopt mathematical models and statistical methods and focus on deduction and empirical observations to construct and test ideas; however, Austrian economists reject this approach; they are instead in favor of deduction and logically deduced inferences. Austrian economists stress deduction because, if performed correctly, it will lead to certain conclusions and inferences that must be true. Though Austrian economists do not discount empirically driven methods, they hold that it does not assure certainty like deduction. Mainstream economists hold that conclusions that can be reached by pure logical induction are limited and weak.

Austrian economists advocate strict adherence to methodological individualism—analyzing human actions from the perspective of an individual agent. They favor this method because it allows them the discovery of fundamental economic laws valid for all human action. Critics of the method argue that it lacks scientific precision since it relies on verbal logic instead of the scientifically accepted empirical methods based on mathematical models.

E. The Akerlof and Shiller View

Apart from the well-known Keynesian remedy of deficit financing to get out of recession, George Akerlof and Robert Shiller (2009) believe that an important but overlooked message of *The General Theory* (Keynes 1997 [1936)]) was his deeper analysis of how the economy works and the role of government within it. Keynes appreciated that most economic activity results from the pursuit of self-interest but also that much economic activity is governed by animal spirits. In Keynes's view, these animal spirits are the main cause of economic fluctuation. They are also the main cause of involuntary unemployment.

According to Akerlof and Shiller (2009), to understand the economy then is to comprehend how it is driven by the animal spirits. Just as Adam Smith's "invisible hand" is the essence of classical economics, Keynes's animal spirits are the door to a different view of the economy—a view that explains the underlying instability of capitalism.

Akerlof and Shiller (2009) look to the emerging field of behavioral economics. Behavioral economics draws on scientific research on human social, cognitive, and emotional factors to get a better understanding of people's economic decisions. Akerlof and Shiller believe the classical and new classical view of free markets fails to take into account the extent to which people are guided by noneconomic motivations. In contrast, Keynes sought to explain departures from full employment and emphasized the importance of animal spirits. He stressed its fundamental role in businessmen's calculations.

In Akerlof and Shiller's (2009) view, when people are uncertain, decisions can only be made on the basis of animal spirits. They are not as rational as economic theory would dictate. Therefore, they believe the economic crisis of 2008 was"…caused by our changing confidence, temptations, envy, resentment, and illusions—and especially by changing stories about the nature of the economy" (Akerlof and Shiller 2009, 4). In their view, there are five different aspects of animal spirits that affect economic decisions.

1. *Confidence*—this is the bedrock of their theory; the feedback loop between it and the economy magnifies disturbances.
2. *Fairness*—issues involving price and wage setting is largely a matter of fairness.
3. *Corrupt and Antisocial Behavior*—the temptation toward these affects the economy.
4. *Money Illusion*—this is also another important factor given that the public gets confused about inflation and deflation and does not fully understand their effect.
5. *Stories*—people's sense of who they are and what they are doing is interwoven with stories of their lives and the lives of others. These stories taken all together are a national or international story and affect the economy significantly.

F. What Does It All Mean?
Some theories point to the indisputable fact that financial crises have been recurring frequently in the last four hundred years although with different time intervals. However, these theories differ as to the causes and the solutions to minimize or eliminate their recurrence and cost. I first assess what I consider to be the key strengths and/or weaknesses of each theory and then express my point of view on which theory offers a potential solution.

Classical and New Classical View

To begin with, there are problems with the classical and new classical approach. First, to economists in this camp, the efficient market hypothesis (EMH), in one of its forms, plays a critical role in understanding how the financial markets work. For them, the importance of efficient markets lies not in the markets' pricing mechanism directly, but rather in the ability of the pricing mechanism to maximize economic output through an optimal allocation of resources. To financial professionals, the emphasis is more directly on the pricing of the items being traded.

Let me focus on the weak form of EMH, where stock prices fully reflect all public information, where future prices cannot be predicted by analyzing past price data, and where excess returns cannot be earned in the long run by using investment strategies based on historical share prices or other historical data. Prices are assumed to follow a random path.

Does this weak form of EMH necessarily imply that there is no room for asset price bubbles or busts? The answer is no.[15] However, in recent years, some finance researchers have returned to a broader conception of economics and have questioned market efficiency's assertion that securities prices are influenced by a powerful correction force. This questioning is based on theoretical arguments that the arbitrage forces acting to improve informational efficiency are omnipotent.[16]

Even some proponents of the efficient market acknowledge that investors frequently make large errors that cause systematic mispricing. According to David Hirshleifer (2001), many or most familiar psychological biases can be viewed as outgrowths of heuristic simplification, self-deception, and emotion-based judgments.

Because efficiency is not instantaneous, sophisticated models may be able to exploit small, short-run anomalies in the market and take advantage of market momentum, either in the upward or in the downward dimension. In combination with the herd instinct, this may propel significant bubbles before the long-run equilibrium eventually reasserts itself. Crucially, rational investors, ex-ante, cannot beat the market on average, in such an environment, though, of course, there will be lucky winners and unlucky losers from an ex-post perspective (Rowley and Smith 2009).

Under this theory, the wild asset price swings or bubbles are consistent with rational investment behavior under EMH conditions, even if non-economists find it difficult to reconcile EMH with the fact that the NASDAQ Composite Index was priced at 1,140 in March 1996, at 5,048 in March 2000, and at 1,140 in October 2002.[17]

One apparent shortcoming of the EMH, nevertheless, is the result one would get by inferring from the manner in which asset prices move under EMH, which in turn allows for the calculation of the entire probability distribution of potential future asset returns (this is the notion that asset prices follow a random path—assuming the market is liquid and deep, i.e., the stock market).

Unfortunately, these theoretical distributions do not necessarily fit with the reality of financial markets, which in practice tend to generate extremes of both positive and negative returns that simply cannot be explained with the statistical models derived from the EMH (Taleb 2007). The clash between the theoretical statistics predicted by efficient markets and those observed within real financial markets is known as the "fat tail" problem[18] (see also Ready and Hu 1995).

A second apparent weakness concerns the bounded rationality of many investors. Experience shows that investors' or participants' interaction with the market influences market prices—their misjudgment and misconceptions affect market prices, and, more important, market prices affect the fundamental values they are supposed to reflect. If this is the case, then a whole new set of problems opens up for the idea of efficient markets; the process through which investors are supposed to maintain the optimum equilibrium is undermined.[19] The important assumption underlying modern financial theories that everyone in the markets has the same and perfect information is not supported by the realities in the financial markets.

The Keynesian, New Keynesian, and Minsky Views of Financial Crises

The process through which borrowing and savings drive economic activity is the essence of Keynes's famous "paradox of thrift" (Keynes 1997 [1936]) and of his recommendation for fiscal stimulus. In the paradox of thrift, if one section of the economy tries to save money, it will reduce the income of another section of the economy. This will likely find its way back to undermine the income of the original savers, leading them to further reduce their spending, causing a self-reinforcing cycle of declining activity. Keynes figured out that the path to escape from the paradox of thrift was for the government to spend more money, thereby boosting profits, encouraging more borrowing, and generating more profits, leading to a virtuous cycle of economic expansion.

My view is that Hyman Minsky's financial instability hypothesis (FIH) is a better theory of how financial markets operate, one that is fully able to explain the credit crunch the world recently witnessed and one that, with a little thought, can explain the erratic behavior of financial markets. The finance and economic community up until recently ignored the FIH, as well as Minsky's refutation of efficient market theory.

The key difference between the efficient market hypothesis and Minsky's financial instability hypothesis comes down to the question of what makes the prices within financial markets move. As discussed, efficient theory says that markets move on naturally toward equilibrium, and after reaching equilibrium, they remain in this state until influenced by a new, unexpected, *external* event. The emphasis here is on the external nature of the force causing financial markets to move.

By contrast, Minsky's instability hypothesis argues that financial markets can generate their own internal forces, causing waves of credit expansion and asset inflation followed by waves of credit contraction and asset deflation. In my view, the implications of Minsky's suggestion are that financial markets are not self-optimizing, or stable, and certainly do not lead toward a natural optimal resource allocation.

In short, Minsky's arguments attack the very foundation of today's laissez-faire economic orthodoxy. This conclusion is supported by the recent startling admission of Alan Greenspan, the former chairman of the Federal Reserve System. Mr. Greenspan stated that his assumption that markets have self-correcting powers was flawed!

Answering the question of whether or not Minsky is correct boils down to the challenge of identifying processes internal to the financial markets that may build upon themselves and become strong enough to push markets away from any equilibrium position. If processes such as these can be identified, the efficient market hypothesis must be rejected and with it, today's accepted wisdom on how to conduct macroeconomic policies.

Austrian Business Cycle Theory of Financial Crises

According to the Austrians, the central bank's policy of intervening in the economy to push interest rates lower than the market would have set them is the single greatest contributor to financial crises. However, there are several problems with this assertion. If intervention by the central banks is what causes financial crises, how can the Austrians explain the case of countries whose central banks intervene in the economy, control the money supply, and set the interest rate and yet do not suffer from asset boom-bust business cycles as predicted. For example, Germany and Switzerland have not suffered from any real estate, stock market, or other asset bubbles in the last thirty or forty years, even though their central banks actively intervene in their economies.

Another problem with the Austrian prescription is that abiding by this remedy is not only politically difficult, such as to do nothing when a country is in a deep recession, but also technically very difficult, because the central bank is not able to observe what the natural rate of interest is and how it might be changing. These challenges of the central bank in preventing a credit-induced boom suggest, as Hayek foresaw late in his career, that a fundamental reform rather than policy prescriptions is warranted. Hayek recommended the *denationalization of money* (Hayek, F. A. 1976).

Hence, the risks were not really moved off the bank balance sheets but rather would come back to banks at the worst possible time—when markets experienced difficulty and asset prices fell. This means conventional banks are more likely to be exposed to banking crises during severe deflationary periods. This problem is less likely to affect Islamic banks because these practices are not allowed under Islamic banking and finance rules.

The Akerlof and Shiller View
Akerlof and Shiller (2009) believe the best way to understand how the real economy works is by taking into consideration both the rational and self-interest of people as well as other ignored behavioral factors, such as psychological, social, and cognitive impulses that influence their economic decisions. Their belief echoes Keynes's view of the role of central banks to ensure the credit conditions that enable full employment. Given the novelty of their theories, it is too early to tell whether the empirical evidence would support their view of what causes financial crises or financial instability.

Endnotes

13.   A good source for an empirical literature of Western financial crises is *Crashes and Panics* edited by Eugene N. White (Homewood, IL: Dow Jones-Irwin, 1990).

14.   According to the classification of Snowdon and Vane in *Modern Macroeconomics* (Northampton, MA: Edward Elgar Publishing, Inc., 2005).

15.   Current theoretical research and literature acknowledges the possibility that investors could be imperfectly rational in situations

when an information cascade occurs (where an individual's actions and observation of others does not depend on his private information signals) and results in either complete or partial blockage of information. Such limitation may pressure individuals to herd—and distort market prices—despite the availability of a rich set of public and private information signals. Other possible occurrences of imperfect rationality and social learning could be found in the evidence of emotional contagion within groups, which suggests that there might be merit to the popular view of contagious manias or fads (see Shiller 2000). For a general discussion about how the rational choice theory has evolved beyond the EMH, see D. Hirsdheifer and S. H. Teoh, "Herd Behavior and Cascading in Capital Markets: A Review and Synthesis," *European Financial Management Journal* 9 (2003): 25–66.

16. See, for example, DeLong et al. (1990), Shleifer and Vishny (1997), and Daniel et al. (2001).

17. See Lubos Pastor and Pietro Veronesi, "Was There a Nasdaq Bubble in the Late 1990s?" *Journal of Financial Economics* 81 no. 1 (July 2006).

18. See "Predators, Prey and the Fat-Tail Problem in Quant," *Wall Street Journal* (August 17, 2007).

19. The problem of two-way causality between financial markets and economic fundamentals is a component of George Soros's theory of reflexivity. Soros takes the argument further by identifying more factors contributing to financial market instability. See *The Alchemy of Finance* by George Soros.

An Analytical History of Western Financial Crises

ooking back at the history of the free-enterprise economy since the seventeenth century, it is easy to see that it is given to recurrent episodes of speculation, or periods of boom followed by periods of bust. Starting with the Dutch tulip mania of 1634–1637, financial crises and bank failures have occurred quite regularly, although at irregular intervals. Over this time span, theories of financial crises were developed subsequent to their occurrence. However, there is no theoretical consensus among economists and financial historians about what causes financial crises or, for that matter, how to prevent one in the future. In hindsight, there are explanations for what triggered a particular crisis (see chapter 2).

A. Are There Specific Features of a Speculative Episode?
Given the recurrent episodes of speculation, are there common features to these episodes that signal their certain return historically? According to John Kenneth Galbraith, in all speculative episodes, there is the thought that there is something new in the world (Galbraith 1990). This new thing can be almost anything.

In the seventeenth century, it was the arrival of tulips in continental Europe. Shortly thereafter, it was the wonderful discovery of the joint-stock company. In more recent U.S. history, it was the miracle of high-risk or junk bonds that fueled the financing of a new generation of corporate raiders and leverage specialists in the 1987 stock market crash (Galbraith 1990). During the savings and loan (S&L) crisis of the 1980s and 1990s, there were 745 failures of savings and loan associations. Ultimately, it cost around $160 billion, about $124 billion of which was paid by U.S. taxpayers.[20]

Another case in point is the bursting of the so-called "dot-com" bubble in 2001. There were significant gains in productivity during the 1990s for U.S. firms due to advances and innovations in computers and telecommunications. These gains played a critical role in America's economic growth during the mid- to late 1990s.[21] There were a lot of dot-com firms with terrific ideas, realistic business plans, great products, and brilliant leaders. However, during the boom phase of the speculative episode, these firms were outnumbered in the rush to get rich quickly (hopefully by the age of thirty) by firms that were based on nothing more than a few Web pages and meager plans with no profitability or cash flows in the foreseeable future. Realization of this fact triggered panic and the bust of the dot-com bubble.

More recently and specifically, in the financial and credit crisis of 2007 to 2009, a total of thirty-nine banks and thrifts failed from the beginning of 2008 with a total of $379 billion in assets.[22] In the investment-banking sector, three out of the seven investment banking firms folded (Lehman Brothers) or were forced to merge with financially stronger banks (Bear Stearns and Merrill

Lynch). Financial instruments, such as mortgage-backed securities (MSB); legal financial structures, such as special purpose vehicles (SPV); and derivative instruments, such as credit default swaps (CDS) played a critical role in leading the way to perhaps the worst financial crisis since the Great Depression.

In all speculative episodes, there is always the element of an alleged discovery of what appears to be a new and greatly rewarding innovative financial instrument or structure. Yet, a historical analytical review of the conventional financial system will show that what has been proclaimed as a new financial innovation involves, in one form or another, the excessive use of debt leverage. Galbraith captured this best:

> This was true in one of the earliest seeming marvels: when banks discovered that they could print bank notes and issue them to borrowers in a volume in excess of the hard-money deposits in the banks' strong rooms. The depositors could be counted upon, it was believed or hoped, not to come all at once for their money. There was no seeming limit to the debt that could be leveraged on a given volume of hard cash... All subsequent financial innovation has involved similar debt creation leveraged against assets with only modifications in the earlier design. (Galbraith 1990, 19–20).

For American economist Hyman Minsky, the speculative episodes observed in the United States in the last few decades are largely due to the self-reinforcing dynamic of speculative corporate finance, decreasing debt quality, and economic volatility that has come to characterize our times (Minksy 2008 [1986]). In Minsky's view, corporate borrowing for the purpose of repaying "speculative finance" debt will mostly drive asset prices. This view of a "bullish rise in employment, investment and profits tends to confirm, in the minds of business leaders and bankers, the soundness of an approach that ultimately fosters volatility and unacceptable risk" (Minksy 2008 [1986]).

B. Historical Banking Crises in Europe and the United States

Prior to the twentieth century, banking panics occurred more frequently. Kindleberger (1993, 264) studied the financial history of continental Europe and discovered that financial crises have occurred at roughly ten-year intervals over the last four hundred years. Panics were generally regarded as a bad thing because they were often associated with major economic downturns.

Over time, eliminating panics and ensuring financial stability have become the major roles of central banks. The first central bank, the Bank of Sweden, was established over three hundred years ago in 1668. The Bank of England was established soon after. It played an especially important role in the development of effective stabilization policies in the eighteenth and nineteenth centuries.

Michael Bordo, examining the period 1870 to 1933, established that there were very few banking panics in the United Kingdom, Germany, and France (Bordo 1986). Many British economists credited the absence of crises in the United Kingdom to the skillful manipulation of discount rates by their central bank (Kindleberger 1993). France also experienced no financial crises from 1882 to 1924.

However, the United States took a different track. Alexander Hamilton was influenced by the British experience with the Bank of England, and after the Revolution advocated a large, federally chartered bank with branches all over the country. This led to the foundation of the First Bank of the United States (1791–1811) and later the Second Bank of the United States (1816–1836).

However, due to the mistrust of the concentration of power these institutions represented, a controversy over the re-chartering of the Second Bank came to a head in 1832. Although Congress passed the bill, President Andrew Jackson vetoed it, and the veto was not overturned. Thus, there was no central bank in the United States from 1836 until 1914.

The creation of the national banking system did not prevent the problem of panics and the associated economic disruption and depressions. There were panics in 1873, 1884, 1893, and 1907. The severity of the recession following the 1907 banking panic led to a debate on whether or not a central bank should be established in the United States.

However, it took another seven years for the Federal Reserve System to be established in 1914. Unfortunately, this appears to have worsened banking panics. In 1933, there was another major banking panic, which led to the closing of banks for an extended period just after President Franklin Roosevelt, took office. The problems faced by the banking system led to the Glass-Steagall Act of 1933, which introduced deposit insurance and wisely required the separation of commercial and investment banking operations. Unfortunately, this act was repealed at the end of 1999 with strong lobbying from the banking and financial industry.

Crises and Stock Market Crashes

In the four hundred years since shares were first bought and sold, there has been a succession of financial bubbles. Time and again, share prices have soared to unsustainable heights only to crash downward again.

Historical events show that generally banking crises and stock market crashes are closely interconnected. In an important study, Wilson, Sylla, and Jones (1990) examined four major banking panics accompanied by stock market crashes in the United States during the National Banking Era (1866–1913). These were the crises of September 1873, June 1884, July 1893, and October 1907. Wilson et al. wanted to know why these banking panics were linked to the stock market crashes. They investigated stock returns and their volatility during the panic and crash periods. The results showed that four of the eight lowest returns that occurred during the period of the study (1866–1913) were during the panic months.

Crises in Different Eras

In an effort to get a better understanding of whether there are certain patterns or fundamental factors that underlie financial crises, Bordo, Eichengreen, Klingebiel, and Martinez-Peria (2001) examined 117 years (1880–1997) and addressed the question of how recent crises, such as the European Monetary System crisis of 1992–1993, the Mexican crisis of 1994–1995, the Asian crisis of 1997–1998, the Brazilian crisis of 1998, the Russian crisis of 1998, and the Argentinean crisis of 2001 compare with earlier crises. They identified four periods.

1. Gold Standard Era (1880–1913)
2. The Interwar Years (1919–1939)
3. Bretton Woods Period (1945–1971)
4. Recent Period (1973–1997)

They considered twenty-one countries for the first three periods and obtained data for the original twenty-one as well as an expanded group of fifty-six for the fourth period. According to Bordo et al., there were a number of similarities between the periods but also some notable differences. The first issue addressed was how to define a crisis. They defined a banking crisis as a "financial distress that is severe enough to result in the erosion of most or all of the capital in the banking system." Similarly, a currency crisis was defined as a forced change in parity, abandonment of a pegged exchange rate, or an international rescue.

Their second issue was how to measure the duration of a crisis. To do this, they computed the trend rate of GDP growth for five years before. The duration was determined to be the amount of time before GDP growth returned to its trend rate. Finally, the depth of the crisis was measured by summing the output loss relative to trends for the duration of the crisis. The Bordo et al. (2001) analysis reached several conclusions.

Banking crises, currency crises, and twin crises (simultaneous occurrences of banking and currency crises) occurred under a variety of different monetary and regulatory regimes. Over the 120-year period, crises were followed by economic downturns lasting on average from two to three years, costing 5 to 10 percent of GDP. Twin crises were accompanied by large output losses. Recessions with crises were more severe than recessions without them.

The following is a list of some recent crises:

- *The Scandinavian Crises*—Norway, Finland, and Sweden experienced a classic boom-bust cycle that led to the twin crises (see Heiskanen 1993 and Englund and Vihriala 2006).

- *Japanese Real Estate and Stock Market Financial Crisis*—in the 1980s, price increases in Tokyo's asset markets seemed like a perpetual motion machine; bank loans to real estate investors led to sharp increases in real estate prices, which in turn pulled up the stock prices. The liberalization of regulation during the 1980s also contributed to the boom cycle of the crisis.

- *The Mexico Peso Crisis of 1994*—After Mexico recovered from the international external debt crisis in 1989, a new international financial regime for developing countries started, one in which portfolio capital and foreign direct investment flowed abundantly to the private sector. These flows came to an abrupt end in December of 1994; Mexico experienced a severe financial crisis when international institutional investors panicked, afraid that Mexico might not be able to service its debt.

- *The East Asian Financial Crisis of 1997–1998*—the "Dragons" (Hong Kong, Singapore, South Korea, and Taiwan) and the "Tigers" (Indonesia, Malaysia, the Philippines, and Thailand), who were considered to be models of successful economic development were caught up in currency crises in late 1997, which eventually led most countries to experience severe economic contractions.

- *The Russian Crisis* and *Long-Term Capital Management (LTCM)*—in 1998, the failure of the LTCM hedge fund triggered Russia to devalue its currency and declare a moratorium on about 281 billion rubles ($13.5 billion) of government debt (Damjanovic and Pastor 2001). Despite the small scale of the default, this triggered a global crisis with extreme volatility in many financial markets.

- *The Argentina Crisis of 2001–2002*—in 1991, Argentina introduced a currency board that pegged the Argentinean peso at a one-to-one exchange rate against the dollar to stop the inflationary episodes and crises that plagued the country during the 1970s and 1980s (IMF 2003). This measure ushered in a period of low inflation and economic growth. However, a gradual decrease in fiscal discipline as well as an explosion of external public debt created a confidence crisis in Argentina's peso, which triggered massive capital flight that resulted in the suspension of convertibility by the government in November 2001. In December 2002, the economy collapsed.

The Bretton Woods period from 1945 to 1971 was quite special. Governments either regulated bank balance sheets to prevent them from taking too much risk or owned them to achieve the same objective. These measures were successful in that there were no banking crises during this time and only one twin crisis.

The interwar period was also unique. Banking crises and currency crises were widespread. Moreover, the output losses from these were severe particularly when they occurred together and there was a twin crisis. The more recent period (1973–1997) seemed more crisis-prone than any other period except for the interwar years. In particular, it seemed more crisis-prone than the Gold

Standard Era, which was the last time that capital markets were as globalized as they are now.

C. What Are the Prospects of Severe Financial Crises?

History is likely to repeat itself as the circumstances that lead to recurrent memory lapses and financial amnesia have not truly changed in operation since the tulip mania of 1636–1637.

Many individuals and institutions, driven by the urge to get rich quickly coupled with the easy availability of credit and fast-rising asset prices, will be hailed as geniuses in innovating new financial products, even though in substance, there is no innovation or increase in productivity that justifies the astronomical increases in asset prices. Instead, a speculative bubble gets under way and will manifest itself largely as a mere redistribution or transfer of existing market and credit risk exposures to unsuspecting and/or naive investors by masking these risks through lack of transparency and complexity—and by the economic community's shunning of those who point out that the emperor has no clothes.[23]

When will the next speculative episode come, and in what venue will it recur—real estate, securities markets, or commodities? Of course no one knows. But one thing is certain. There will be more episodes, and naive or unsuspecting investors will again be separated from their money.

Endnotes

20. U.S. Government Accounting Office, "Financial Audit: Resolution Trust Corporation's 1995 and 1994 Financial Statements" (July 1996), 8, 13.

21. For a detailed analysis explaining how the foundation of the resurgence of economic growth in the United States during the mid- to late 1990s was due to the development and deployment of semiconductors, see Dale Jorgenson's annual presidential address to the American Economic Association, "Information Technology and the U.S. Economy," *American Economic Review* 90 no. 1 (2001):1–32.

22. Federal Deposit Insurance Corporation, "Failed Bank List," http://www.fdic.gov/bank/individual/failed/banklist.html (retrieved January 15, 2009).

23. Strongly reinforcing the vested interest in euphoria is the condemnation that the reputable public and financial opinions direct at those who express doubt or dissent either by accusing them of lack of imagination or deeming suspect their motivation. In 1929, Paul Warbug, the most respected banker of his time and one of the founding members of the Federal Reserve System, was critically condemned when he spoke against what he termed "unrestrained speculation" in Wall Street (Alexander Dana Noyes, *The Market Place* (Boston: Little, Brown & Company, 1938), 324).

Differing Characteristics of Conventional and Islamic Banks

A. Traditional Financial Intermediation

For most economies in the world, there is always a need to transfer funds from savers to investors since the people who save are usually different from those who can take advantage of profitable investment opportunities. This transfer is the result of either direct finance through the securities market or through means of financial intermediation in the financial markets, with the latter being more important.

The main functions of a financial intermediary are asset transformation, conduct of order payments, brokerage, and risk transformation. The importance of financial intermediation is underscored by the fact that around two-thirds of new investments go through this process in most countries, particularly in emerging economies.

Financial intermediation improves the efficiency and savings/investment process by reducing transaction costs and eliminating the mismatches inherent in the needs of surplus and deficit units of an economy. Given the fact that those who save and invest are from different units, they would require a great deal of information about each other. Since this information is not free, the transfer of funds from savers to investors entails transaction costs.

Furthermore, the existence of asymmetric information will also give rise to moral hazard and adverse selection. Unlike an individual or a firm, financial intermediaries, given their size, have the ability to take advantage of economies of scale and therefore minimize the transaction costs of channeling funds from surplus units to the deficit units. Due to this comparative advantage, financial intermediaries are also in a good position to deal with the problems emanating from asymmetric information.

The financial intermediation process also gets rid of differences in the maturity terms, tastes, and sizes of the funds needed by both sides. In general, the units with excess funds are small households who save relatively small amounts while the units in shortage of funds are often firms who need large amounts of cash. Financial intermediaries reduce the size mismatch by lumping together small savings and deliver them in a form suitable to the needs of users.

In addition, users of funds, in general, need funds for relatively long-term deployment, which cannot be met by individual suppliers of funds. This creates a mismatch between the maturity and liquidity preference of individual savers and users of funds. The intermediaries resolve the conflict again by pooling small funds. Moreover, the risk preferences of small suppliers and large users of funds may differ. Small savers are generally considered to be risk-averse and prefer safer placements while the fund users deploy the funds in risky projects.

Therefore, the funds cannot be directly supplied. The role of the intermediary again becomes crucial.

They can substantially reduce this risk through portfolio diversification. Furthermore, small investors cannot efficiently gather information about investment opportunities. Financial intermediaries are in a much better position to collect such information, which is crucial for making the investment successful.

Many current theories of financial intermediation put heavy emphasis on functions of institutions that are no longer crucial in many developed financial systems (Allen and Santomero 1996). These theories focus on products and services that are of decreasing importance to the intermediaries but are unable to account for those activities that have become the central focus of many institutions.

Most literature stresses the role of financial intermediaries in reducing the frictions of transaction costs and asymmetric information and says very little about the increasing roles of financial intermediaries as facilitators of risk transfer and the proliferation of complex financial instruments and markets.

For example, risk management is an important area in which banks and other financial institutions are heavily involved; however, intermediation theory says very little about this. These new functions of intermediation are the result of a dramatic transformation in the financial system of many countries in recent years. More particularly, the rapid rise of major financial innovations in the 1970s and 1980s coupled with the revolution in computer technology and telecommunications played an important role.

New financial products that came into existence included mortgage-backed securities and other securitized assets; derivative instruments, such as interest rate and currency swaps; and complex options. The net impact of these innovations and complex financial derivative securities has been *less* transparency and a significant shift in risk assumption.

B. Other Unique Aspects of Intermediation

Brokerage

When functioning as a pure broker, a financial institution acts as an *agent* for the saver by providing information and transactions services. In fulfilling a brokerage function, the financial institutions play an extremely important role by reducing transaction and information costs or imperfections between households and corporations due to economies of scale. Thus, the financial institution encourages a higher rate of savings than would otherwise exist.

Transmission of Monetary Policy

The highly liquid nature of bank deposits has resulted in their acceptance by the public and resulted in their status as the most widely used medium of exchange in the economy. At the core of the three most commonly used definitions of the money supply—M1, M2, and M3—lie the depository institutions' deposit contracts. Because the liabilities of depository institutions are a component of the money supply that impacts the rate of inflation, they play a key role in the transmission of monetary policy from the central bank to the rest of the economy. That is, depository institutions are the conduit through which monetary policy actions impact the rest of the financial sector and the economy in general.

There may be a need for regulation given the special role banks play in the transmission of monetary policy from the central bank to the rest of the economy. The problem is that the central bank directly controls only the quantity of notes and coins in the economy, whereas the bulk of the money supply consists of deposits. In theory, a central bank can vary the quantity of cash and directly affect a bank's reserve position as well as the amount of loans and deposits it can create without formally regulating the bank's portfolio.

In practice, regulators have chosen to impose formal controls. In most countries, regulators commonly impose a minimum level of required cash reserves to be held against deposits. Central banks may also act as lenders of last resort during banking and financial crises and thus provide the needed liquidity to avoid a slowdown in economic activities.

Credit Allocation

Another reason why financial institutions (FIs) are usually viewed as unique is that they are the major and sometimes the only source of finance for a particular sector of the economy pre-identified as being in special need of finance. Policy makers in many countries have identified *residential real estate* as needing special subsidies. This has enhanced the specialness of FIs that most commonly service the needs of that sector.

In the United States, savings associations and savings banks have traditionally served the credit needs of the residential real estate sector. In a similar fashion, farming can be considered an especially important area of the economy in terms of the overall social welfare of the society and thus deserving of more credit.

Payment Services

Depository banks and thrifts are special in that the efficiency with which they provide payment services directly benefits the economy. Two important payment services are check clearing and wire transfer services.

Safe and Sound Regulation

To protect depositors and borrowers against the risk of financial institution failure, regulators have developed different levels of protective mechanisms. The objective of these mechanisms is to ensure the safety and soundness of financial institutions and credibly gain the confidence of borrowers, lenders, and the public at large.

Among these levels of protection is the need for financial institutions to diversify their assets, to establish minimum levels of capital or equity funds that owners of the financial institutions need to contribute to the funding of their operations, to guarantee the safety of certain amounts of customer deposits (deposit insurance), and to regularly monitor and supervise the operations of financial institutions.

C. Conventional Banks

Commercial Banks

Commercial banks comprise the largest group of depository institutions in most countries. They perform functions similar to those of savings institutions and credit unions; that is, they accept deposits (liabilities) and make loans (assets). However, they differ in their composition of assets and liabilities, which are much more varied. Their liabilities usually include several types of non-deposit sources of funds, and their loans are broader in range, including consumer, commercial, and real estate loans.

As the consolidated balance sheet of all U.S. commercial banks shows (see table 4.1), a major inference we draw from their asset structure is that credit or default exposure is a major risk faced by modern commercial bank managers. Since commercial banks are highly leveraged and have little equity compared to total assets, even a relatively small amount of loan defaults can wipe out the equity of a bank, leaving it insolvent.

Commercial banks have two major sources of funds besides the equity provided by owners: deposit and borrowing or other liability funds. Transaction accounts are checkable deposits that bear no interest (demand deposits) or are interest bearing, such as the NOW accounts.

Investment Banks

Investment banking involves the raising of debt and equity securities for corporations or governments. This includes the origination, underwriting, and placement of securities in money and capital markets for corporate or government issuers. Because of the emphasis on securities trading and underwriting, the size of the industry is usually measured by the equity capital of the firms participating in the industry.

Table 4:1

Balance Sheet (All U.S. Commercial Banks) as of December 31, 2010

Assets:	USD
	(in billions)
Cash and Due from	368.4
Investment Securities	1,058.3
Total Loans and Leases	3,786.6
Allowances of Losses Loans and Leases	(63.7)
Other Earning Assets	583.4
Bank Premises and Equipment	75.1
Other Real Estate	3.2
Intangible Assets	103.6
All Other Assets	277.3
Total Assets	**6,192.2**

Liabilities and Equity Capital

Total Deposits	4,149.0
Borrowed Funds	1,029.1
Subordinated Loans	86.8
Other Liabilities	400.6
Total Liabilities	**5,665.5**
Perpetual Preferred Stocks	3.2
Common Stock	30.9
Surplus	259.5
Undivided Profits	233.1
Other Capital	0.0
Total Equity	**526.7**
Total Liabilities and Equity Capital	**6,192.2**

Source: FDIC, December 2010 (www.fdic.gov)

D. Islamic Banks

For Islamic banks and Islamic financial institutions in general, the nature of financial intermediation is different from that of non-Islamic financial institutions. Understanding this difference is crucial to appreciating how the nature of the risks differs between conventional and Islamic banks.

An Islamic bank, like any other bank, is a company whose main business is to mobilize funds from savers and supply these funds to entrepreneurs. It is generally organized as a joint-stock company with the shareholders supplying the initial capital. Conventional or non-Islamic banks use the rate of interest to obtain funds from savers and supply these funds to businesses or entrepreneurs; an Islamic bank performs similar functions but uses financing modes compatible with Islamic law or the *Shari'a*.

The activity of a typical Islamic bank is a combination of commercial and investment banking, as shown in figure 4.1 in the boxes on both sides of the balance sheet. The boxes on the assets and liabilities side represent the specialized functions of an Islamic bank. Each box also highlights the separation of assets and liabilities based on their maturity structure, risk exposure, and related market. The arrows across liabilities and assets indicate how assets and liabilities can be maturity matched.

On the resource mobilization side (liabilities), Islamic banks use the contracts of *amana, mudaraba,* or *wakala* with the fund owners. Under the first contract, the net income of the bank is shared between shareholders and investment deposit holders according to a predetermined profit-sharing formula.

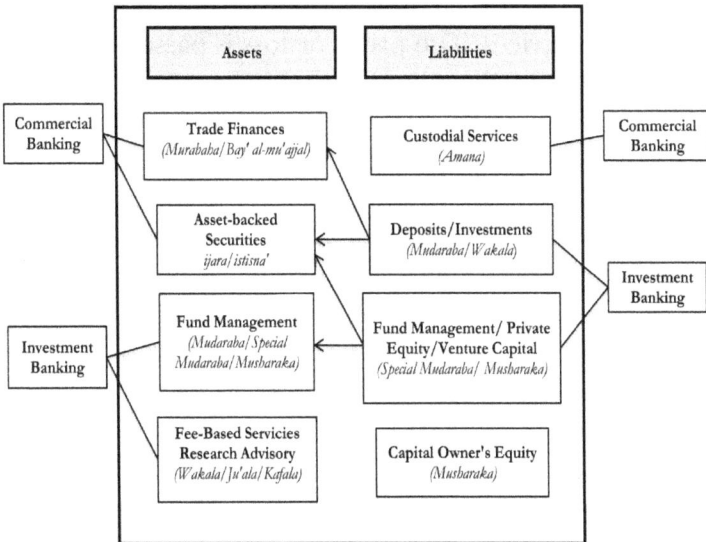

Source: El-Hawary, Grais & Iqbal 2004

Figure 4.1 Anatomy of the Balance Sheet of an Islamic Bank.

The investment deposits could be either *unrestricted* investment deposits that enter into a pool of investment funds or *restricted* investment accounts in which deposits are made for investment in particular projects.

In addition, there are demand deposits or current accounts that are like an interest-free loan to the bank. The bank guarantees the principal but pays no profit on these accounts. The bank is allowed to use these deposits at its own risk. Like conventional banks, demand deposits can be withdrawn without notice. The reason to justify the capital value guarantee is the assumption that demand deposits are placed in banks as an *amana*, that is, for safekeeping.

In the case of a *wakala* (representation) contract, clients give funds to the bank that serves as their investment manager. The bank charges a predetermined fee for its managerial services. The profit or loss is passed on to the fund providers after deducting such a fee.

On the asset side, Islamic banks have more choice of instruments with differing maturities and risk-return profiles. For short-term maturities, trade financing from a sale contract—that is *murabaha*—are available. For medium-term investments, leasing (*ijara*), manufacturing contracts (*istisna'*), and various partnerships are possible. For long-term investments, partnerships in the form of *musharaka* are possible.

An Islamic bank can also provide capital to an outside entrepreneur on the basis of *mudaraba*, in which the bank acts as a principal and the entrepreneur acts as an agent. In this capacity, an Islamic bank can form a syndicate with other financial or nonfinancial institutions to provide entrepreneurs with medium to long-term capital. Finally, like non-Muslim banks, Islamic banks also provide customized services, guarantees, and underwriting services (*wakala/ju'ala/kafala*) for a fee.

Islamic banks use a number of financial instruments, none of which involves interest, for providing finance to businesses. A wide variety of such modes of financing are now available (see table 4.2).

Shown on table 4.3 at the end of this chapter is the balance sheet of Bahrain Islamic Bank. The composition of the assets and liabilities reflect maturity profile, risk profile, and functions of a typical Islamic bank.

Table 4.2

Categories of Modes of Islamic Financing

Profit-Loss Sharing (PLS) Contracts	Non-Profit-Loss Sharing Contracts
mudaraba (financing by way of Trust) *musharaka* (partnership)	*murabaha* (mark-up) *ijara, ijara wa iqtina'* (leasing, leasing to purchase) *istisna'* (commissioned manufacture) *bay' al-salam* (advance purchase) *bay' al-mu'ajjal* (deferred payment sales or credit sales) *ju'ala* (service charge) *qard hasan* (beneficence loans)

Other Unique Features of Islamic Banks

A Limited Ability to Require Collateral
As a general rule, when financing customers through profit-and-loss-sharing (PLS) modes, Islamic financial institutions are not expected to require collateral to reduce credit risk. Owing to the structure of their balance sheet and the use of profit-and-loss-sharing arrangements, Islamic banks may be better suited than conventional banks

to absorb external shocks. In the event of operational losses, unlike conventional banks, Islamic banks have the ability to reduce the nominal value of investment deposits, that is, reduce the nominal value of a portion of their liabilities. As a result, solvency risks that may arise from an asset-liability mismatch are typically lower in Islamic banks than in conventional banks.

Theoretical Models for the Structure of Islamic Banks

There are two formal conceptual models for the structure of Islamic banks: the "two-tier *mudaraba*" and the "two-windows" models.

Two-Tier Mudaraba Model

Using the concept of profit-and-loss sharing (PLS), this model links the assets and liabilities sides on the basis of how funds are mobilized and utilized. The first tier is a *mudaraba* contract between the investor of funds and the bank. This transaction will be reflected on the liability side of the bank. The investor will share in the profits and losses the bank earns on the business ventures it finances with the investor's funds.

The second tier is a *mudaraba* contract between the bank and the entrepreneurs, whom it funds and with whom it agrees to share profits and losses according to the terms stated in the contract.

Islamic banks operating according the two-tier *mudaraba* model (the norm in practice) are still subject to the risk of an asset-liability mismatch because:

1. demand deposits are guaranteed in capital value and are redeemable by depositors at par and on demand;

2. demand deposits can be used to finance long-term risk-bearing investment projects; and
3. there are no mandated specific reserve requirements on demand and investment deposits.

Two-Windows Model

This model separates the liabilities side of the balance sheet into two windows, one for demand deposits (transaction balances) and the other for investment balances. It is up to the depositors to decide which window to use. There will be a 100 percent reserve requirement for the demand deposits since it is only for safekeeping (*amana*) purposes. However, there will be no reserve for the second window of the investment because the depositor is fully aware that the funds will be invested in risky projects. For the demand deposit accounts, the bank charges a fee for undertaking the safekeeping function.

An Islamic bank's operation on the demand side of the window ("Narrow Banking," also has similar characteristics) is virtually insolvency proof. Islamic banks' operational activity in the investment window shows similarity with non-Islamic investment companies, including mutual funds, owing to the fact that they do not guarantee either the capital value or the return on investment deposits and they basically pool depositors' funds to provide them with professional management.

There is, however, a fundamental conceptual difference between the two that also needs to be recognized. It lies in the fact that the investment companies sell their capital to the public, while Islamic banks accept deposits from the public. This implies that shareholders of an investment company own a proportionate part of the company's equity capital and are entitled to a number of rights, including receiving a regular flow of information on developments of the company's business and exerting voting rights on important matters (such as changes in investment policy) corresponding to their shares.

Hence, they are in a position to make informed decisions, monitor the company's performance, and influence strategic decisions. By contrast, (investment) depositors in an Islamic bank are only entitled to share the bank's net profit (or loss) according to the PLS ratio stipulated in their contracts.

Investment deposits can be withdrawn only on maturity and at best case, at par value. Moreover, depositors have no voting rights, because they do not own any portion of the bank's equity capital. Hence, they cannot influence the bank's investment policy. In fact, their relationship with the bank is regulated according to an *unrestricted mudaraba* contract.

Risk Aversion
Contemporary Islamic banks are organized as companies rather than on a mutual basis; hence their shareholders are distinct from their depositors. The former have the ownership rights and responsibilities, but the latter do not. Islamic banks contain potential conflicts of interest between the bank's management and its shareholders: the classical principal-agent problem.

For example, higher pay or bonuses for the bank's management, unless matched by efficiency gains, may be at the expense of dividends paid to shareholders. This two-way conflict may become a three-way conflict in Islamic banks, as customers with investment deposits on a *mudaraba* profit-sharing basis may have their payouts reduced if management rewards itself more, their position being similar to that of the shareholders as principals.

At the same time, however, there may also be a trade-off between the interests of shareholders and clients with *mudaraba* deposits, as higher dividends for the former may be at the expense of the profit shares of the latter.

Role of the Central Bank

The central bank should be the nerve center of the Islamic banking system, because only through its efforts will the Islamic money and banking system be able to achieve its goals. Ideally, it should be an autonomous government institution responsible for the realization of the Islamic economic and social objectives. Its responsibilities, like all central banks', should primarily be the issuance of currency, the clearance and processing of checks, and acting as a lender of last resort. Equally important, it should supervise and regulate the commercial banks, as well as the nonbank and specialized financial institutions.

In implementing monetary policy, the central bank should use instruments and methods it deems appropriate provided they do not conflict with the teachings of the *Shari'a*. Similar to conventional central banks, Islamic central banks should act as lenders of last resort during liquidity crises.

A liquidity crisis may arise in a profit-and-loss transaction where the bank may not be able to withdraw its equity-oriented loan until the project venture is completed. In any case, a solvency crisis may tend to be of less gravity in the Islamic system because of the relatively large equity base of the bank along with a substantial volume of *amana* (safekeeping) deposits. These might be adequate to protect demand depositors. However, insurance demand deposits should be instituted to prevent any runs on banks and the central bank should be prepared to act as a lender of last resort.

Table 4.4 at the end of this chapter summarizes key differences between Islamic and commercial banks.

Table 4.3

Consolidated Balance Sheet of Bahrain Islamic Bank—
December 31, 2010

	In Bahrain Dinars (BD) *(in thousands)*
Assets:	
Cash and Balances with Banks and Central Bank	45,831
Due from Banks and Financial Institutions	208,006
Murabaha Receivables	230,919
Musharaka Investments	81,159
Investments	127,383
Investments in Associates	6,778
Investments in *Ijarah* Assets	9,635
Ijarah Muntahia Bittamleek	101,884
Investment Properties	105,192
Ijarah Rental Receivables	7,569
Other Assets	11,318
Total Assets	**935,674**
Liabilities	
Customers' Current Accounts	81,660
Other Liabilities	12,571
Total Liabilities	**94,231**
Equity of Investment Accountholders	
Financial Institutions' Investment Accounts	141,859
Customers' Investment Accounts	599,523
Total Equity of Investment Accountholders	**741,382**
Owner's Equity	
Share Capital	72,859
Treasury Shares	(307)
Share Premium	43,936
Reserves	(16,594)
Proposed Appropriations	167
Total Equity	**100,061**
Total Liabilities, Equity of Investment Accountholders and Owner's Equity	**935,674**

Source: 2010 Annual Report of Bahrain Islamic Bank

Table 4.4

Fundamental Differences between Islamic and
Conventional Banking

	Islamic Banking	Conventional Banking
1	An advanced step toward achievement of Islamic economics	Part of the capitalistic interest-based financial system
2	Interest and usury avoided at all levels of financial transactions	The basis of all financial transactions is interest and high-level usury
3	Depositors bear the risk, no need for deposit insurance	Depositors do not bear any risk; moreover, the bank is inclined to pay back principal with a guaranteed interest amount
4	The relationship between depositors and entrepreneurs is friendly and cooperative	Creditor-debtor relationship
5	Islamic banks become partners in the business of the client after sanctioning the credit and bearing loss	Do not bear any loss of client
6	Islamic bank is likely to absorb any endogenous or exogenous shock	Less likely to absorb any shock because of the ex-ante commitment
7	Interbank transactions are on a profit-and-loss-sharing basis	On interest basis and more likely to cause credit or asset bubbles that burst afterward
8	Islamic banks work under the surveillance of the *Shari'a* supervisory boards	No such surveillance
9	Avoids speculation-related functional activities	Main functions are susceptible to speculation
10	Islamic banks sell and purchase foreign currency on an on-the-spot basis, not a forward-looking or future basis	On-the-spot and forward-looking bases are both used

Source: (Brown, Hassan, & Skully, 2007)

The Nature of Islamic Finance

Islamic laws (*Shari'a*) fundamentally forbid "interest" but do not prohibit all gains on capital. *Shari'a* law simply requires that the performance of capital must be taken into consideration when rewarding capital. Therefore, in financial terms, the use of capital must add value and not be devoid of risk (Arberry 1964, 4). Prohibition of interest or usury is stated in the Holy *Qur'an* in the following verses:

> Those who devour usury
> Will not stand except
> As stands one whom
> The Evil One by his touch
> Hath driven to madness.
> That is because they say:
> "Trade is like usury,"
> But Allah hath permitted trade
> And forbidden usury.
> Those who after receiving
> Direction from their Lord,
> Desist, shall be pardoned
> For the past; their case
> Is for Allah (to judge);
> But those who repeat

(The offence) are Companions
Of the fire; they will
Abide therein (forever).
(*Holy Qur'an*, Surah al Baqarah, 2:275)[24]

O ye who believe!
Devour not Usury,
Doubled and multiplied;
But fear Allah; that
Ye may (really) prosper.
(*Holy Qur'an*, Surah al-Imran, 3:130)

It is important to remember that *Shari'a* principles are not simply a prohibition of interest; they are also designed to prevent unethical practices, ensure that investments be undertaken on the basis of *halal* (permitted) activities, and benefit society through the collection of *zakat* (almsgiving).[25] Other prohibitions of *Shari'a* laws include *maysir* (gambling, speculation) and *gharar* (unreasonable uncertainty).

Islamic finance starts from one basic concept, that is, to avoid trading directly present for future money. Finance is provided in the form of money in return for either equity or rights to share proportionately in future business profits. It is also provided in the form of goods and services delivered in return for commitment to repay their value at a future date.

This is an obvious option in addition to the conventional practices of interest-based finance through which people borrow money and pay it back in the future in addition to interest. The following are important questions one might ask:

- Is there an economic rationale for interest?
- What is the alternative to *interest-based* debt financing?

- What are the advantages and challenges of Islamic finance?

Answering these questions, I hope, will give us an insight into the unique features of Islamic banking and finance.

A. What Is an Interest Rate?

Iqbal and Mirakhor (2007) defined *riba* (interest) as the "premium" that must be paid by the borrower to the lender along with the principal amount as a condition for the loan or for an extension in the duration of the loan. Furthermore, at least four characteristics define the prohibited interest rate:

1. it is positive and fixed ex-ante;
2. it is tied to the time period and the amount of the loan;
3. its payment is guaranteed regardless of the outcome or the purposes for which the principal was borrowed; and
4. the state apparatus sanctions and enforces its collection.

As stated earlier, the prohibition of interest is not due to any formal economic theory as such; it is directly prohibited by divine order in the *Qur'an.* Yet, *riba* or interest is not precisely defined in the *Qur'an* at the time of its prohibition (Algaoud and Lewis 2001, 18–19). A great deal of confusion is created in trying to define *riba* in modern times in a language other than Arabic. Thus, the actual meaning of *riba* has been debated since the earliest Muslim times. Umar, the second caliph, wished that the

Prophet died after having given a more detailed account of what constituted *riba* (Algaoud and Lewis 2001).

Islamic scholar Joseph Schacht (1964) expressed the widely shared view that *riba* is simply a special case of unjustified enrichment or, in terms of the *Holy Qur'an*, consuming (that is, appropriating for one's own use) the property of others for no good reason, which is prohibited. More formally, he defined *riba* as "a monetary advantage without a counter value which has been stipulated in favor of one of the two contracting parties in an exchange of two monetary values." p. 145.

Contemporary economist Gregory Mankiw defined an interest rate as "the market price at which resources are transferred between the present and the future; the return to savings and the cost of borrowing" (Mankiw 2007).

B. Islamic Law and the Concept of Interest

The purification of sources of income is a very important subject in Islam and according to the *Qur'an* and *Sunna*, those whose income is not pure must face the consequences in both this world and the hereafter (Yaquby 2002). The prohibition of interest is generally understood to refer to any increment over and above the principal. It represents the return on transactions involving exchange of money for money, or an addition, on account of delay in payment, to the agreed-upon price in sales/debts.

One of the primary rationales espoused by Muslim scholars is that the existence of *riba* (interest) in the economy is a form of economic exploitation, which violates the core Islamic teaching of social justice (Khan 1987). Therefore, the elimination of interest from the economic system would be "fairer" and ethically and morally a more appropriate economic behavior.[26]

From an Islamic point of view, under one concept of fairness, there are two dimensions: the supplier of capital possesses a right to reward, but this reward should be commensurate with the risk and effort involved and should be determined by the return realized on the individual project for which funds are supplied (Presley 1988). What makes profit-sharing permissible in Islam, while interest is not, is that in the case of the former, it is only the profit-sharing ratio, not the rate of return itself that is predetermined.

C. Islamic Law and Restrictions on the Contract Set

The conventional financial system allows individuals and businesses with heterogeneous risk preferences to enter into a large set of business and financial transactions and form the contracts they wish to, as long as it is not fraudulent or coercive. However, Islamic law is more restrictive in this regard.

Islamic finance is broadly based on some prohibitions and encouragements. The prohibition of interest (*riba*) and permission of trade drive the financial activities in an economy toward asset-backed businesses and transactions. This implies that all financial transactions must be representative of real transactions for the sale of goods, services, or benefits (Ahmed and Khan 2001, 22).

This means that the structure of Islamic finance revolves around the prohibition of pre-fixed returns derived from loans/debts (*riba*) and the encouragement of profit-and-loss activities whose return is variable. However, this does not mean that all pre-fixed returns are prohibited under Islamic law.

To ascertain the *Shari'a* position on any type of transaction, you have to look at its nature. If it is a loan or credit transaction culminating in a debt, such loans or debts cannot fetch any increase whatsoever because it would be considered interest. In the sale of goods or their usufructs, however, one can make a profit as per the rules of *Shari'a* relating to the respective transactions.

For example, in trade, a person can sell any commodity, not including money, for one price on a cash-and-carry basis and for a higher price on a deferred payment basis as long as market forces determine the price. However, this is subject to certain conditions, the fulfillment of which are necessary to differentiate between interest and profit. More specifically, let us examine the case of *bay'* (sale / purchase of goods) and *ijara* (leasing).

Under *bay'* (sale / purchase of goods), there is a definite transfer of ownership of the goods to the buyer against the payment of a price that can be on the spot, delayed (in credit sale), or in advance (*bay' al-salam*). The risk and reward relating to the sold goods will belong to the buyer, who will be required to pay the price irrespective of the manner in which he has used them or the profit/loss to him in business. As such, Islamic banks will have no recourse to the sold goods. The bank prices the goods, and the debt is created; the goods belong to their clients, and they have no right to reprice them.

Ijara (leasing) refers to the transfer of the usufruct of assets against payment of rent. Technically, it is a contract of sale, but it is not the sale of a tangible asset; rather, it is a sale of the usufruct (right to use the object) for a specified period of time (Iqbql and Van Greuning 2008). Islamic law allows rentals subject to the condition that the lessor bears the risk and expenses related to ownership of the leased asset. There should be no confusion in this regard vis-à-vis the concept of rent in *ijara* (leasing). It might be argued, for example, that as per approved *Shari'a* principles, predetermined rent including a time value of money is allowed; therefore, a predetermined time of value of money in loans/debts should also be permitted by analogy.

This argument does not apply because the rent in leasing is calculated on the basis of the capacity of the asset to give usufruct, which is, in principle, uncertain (Ayub 2007). Hence, it remains uncertain how much time value of money is actually realized until the asset has completed its economic life. The lessor, as owner of the leased assets, is also the owner of the risk and reward associated with the asset.

Further, another reason given for why the analogy does not hold is that anything that cannot be used without consuming its corpus during its use cannot be leased out, like money, edible goods, fuel, etc., because when an asset no longer exists, how can the lessor bear the ownership-related risk (Ayub 2007)? All such assets, the corpus of which is not consumed with their use, can be leased out against fixed rentals. As such, one leases out his asset to others for use against fixed/stipulated rental(s).

Risk Preferences
Islamic law leaves it up to individual investors to decide what level of risk they want to assume as long as the underlying economic activity is permitted (*halal*), the obligations and rights under the contract are well defined, and the nature and risk exposure of the investment project are clearly understood by all parties. Riskier business ventures offer higher potential rewards, and the reverse holds as well.

As was shown on the liability side of a typical Islamic bank in chapter 4, depositors have the choice of putting their money in safekeeping or investment accounts. Furthermore, under investment accounts, depositors have the choice of selecting "restricted" or "unrestricted" investment accounts. Restricted investing means the depositor could invest in the trade financing transactions, leasing transactions, or profit-and-loss based transactions (equity) of a particular industry.

For example, a widow may require an Islamic banker to invest her money in less risky but *Shari'a*-compliant business because she is not in a position to bear the risk of loss that could arise in equity-based businesses. The bank, as a trustee, would be bound to invest the funds of such a risk-averse investor in trade and *ijara*-based activities.

On the other hand, a more risk-tolerant investor might choose to invest in *mudaraba* contracts. Under *mudaraba*, an economic agent with capital develops a partnership with another agent who has expertise in deploying the capital to undertake a business venture into real transactions with an agreement to share the profits (Vogel and Hayes 1998). Any loss in the investment or business will be borne solely by the capital owner, unless such a loss is caused by the misconduct or negligence of the economic agent who deploys the capital. Note that the profit-sharing ratio may differ from the capital contribution; however, it must be made specific beforehand and must be clearly stated.

In situations where the agent acted in good faith, but the investment resulted in a loss, the capital owner loses his capital and the entrepreneur agent loses the time and effort deployed during the business venture (the opportunity cost of what he might have earned otherwise).

Debt Versus Equity

From the above discussion, it is clear that debt could arise from credit sales or leasing activity. Islamic financial institutions, while providing a financial facility through trading activities, create debt, which is reflected in their balance sheets. So, the issue is not one of debt versus equity, but one of putting together reliance on equity and subjecting the debt to the principle of *Shari'a* so that debt, once created, should not increase (Iqbal and Llewellyn 2002).

It is important to point out that the debt financing under non-Islamic banking is found to be preferable to equity financing for several reasons. First, debt financing is found to be more efficient in the presence of asymmetric information, given how excessively high the cost involved in verifying the return on a project becomes compared to the potential benefits (Aoki 1994). Second, debt contracts have lower monitoring costs since the lending bank is not interested in the degree of success of the project as long as it does not fail to an extent that causes the borrower to default. Finally, debt contracts also have lower transaction costs.

For the above-stated reasons, non-Islamic banks naturally prefer debt contracts. However, there are several disadvantages to debt financing. One major disadvantage is that banks do not share in potential upside gain (the return is fixed in the unexpectedly successful project) but does share in the extreme downside if the borrower goes bankrupt. Equally important is the potential instability from debt leveraging and speculation that makes the financial system susceptible to financial crisis.

To summarize, Islam does not object to the use of debt in its modes of financing—allowed debt contracts include those that arise from trade financing, the so-called cost-plus contracts that are payment-deferred sales transactions (*murabaha*) and leases (*ijara*)—however, creating debt is constrained only to that which arises from real transactions. With regard to profit-sharing contracts, return on investment is unknown ex-ante but will vary, depending on the performance or profitability of the project or business venture.

Of course, even though the return on investment is unknown ex-ante, it is probable that riskier transactions or business ventures (depending on the industry or project or on the experience and managerial skills in the case of an entrepreneur) would likely have higher expected returns, all else being equal. In other words, it is the bank's responsibility to analyze potential investments or projects and perform the necessarily required due diligence before deciding whether to partner with an entrepreneur or fund a project. Rational investors are less likely to accept a profit-sharing ratio that is not commensurate with the risk they will bear. In particular, no investor would accept a zero expected return to any part of his portfolio.

D. Types of Islamic Contracts
To gain a broader understanding of how economic activities are conducted under the Islamic economic system, one has to understand the nature and types of contracts that are used. Islam requires that all material economic activity should be based on written contracts from those with excess funds to those who are in need of funds for potentially promising investment projects, new business ventures, or expansion of existing businesses. There are four basic contracts that encompass all the economic activities under Islam. These contracts are not explicitly defined or classified under the Islamic legal system; however, they are an effective way to classify economic activities logically and by function. As figure 5.1 shows, these contracts are:

     i. transactional contracts,
     ii. financing contracts,
     iii. intermediation contracts, and
     iv. social contracts

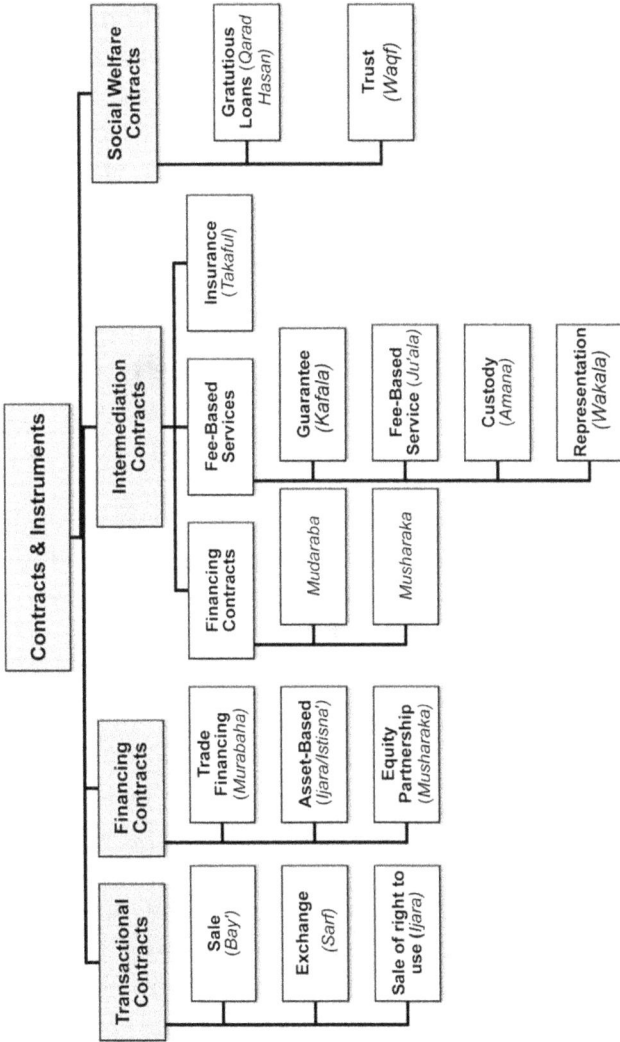

Figure 5.1 Contracts and Instruments

Source: Iqbal and Mirakhor, 2007

Transactional contracts reflect all economic transactions in the real sector of the economy, such as the buying and selling of goods and services, exchange and trade, and the sale of the rights to use assets. Contracts of sale and exchange transfer ownership, whereas contracts for the sale of the right to use assets (i.e., leases, or *ijara*) transfer rights from one party to another.

Financing contracts, on the other hand, deal with extension of credit to finance the purchase of physical assets, trade transactions, and partnership business ventures or projects. Debt created under these contracts is nonnegotiable and therefore cannot be traded.

Intermediation contracts are the essence of all banking and finance activities as explained in detail in chapter 4. This covers the efficient mobilization of savings.

E. Modes of Islamic Finance

Islamic modes of finance can be grouped into three categories: equity and profit-and-loss sharing, credit purchase, and leasing (Jobst 2007, 5).

Profit-and-Loss Sharing (Equity-Based)

In profit-sharing contracts, lenders (investors) and borrowers (entrepreneurs) agree to share any profits from financed projects at an agreed-upon ratio in advance. However, losses will be shared based on contributed capital (Iqbal and Llewellyn 2002). Generally, in equity financing under conventional finance, savers would provide funds to enterprises in return for a share in their prospective net returns as well as a share in their management. However, in contrast, profit-sharing funding of projects under Islamic finance is not for the whole life of the financed enterprise, but for a shorter period, as in the case of providing working capital. Profit-sharing finance may be provided with or without a share in management.

Linked with profit sharing is the notion of risk sharing. This is based on the principle of liability, which states that profit is justified on the basis of one's obligation to take a loss. This legal maxim is said to be derived from a saying of Prophet Mohammad that "profit comes with liability" implying that *Shari'a* distinguishes lawful profit from all other forms of gain. One becomes entitled to profit only after one bears the liability, or risk, of loss (Ayub 2007).

Credit Purchase

Credit purchase implies that the financing institution provides the goods or services for immediate or future delivery in return for a debt instrument that promises payment of their value at a specified future date. That value differs from on-the-spot prices by a certain margin called *markup*. The most common and widely used contract of this form is the *murabaha* (cost plus sale), and the debt instrument created under this contract is *non*-negotiable (Jobst 2007). In the case of temporary insolvency, the debtor is granted an extension with no increase in maturity value.[27] Only delinquent debtors with no valid excuses can be subjected to penalty (Ahmed 2002, 40–56).

Alternatively, the financing institution can pay the value of the goods and services on the spot and get them delivered at some specified time in the future. In this case, the debt instrument would be written in terms of goods and services. Some might think that this type of *sales finance* is no different from interest. They might argue that trading present against future money involves explicit interest, while trading goods against future money involves *implicit interest*. While both interest and markup reflect time preference, the latter is far from similar to the former. Several differences can be cited in this regard.

First, the nominal value of the debt involved in sales finance cannot grow by itself. The value of debt is set at the time of sale and cannot be increased. In contrast, interest is set as a compound rate per unit of time, allowing the nominal value of debt to grow until it has been repaid. Second, finance is provided in conjunction with acquiring goods and services. This has serious implications with regard to the relationship between the real and the financial sectors, which will be taken up further below.

Leasing, or Ijara (Operating Lease)

Under *ijara*, the financing institution purchases a durable asset and leases it to a customer in return for regular payments reflecting the cost of holding and maintaining the asset in addition to the transfer of property from the financing institution (lessor) to the receiving agent (lessee) (Mirakhor and Zaidi 2007, 52).

Compared to non-Islamic forms of financing, where financing usually takes the form of debt, leasing is based on a specific asset. In essence, it combines financing and collateral, because the ownership of the asset serves as collateral and security against any future loss. In addition, unlike non-Islamic leasing, financing is not dependent on the capital base of the lessee but on his or her ability to pay the rental charges.

An important difference between *ijara* under Islamic law and the non-Islamic leases is that the leasing agent must own the leased asset for the duration of the lease. Another difference is that no compounding interest may be charged under Islamic leases in the event of default or delay in the installment payments.

F. Conclusion

The universe of contracts feasible under Islamic finance is, at least in principle, smaller than under the conventional financial system. The types of fixed, predetermined returns available for Islamic investors is limited, again in principle, only to real transactions that arise from the credit purchase / sale contracts, trade financing, and leases that give rise to the creation of debt. However, debts created under these contracts are nontradable (again, in principle). In practice, as I have indicated, breaches of Islamic *Shari'a* are widespread.

The benefit of limiting, to the extent possible, debt-creating transactions to only these sets of contracts is preventing the potential instability that arises from the proliferation of debt-leveraging transactions that do not arise from real transactions but from speculative ones. The determinant from an economic point of view is reflected in the limitation of the contract set that prohibits loans with interest. The extent to which this will benefit Islamic banks and the determinant trade-off will be important to the relative economic success of true Islamic banks in contrast to conventional banks.

Inevitably, certain Islamic banks will fail to be compliant with *Shari'a* law and will engage in conventional banking, either secretly or in name only for marketing or public relations purposes, by making loans with interest.

The extent to which they do so will vary from country to country or within the same country, depending on how rigorously they adhere to the Islamic religion. Specifically, we might expect loans bearing interest to be frequently available in countries like Bahrain and Malaysia, where economic gain is weighed more heavily as opposed to countries that are religiously more conservative and observant, such as Qatar or Saudi Arabia.

Whether Islamic banks in practice adhere to the restrictions in the type of activities they undertake in substance will have an implication on their claim of being more stable because of less leveraging and speculation. This will be an important issue of note in examining and analyzing the empirical evidence of Bahrain and Malaysia in this book.

An implication of the narrower set of contracts under Islamic finance might be that many transactions between people with heterogeneous risk preferences that are potentially profitable under conventional banking and finance would not be undertaken. Thus, in essence, under Islamic finance, a system prone to booms and busts is traded for a higher degree of financial stability with a steady growth.

Endnotes

24. Source: *The Meaning of the Holy Qur'an*, 9th ed., trans. Abdullah Yusuf Ali (Beltsville, MD: Amana Publications, 1997).

25. The institution of interest was originally repugnant to followers of the teachings of Judaism, Christianity, and Islam. However, Judaism and Christianity evolved, and a degree of pragmatism has crept in over time, which made them tolerant of the practice of charging interest. It is worth noting that none of the revealed religions has accepted "interest" as the cost of using capital as commonly understood in conventional economics.

26. Non-Muslims might not share this concept of fairness. However, Islam considers interest as unfair in the sense that a lender is being guaranteed a positive return without assuming a share of the risk with the borrower, whereas the borrower takes upon himself all sorts of risks in addition to putting in his skills and labor.

27. Some observers have argued that this mode of financing is not that different from the non-Islamic interest-based lending operation. However, a major difference between *murabaha* and interest-based lending is that the markup in *murabaha* is for the services the bank provides (for example, seeking and purchasing the required goods at the best price) and is not stipulated in terms of a time period.

Advantages and Challenges of Islamic Finance

In the absence of externality, economic activities undertaken would be efficient. As explained in chapter 2 "Theories of Western Financial Crises," the international financial system has suffered from recurring financial crises over the last four hundred years, which continue into the present as the recent global financial crisis attests.

The externalities from these financial crises manifest in different forms, such as the failures of banks and other financial institutions, crashes of stock markets, and liquidity crises that usually culminate in a severe economic recession and expensive bailouts of financial institutions by taxpayers. Investors and depositors under this financial system have the potential risk of losing their savings and investments in addition to sustaining losses in output and employment.

As will be explained later in this chapter, Islamic finance offers the opportunity to reduce these externalities that are inherent in the modern international financial system. Following Coast (1960), many economists would argue externality could be eliminated through trade if transaction costs do not prevent it. In my judgment, externalities arise as a consequence of systemic risk and become exacerbated by contagion, and they cannot be traded away as explained in this chapter.

A. Advantages of Islamic Finance

Islamic finance offers several advantages in comparison to conventional finance, but there are challenges as well. However, on balance, the benefits outweigh their associated costs. My analysis focuses on four key advantages.

1. Islamic Finance Makes the Financial System More Stable

The Evolution of Money

The first big breakthrough in finance came when everyone agreed that barter exchange was too costly and time-consuming. Under the new system, everyone agreed to accept gold in return for whatever they were selling. However, once gold took the role of a recognized means of exchange, it also inadvertently became a store of value.[28]

With gold functioning secondarily as a store of value, it allowed demand to be transferred through time. Under a gold exchange system, there would be the possibility of inflation and deflation cycles.[29] However, these would have been cycles—that is to say, prices would have gone up and then down but on average stayed more or less the same over very long periods of time (Fischer 1996).

The next major change in the development of money was revolutionary and came with the invention of certificates of gold deposits (Eagleton and Williams 1997). Debasement, coin clipping, and the larger monetary transactions, because of economic expansion, meant that gold coins became difficult to deal with. Each transaction required that the coins be counted, weighed, and checked for purity and authenticity besides the constant problem of security (Davies G. , 2002)

These problems led to the creation of gold depository banks. On the face of it, the development of gold depository banks and the use of gold certificates of deposit for trade appeared to be merely a mechanical change in how gold was moved between merchants. But this technical change led to an entirely new financial system and the emergence of modern-day financial instability (Ferguson 2008).

The depository banks soon observed that people did not usually redeem all their certificates at the same time and saw the opportunity to make money by issuing their own certificates of gold deposit and lending them to merchants, who in turn would buy goods and sell them at a profit and share it with gold-deposit banks. This generated income for the depository banks but left them with more gold deposit certificates on issue than reserves with which to pay them. A process was started that altered the role of the depository banks from passive guardians of bullion, charging fees for safe storage, to interest-paying and interest-earning banks. Thus fractional-reserve banking was born.

The invention of the credit creation system associated with certificates of gold deposit allowed the amplification of inflation and deflation cycles, but in the end, the certificates would be tied to a fixed quantity of gold; price volatility would increase, but there would be no trend toward ever higher prices (Eagleton and Williams 1997).

The Classical Gold Standard (1870–1914)
The stability of the pre–World War I gold standard was the result of two very different factors: credibility and cooperation (Eichengreen 1995). The credibility stemmed from the public's confidence in the government's

commitment to this policy. This credibility was further derived from the priority attached by governments to the maintenance of balance-of-payments equilibrium.

The core countries in the classical gold standard were Britain, France, and Germany. There was little doubt that the authorities in these countries would take whatever action was necessary to defend the central banks' gold reserves and maintain the convertibility of the currency into gold.

What are the main reasons for the success of the classical system? According to Gallarotti (1995), one reason is the dominant political philosophy of the day: laissez-faire, which allowed markets to "work," discouraged fiscal deficits, and favored monetary discipline. Also, the United Kingdom, as the world's dominant economic and financial power, acted beneficially for the international monetary system.

The United Kingdom also practiced free trade, allowing other countries to repay international debts in commodities rather than gold. Thus, Britain did not drain gold from debtor nations; rather, she promoted the reflow of international finance (Morgan-Webb 1934). This contrasts with the experience of the interwar gold standard when both the United States and France drained gold from other members of the system.

Understanding how the United Kingdom did not drain gold during this era starts with recognizing the City of London's role as a clearinghouse for other nations. This development emerged in light of the fact that Britain was the world's foremost trading nation coupled with the fact that other exporting countries were able to obtain trade credit from it. Furthermore, the Bank of England's willingness to rediscount the bills on behalf of discount houses—both domestic and foreign—and provide gold on demand was important for the development of England as an international financial center (Eichengreen,1995).

Exporters and importers of other nations maintained sterling balances that they converted into gold or foreign exchange as needed to settle commercial transactions. This created in London a pool of liquid assets greatly in excess of those in any foreign center (Morgan-Webb 1934). Since there was no question of the ready availability of gold at the Bank of England, foreign governments held a portion of their reserves in interest-bearing assets, to be converted into gold upon demand. London was not the only reserve center—Paris and Berlin were her chief rivals—but sterling reserves matched or exceeded the combined value of reserves denominated in other currencies (Lindert 1969, 12).

The implications of London as the center of exchange reserves was that when Britain ran a payments deficit, foreign central banks accumulating sterling claims might deposit them in London rather than presenting them to the Bank of England for conversion into gold. A balance-of-payments deficit did *not* automatically drain reserves from the Bank of England.

The Gold Standard during the Interwar Period
As I explained earlier, the two pillars for the success of the gold standard during the classical gold standard era were the credibility and the official commitment to the gold standard and international cooperation. Credibility induced financial capital to flow in stabilizing directions, supporting economic stability. Cooperation signaled support for the gold standard in times of financial crisis and transcended the resources any one country could

bring to bear. Both of these two pillars were eroded by the economic and political consequences of World War I. The decline in credibility made it virtually impossible to cooperate.

The credibility of the gold standard was based on the confidence the public had in the government's commitment to its policy. Moreover, the credibility of the gold standard was derived from the priority attached by governments to the maintenance of the balance-of-payments equilibrium (Hallwood and MacDonald 2000). There was little doubt, particularly in the core countries (Britain, France, and Germany) that governments would ultimately take whatever action was necessary to defend the central bank's gold reserves and preserve the convertibility of the currency into gold.

For example, if one of the central banks in the core countries lost gold reserves and its exchange rate weakened, funds would flow in from abroad in anticipation of the capital gains investors in domestic assets would realize once governments took measures to stem reserve losses and bolster the exchange rate (Hallwood, MacDonald, and Marsh 1996).

In the realm of domestic politics, disputes over distribution and the proper role of the state became increasingly contentious. In the international political sphere, quarrels over war debts and reparations soured the prospects of cooperation. Economics and politics together ultimately undermined the independence of central banks. This result set the stage for the Depression of the 1930s by heightening the fragility of the international financial system.

Central Banks as Lenders of Last Resort

As explained earlier, once the banking system started moving toward credit creation and fractional-reserve banking, there was no longer enough gold in the system to honor all of the outstanding certificates of gold. It soon became apparent, through repeated waves of financial crises (1873, 1884, 1893, and 1907) that this new credit generation system was highly unstable (Allen and Gale 2000). Therefore, it was clear a solution to the problem of bank runs was required.

The logical thing to do was to create an institution that would prevent trouble at one bank from spreading as a general panic throughout the entire system. The answer was a bank for banks—a central bank.[30] For the United States, after the 1907 financial crisis, the solution was the creation of the Federal Reserve System in 1913.

The idea of central banking was that in the event of a crisis, this institution would lend to a failing bank suffering from a confidence crisis, which otherwise retained a sound loan book. The role by which central banks lend to troubled private sector banks is referred to as "lender of last resort" (LLR).[31] Under this doctrine, the LLR will lend to "solvent but illiquid" banks under certain conditions.

The Bretton Woods System 1944 to 1971

As early as 1941, plans were being prepared in Britain and the United States for the postwar economy. These were heavily influenced by the experience of the 1930s, in which they had witnessed the collapse of the gold standard, the Great Depression, volatile exchange rates, trade protection, and competitive devaluations. The main monetary institution created at Bretton Woods in 1944 was the International Monetary Fund (IMF). The main objectives of the IMF were to promote exchange-rate stability and to give confidence to member countries by making available the IMF's resources with adequate safeguards (Hallwood and MacDonald 2000).

Members were required to state par values for their currencies in terms of gold and then to intervene in the foreign exchange market to keep the market exchange rate within 1 percent of the par value. In practice, members expressed par values against the U.S. dollar and the United States stood ready to convert dollars into gold at the price of $35 per ounce. This system had the characteristic of a gold exchange standard.

The main conditions necessary for the operation of the Bretton Woods System lasted only from about 1944 to 1971. The convertibility of the dollar into gold ceased in 1971, and by 1973, most major countries had renounced par values for their currencies.

The revocation of the convertibility of the U.S. dollar into gold occurred because the United States government financed its fiscal deficits accrued from the Vietnam War and the social programs of the Great Society by borrowing heavily through the open markets. This truly opened the way of literally creating money out of thin air without limitation, which made inevitable bouts of inflation and financial crises much more likely. The great inflations of the 1970s are a result of this deficit financing as well as the oil shocks from OPEC.

Fractional-Reserve Banking
Under the commercial fractional-reserve banking system, reserve requirements contain key features that determine the possibility of both contagion and systemic banking crisis (Cibils, Garcia, and Maino 2004). Credit expansion

through monetary policy can be produced through small changes in base money. This is possible because fractional-reserve requirements create an inverted pyramid—i.e., a small reserve base supports a large quantity of deposits and credit (Bordo 1985, 7).

When monetary policy authorities want to avoid recession, they reduce short-term interest rates by decreasing the reserve requirement for the deposits of commercial banks. This intervention generates confidence and euphoria, which results in greater expansion of credit and the money supply through the multiplying power of the small change in the reserve ratio.[32]

Conversely, when the phase of increase in the credit expansion reverses, the inverted pyramid plays havoc with the system because, in turn, a small fraction reduction on the monetary base reduces credit and money supply by a multiple (Mishkin 1995). This inherent instability in the system of fractional-reserve requirement, coupled with easy credit availability, debt leveraging, and speculation will most likely culminate in recurring financial crises.

The solution for this inherent instability of the fractional-reserve systems in the commercial financial system has been more strict regulation through the central banks.[33] However, this merely delays resolution of the crisis. This dilemma was best expressed by Sjaastad (1997): "Both deposit insurance and the lender of last of resort facility offered by central banks have evolved as devices to stabilize an inherently unstable institution: fractional reserve banking." Most of the banking systemic problems are due to a combination of fractional-reserve requirements, deposit insurance, and moral hazard (Merton and Bodie 1993).

There are, however, several advantages the fractional-reserve banking offers. First, the fractional-reserve system allows banks to act as intermediaries that facilitate the movement of funds from savers to investors in a society.[34] There are also significant economies of scale in banks making investment and lending decisions, as they have access to knowledge and expertise that individual investors or lenders generally do not (Whelan 2009). Without fractional-reserve banking, a great deal of money would sit idle, as savers stored up their money, while entrepreneurs went without much-needed capital.

Secondly, fractional-reserve banking provides regulators with power tools for manipulating the money supply and interest rates, which is essential for conducting monetary policies (Mankiw 2007).

Lastly, fractional-reserve banking permits either the central bank or commercial banks to create money at will, allowing the money supply to adjust to changing demand for money.

Less Speculation

Islamic finance does *not* allow trading present money in return for future money. All Islamic modes of finance involve money on one side and goods or services on the other side of a transaction. Put differently, Islamic finance removes the classical dichotomy between monetary and real economic activities. This naturally leaves little room for excessive credit expansion. Speculative activities related to interest rate expectations would no longer be a factor.

According to one of the leading scholars of Islamic finance, Dr. Umer Chapra, this debt-constraining feature of Islamic finance is the most persuasive argument for Islamic banks being more stable in comparison to conventional banks (Chapra, U. M. 2002). This means that the consequences from the impact of debt leveraging during periods of boom and bust would be more intense.

In particular, with regard to the impact from financial deleveraging when the bubbles burst, the debt- and speculation-constraining features of Islamic finance will mitigate the resultant price deflation of financial assets and cushion equity capital during periods of liquidity and financial crises when it is needed the most.[35] The *Shari'a* law discourages the use of financial derivatives—since the activities of Islamic finance are limited to real transactions—so the adverse magnifying effect of financial derivatives would be significantly mitigated under Islamic finance.

Critics of the ban of derivatives by Islamic finance point to the inability of Islamic financial institutions to *hedge* against certain uncertainties as a hindrance compared to a non-Islamic or conventional financial institution. They argue, strictly limiting speculation could be counterproductive, because speculation may help to stabilize markets or even be necessary for stabilization. For example, if prices for a particular market are plummeting, speculators expecting a recovery at a later date might help to reverse the price movement. However, advocates of Islamic finance, even in the narrow case of hedging, are firm in their belief that the use of derivatives is a form *gharar.*

This type of destabilizing speculation that Islamic finance prohibits was evident during the global financial crisis of 2007 to 2008 when the Securities and Exchange Commission (SEC) issued a temporary ban on short sales of 799 financial stocks on September 19, 2008.[36] The SEC took this unusual action to mitigate the speculative trading of large hedge funds by people who wanted to profit from the financial crisis by betting against bank shares. Incidentally, the United Kingdom also issued a similar temporary ban on shorting bank stocks a day earlier than the SEC.

Overall, it seems the conservative approach of Islamic finance makes booms and busts less likely. Adoption of this approach entails the suboptimal ability of Islamic banks to manage credit and market risks.

Protection from Financial Crises

Islamic banking eliminates the problem of fractional-reserve requirements by mandating a 100 percent reserve requirement for all current or demand deposits (demand deposits are mainly for safekeeping purposes, and the banks guarantee the principal because of the 100 percent reserve provision). However, investment deposits are placed on a profit-and-loss sharing (PLS) basis. When such a bank faces macroeconomic or bank-specific shocks, investment depositors automatically share the risk. The bank is less likely to fail, and bank runs are less probable.

Yet, despite the benefit of risk reduction that PLS offers, Islamic banks are not immune to financial crises or failure. PLS banking can to some extent protect a bank against interest rate risk and credit risk, but not against operational risk. Problems from computer systems/software or fraudulent behavior of a bank's officers can cause serious losses. Even if insolvency is less of a problem for PLS banking, there is little to prevent liquidity problems.

For example, if a bank's liabilities have on average a shorter duration than its assets, and depositors decide to move their funds to other banks because of poor yields, rumors about investments turning sour or doubts about the integrity of the bank's management could trigger a liquidity crisis.

Bank failures in Islamic banking occurred when a number of less-than-trustworthy individuals lured many unsuspecting investors—touting the banner of Islamic banking—to deposit their money with them and then used those funds for risky non-*Shari'a*-compliant investments. The Bank of Credit and Commerce International (BCCI) had promised to invest the funds deposited by other Islamic financial institutions in *Shari'a*-compliant commodity contracts. After the collapse of the BCCI, it turned out that they had failed to do so (Grais and Pellegrini 2006, 8). Apparently, this also escaped the attention of their *Shari'a* board.

Non-Islamic banks are also more vulnerable because they carry liabilities, including demand, time, and savings deposits, which they fully guarantee. Their assets, however, are mainly risky debt. Default on the asset side of a bank, if it happens on significant proportions, would imply an inability to meet the bank's obligations on the liability side. Such a default can be expected at times of crisis, whether bank-specific or macroeconomic in nature.

Unlike non-Islamic banks, Islamic banks cannot create credit out of thin air.[37] Money cannot be issued without a link to production of goods and services. Investment is equal to savings, and the aggregate supply of goods and services is always equal to the aggregate demand. Under this setting, bank runs and wild speculations are highly unlikely since the credit creation process is severely curtailed.

The liabilities of Islamic banks correspond to tangible real assets directly owned by the banks and not to financial assets.

The end result is lower risks for Islamic financial institutions since their investment returns are from investment operations and not from their capital (Khan 1987).

Under the commercial fractional-reserve banking interest-based system, the financing of investment and ownership of capital assets, as well as of consumer spending, is carried out primarily through borrowing and lending, whereby a structure of anticipated cash flows represents the various commitments to make payments on existing debt. The liabilities on the books of an economic entity at any time are the result of past financing positions that are taken on the basis of various margins of safety, one of which is that anticipated receipts will exceed expected payment commitments.

Therefore, given this premise, there are three likely possibilities. One is an economic entity that in every period of its operations will have cash flows that are expected to exceed its contractual commitments of outstanding debt and interest payments.

Another possibility is the case where an economic entity's short-term payment commitments exceed its expected cash flow receipts even though the total expected cash flow (totaled over the foreseeable future) exceeds the total payments on outstanding debt and the net income position of the short-term cash flow exceeds the short-term interest payments on debts.

Lastly, a third situation may arise in which, not only do the short-term payment commitments exceed the cash flow, but the short-term payment commitments on outstanding debt also exceed the income components of the short-term cash flow.

Under the commercial interest-based financial system, there is a tendency on the part of the economic units (i.e., consumers, firms, banks, and governments) to increasingly assume the scenarios of the last two cases, where economic entities can meet their payment commitments by borrowing or selling assets. Since appreciation of an asset constitutes a portion of returns on that asset, the tendency is to refinance or roll over debt rather than sell assets (assuming this is an environment of rising asset pricing—which is likely to be the case in an expansionary phase).

Hyman Minsky labeled the three cases I described as *hedge, speculative,* and *Ponzi finance* respectively.[38] Hedge financing units are those that can fulfill all of their contractual payment obligations with their cash flow. Speculative finance units are units that can meet their payment commitments on "income account" on their liabilities, even as they cannot repay the principal out of income cash flows. For Ponzi units, the cash flow from operations is not sufficient to cover either the repayment of principal or the interest on outstanding debts. The financial difficulty economic units will face will be much worse than when the economy is in recession or during a deflationary period.

Finally, and more important, no debt refinancing takes place on an interest basis. If there is any refinancing, it must be on the basis of profit sharing of future income expected from assets. In an Islamic system, the danger of insolvency arises from economic units only if their revenues fall short of their out-of-pocket expenses and commitments. Such a situation is likely to occur due to poor management or extraneous economic factors but is not inherent in their financial system.

It is interesting and noteworthy that in response to the Great Depression, during the 1930s, a group of economists mostly affiliated with the University of Chicago, launched a proposal for an alternative banking reform currently known as "narrow banking."[39]

The global financial crisis that started on August 2007 crippled the economies of many advanced countries. Trillions of taxpayer dollars were used to bail out long-established banking institutions that were considered too big to fail because of the systemic risk such failure posed. The price paid for this financial crisis also included frozen credit markets that triggered an unexpected crash in stock markets, wiping out trillions of dollars in equity values and severely impacting the wealth and retirement investments of hundreds of millions individuals and firms.

Even though there is an ongoing debate as to the causes of the recent global financial crisis, there is wide consensus that loose money supply, excessive debt leverage, and speculation from the securitization of complex derivative financial instruments were among the key factors responsible for the crisis. Strict adherence to the principles of Islamic finance, as stated earlier, is less likely to have allowed the conditions that enabled most of the occurrence of the financial crisis.

This does not mean that Islamic finance is immune to financial crises. For example, the speculative boom in real estate financed by many Islamic banks in the United Arab Emirates and Qatar adversely impacted these banks during the financial crisis in 2008 (IMF 2009, 11). Furthermore, many Islamic banks in the GCC countries suffered from concentration risk because most of their portfolios were predominately in real estate and construction activities. Despite these losses suffered by Islamic banks, they were relatively and significantly less costly to investors and taxpayers of the countries in comparison to losses suffered in Europe and the United States.

Because Islamic banks would focus on profit-and-loss sharing investments rather than loaning money upon interest, for any given risk, theoretically, Islamic banks would be more experienced in profit-sharing investments than comparative commercial banks. (Here, I am focusing on commercial banks.) In so far as economies of scale are important, Islamic banks should be attractive to customers, whether Muslim or non-Muslim, who wish to obtain a relatively higher return on their investments.

2. Islamic Finance Promotes Efficiency

Conventional finance allocates financial resources with paramount regard to the borrower's ability to repay loan principal and interest. In modes of Islamic finance that are based on equity and profit sharing, the focus would be on the profitability and rate of return of the concerned investment. This type of finance for long-term projects conceptually has the potential to direct financial resources to the most productive investments.

Defining Efficiency

Efficiency is an important factor for banks to take into consideration to remain competitive. Islamic banks are no exception, with increased competition from non-Islamic banks, despite often only having a few Islamic banks within any one country. Efficiency can be defined as the relative performance of a bank given its input or output compared to other banks with the same input or output limitations.

Thus, we expect more efficient firms will produce more output from a given set of inputs.

One way to measure the efficiency of a bank is to give the most efficient bank in a sample a score of 1 (or 100 percent). Other banks in the sample are compared relative to the best bank and will often have an efficiency score of less than 1. However, the traditional measurement of efficiency for banks is the cost-to-income ratio. For banks to maximize efficiency, they have to minimize costs as much as possible.

Using this traditional method, a recent study found Islamic banks had higher cost-to-income ratios (Brown, Hassan, and Skully 2007; table 7.1 is a reproduction of their findings). For the years 2001 to 2003, Islamic banks had higher cost-to-income ratios of approximately 70 percent. According to Brown at el. (2007), this could be due to the higher costs Islamic banks are expected to incur in the initial years of equity investments in new projects compared to conventional banks. However, over time, the expected returns will, one hopes, be higher and related costs lower. For conventional banks, the measure attained for this ratio was around 55 to 60 percent, which is considered quite low.

This conservative structure is due to the requirement of Islamic *Shari'a* as well as the fact that Islamic banks are more exposed to business risks than conventional banks (since Islamic banks predominately focus on profit-loss-sharing activities). The equity/total assets ratio from 2003 to 1998 has a constant difference of approximately 4.5 percent. Because of this higher equity capital, Islamic banks generally have lower profitability and return on average assets.

Table 6.1

Aggregate Performance Data for Eleven Countries: Islamic Versus Conventional Banks 1998–2003

			2003	2002	2001	2000	1999	1998
Structure	Capital funds/ Liabilities	Islamic	20.10	23.64	62.26	35.98	42.90	46.00
		Conventional	13.50	18.66	16.29	17.22	15.93	15.54
	Equity/Total Assets	Islamic	15.40	18.49	20.77	20.22	21.62	20.08
		Conventional	10.88	11.60	11.48	11.80	10.55	12.34
Liquidity	Liquid assets/ customer and ST funding	Islamic	33.46	35.52	66.83	42.13	40.31	42.93
		Conventional	46.00	52.92	63.68	55.06	55.45	54.60
Lending	Net loans/ total assets	Islamic	54.28	50.71	53.58	53.81	50.52	50.79
		Conventional	44.28	39.96	40.72	42.18	43.41	44.38
	Net loans/ Customer and ST funding	Islamic	74.30	66.72	99.09	85.85	81.09	111.04
		Conventional	56.81	50.46	50.60	51.85	54.51	58.30
Performance	Cost to Income ratio	Islamic	81.06	60.71	73.30	54.12	58.38	58.94
		Conventional	52.89	60.23	67.53	63.47	62.42	58.29
Profitability	Return on average equity	Islamic	12.04	12.44	6.76	17.48	14.82	13.05
		Conventional	15.04	8.42	1.46	9.76	11.56	12.78
	Return on average assets	Islamic	2.22	2.37	2.35	2.96	1.76	1.47
		Conventional	1.63	1.00	0.22	0.74	(0.02)	0.98

Other Empirical Studies on the Efficiency of Islamic Banks

An efficiency study on the Sudanese Islamic banks alone (note that the Sudanese financial system is Islamic in nature) found that the decline in efficiency was attributed to poorer use of technology and not operating at sufficient size or scale to be optimally efficient in the presence of scale economies (Hassan and Hussien 2003).[40]

Another study using a panel of Islamic banks from twenty-two countries and multiple efficiency techniques, including parametric and nonparametric methods, found that the average cost efficiency of Islamic banks was 74 percent for the twenty-two countries in the study, whilst the average profit efficiency was 84 percent (Hassan, M. 2005). This suggests that the Islamic banks could improve efficiency mostly through cost cutting.

Furthermore, this study examined allocative efficiency (Hassan, M. 2005) and found empirical support that Islamic banks were less efficient than conventional banks in relation to the way resources were allocated rather than the use of technology. Reasons suggested for such results were that Islamic banks often face regulation not conducive to Islamic transactions in most countries. This further weakens the potential comparative advantage in efficiency Islamic banks expect.

Taking into consideration specific environmental differences for each country, Brown and Skully (2004) conducted a cost-efficiency study. They found Sudanese banks had the lowest cost efficiency, as could be expected, which related to agricultural financing rather than cost-plus-type transactions for retail expenditure; however, they had higher compensating net margins. At the regional level, Middle Eastern Islamic banks were the most cost-efficient followed by Asian and then African banks.

So, even though conceptually, Islamic banks should have an efficiency advantage in comparison to non-Islamic banks, in reality, they face many obstacles that hinder the realization of their potential.

3. Islamic Banks Reduce Moral Hazard and Adverse Selection
As discussed in chapter 4, Islamic banks take equity positions in *musharaka* contracts and trade in goods and services in their non-profit-and-loss contracts (see figure 4.1) and therefore are similar in operation to universal

banks, which are a hybrid between commercial and investment banks. Universal banks are defined as "large-scale banks that operate extensive networks of branches, provide many different services, hold several claims on firms (including equity and debt), and participate directly in the corporate governance of the firms that rely on the banks as sources of funding or as securities underwriters" (Calomiris 2000).

A bank can be exposed to a *moral hazard* when the firm obtaining finance uses the funds for purposes other than those for which finance was advanced. This could lead to business failure and inability to repay on the part of the debtor firm. The bank would be exposed to *adverse selection* when it fails to choose finance applicants who are most likely to perform.

Obviously, adverse selection can be avoided by careful screening of finance applicants. When a bank provides equity and debt finance simultaneously, it will have more access to information than when only debt finance is provided. So, it is more likely that Islamic banks would be more effective in screening investment projects or proposals and reduce adverse impact from moral hazard and adverse selection.[41]

Monitoring the activities of firms is a prerequisite for reducing the possibilities of a moral hazard for a firm seeking financing (Aoki 1994). Equity finance provides the bank with access to information necessary to practice monitoring at all intervals. It also reduces firm incentives to substitute riskier for safer assets. Meanwhile, debt finance would reduce the firm's incentives to hide its profits. Furthermore, when the firm faces problems, the bank, as an equity holder, will assist in order to protect its investment. In short, banking theory indicates that universal banking is more likely to be exposed to lower levels of moral hazard and adverse selection in general.

On the other hand, companies depend upon banks for short-term funding either because banks hold equity shares or sit on their board of directors, which could insulate these firms from short-term financial pressures. However, as it turned out, in Japan in the 1990s, the root of the economic malaise was the easy credit given by government-guaranteed banks to businesses with whom they had cozy relationships (Krugman 2009).[42]

Empirical evidence has shown that when insiders control the investment decision making of a firm, increases in a bank's ownership of the funded firm's equity increased investment efficiency and reduced the risk of the bank's portfolio (John, John, and Saunders 1994).[43] The risk from increasing the bank's equity investment in the firm is offset by the likely reduction in debt-leverage ratio because of cash infusion from the bank's additional investments.

This empirical evidence is in support of the profit-loss-sharing Islamic mode of financing—equity partnership (*musharaka*)—where the bank has access to information about the operations of the firm and is able to monitor its activities at a lower cost and yet offer advice to the firm's management without dictating how it should be run. Of course, the caveat here is the assumption that monitoring costs are outweighed by the reduction in the risk exposure from moral hazard and adverse selection.

4. The Growth Implications of Islamic Finance
The essential characteristic of Islamic modes of financing is their direct link to real economic activities or transactions. Mirakhor (1988) defined an Islamic financial system as

one in which there are no risk-free assets and where all financial arrangements are based on risk and profit-loss-sharing (PLS). Thus, all financial assets are contingent claims and there are no debt instruments with fixed or floating interest rates.

In his seminal working paper, Abbas Mirakhor modeled the financial system as nonspeculative equity shares and showed that the rate of return to financial assets is essentially determined by the return to the real sector (Mirakhor 1988). This means that in a growing economy, Islamic banks will have positive net returns, at least in theory.

Another theoretical factor in support of higher growth under Islamic finance is the moral inculcation from the *Qur'an* and *Sunna* that discourages engagement in speculative economic activities, debt leveraging investment in financial assets, short-selling, leverage buyouts (LBOs), and speculative trading of complex derivative instruments also known as "proprietary trading"—Goldman Sachs and J.P. Morgan Chase being the best known firms engaged in this activity. So, the teachings of Islam that instill in Muslims superior values have the potential of directing their behavior toward more productive economic activities—real transactions, hence allowing them to avoid transactions that are exclusively financial in nature (Kuran 1995).

Expressed differently, Islamic finance is a smaller subset of the contracts than is possible under conventional finance. In general, agents with no restrictions in their economic decision-making are more likely to be sub-optimally prudent. This tendency is a form of bounded rationality that is likely to occur under laissez-faire because, in general, people cognitively use heuristics to make unrestricted decisions. Niall Ferguson aptly expressed this tendency in his best seller *The Ascent of Money* as follows:

> If the financial system has a defect, it is that it reflects and magnifies what we human beings are like. As we are learning from a growing volume of research in the field of behavioral finance, money amplifies our tendency to overreact, to swing from exuberance when things are going well to deep depression when they go wrong. (Ferguson 2008, 13)

One of the heuristics associated with conventional finance is excessive risk-taking. This means that left on their own, agents under conventional financial systems would be more likely to shun, sub-optimally, the prudence instilled by Islamic finance.

In contrast to conventional finance, Islamic finance is not centered only on creditworthiness and ability to repay loans and their return. The key in Islamic financing is the worth and profitability of a project and the exchange of goods and services. On the other hand, the ability to recover the financing principal becomes a by-product of the profitability and value of the project itself. It is a necessary condition in Islamic financing, but not sufficient.

Increase in Participation of the Official Financial System
There are many people in Islamic countries who, because of their strong religious orientation, would avoid using interest-based banking systems. So, if an Islamic bank opens a branch in their neighborhood, this might be all the incentive they need to enter the world of formal finance (Scheepens 1996). This was in fact the underlying reason for the creation of Turkey's Islamic Finance Houses in 1983 (Jang 2005, 141).

In this way, Islamic banks in these countries can contribute to a higher degree of financial intermediation, which both economic theory and econometric research say generally fosters economic development (Levine 2004; Ang 2008). Islamic investment funds may fulfill a similar role. These banks also offer an alternative for non-Muslims seeking ethical investment opportunities.

Other empirical studies similarly support the theory that development of financial markets and increased financial intermediation promote real economic growth by enhancing the quantity, quality, and efficiency of investments (Greenwood and Smith 1997). Many economists have maintained that the development and efficiency of the financial system are closely linked to economic growth and have pointed out various channels through which the financial system affects economic growth (Levine 2004).

Most of the empirical studies on the subject find a positive relationship between the development of the financial sector and economic growth (see King and Levine 1993a; King and Levine 1993b; Levine, Loayza, and Beck 1999). One way to study the role of the financial sector in the economy and its impact on growth is to examine the functions the sector performs and the implications these functions have on growth.

Ross Levine (1997) identified the functions of a financial system that generate economic growth as those that "facilitate the trading, hedging, diversifying, and pooling of risk; allocating resources; monitor managers and exert corporate control; mobilize savings, and facilitate the exchange of goods and services." p. 691. These functions enhance growth through innovation. Even though financial systems and structures may differ, these basic functions are common to all systems and spur growth in the economy.

A financial system can be analyzed at four levels (Merton and Bodie 1995, 16–20). The first is the system level: that is, a country's entire financial system. The second is at the institution level. At this level, different services are identified. The third level relates to the *activity* level in which the activities of financial institutions are elaborated. Activities would, for example, include lending, leasing, or equity financing. The fourth level concerns products; this is where the financial products or instruments are identified and discussed. At this level, the specific contracts used for financial transactions in different activities are studied.

Islamic Banks' Close Similarity to Universal Banks
The nature of financial intermediation and the style of financial products and services offered by Islamic financial institutions make them a hybrid between commercial and investment banks and similar to universal banks. Universal banks are known to benefit from the economies of scope because of information obtained in their close relationship with clients.

Several economists believe that universal banking can be credited in part for industrial development and economic growth in Germany and Japan, thanks to the economies of scope and greater efficiency that allowed more finance at lower costs (Folin 1998).

Calomiris (2000), through his study of pre-First World War Germany, has found that universal banking served to reduce the cost of financing industrialization in Germany relative to the corresponding levels in other countries where commercial banking was prevalent. He also found that the financial sector reached a higher level of allocative efficiency in universal banking than in commercial banking. So, Islamic banks, if efficiently operated and managed, could potentially attain higher levels of economic growth.

This does not mean that all countries with universal banks are more likely to have higher economic growth. The case of Japan is an example of what can happen when the banking supervisory authorities fail to write off nonperforming loans on a timely basis. The end result is the creation of the so-called "zombie banks." This was a major contributing factor to Japan's bad economic performance in the 1990s. Some economists refer to this phenomenon as the "lost decade" (Krugman 2009).

This means that banks operating under universal banking can lead to suboptimal economic performance if timely and prudent supervisory measures are not taken. The East Asian financial crisis in 1997 was triggered in large part by lax supervision and the authorities' failure to properly close many banks carrying large amounts of bad loans in their books. Oppressive or stifling banking regulations could also lead to inefficient resource allocation and lower economic growth. Attaining an optimal level of supervision is an art, which requires skill, experience, and constant reevaluation and research.

B. Challenges of Islamic Finance
Just as the role and basic functions of financial systems are universal, so too are the problems that are encountered in performing these functions. However, there are differences in the way they are handled.

1. High Monitoring and Verification Costs
As I explained in section A.2, the need to monitor the activities of entrepreneurs funded by Islamic banks under a profit-and-loss-sharing basis exposes them to the

risks of moral hazard and adverse selection because of asymmetric information. Reducing these risk exposures imposes additional costs on Islamic banks. The moral hazard problem arises when the entrepreneur's conduct changes after the receipt of the funds from the bank. In the profit-and-loss-sharing mode of financing, moral hazard problems are similar to those found in agency relationships (Iqbal and Llewellyn 2002). In particular, the moral hazard problem arises in this setup if the agent misuses the funds, slacks off on the management of the firm, or deceptively understates the profit of the enterprise (Mishkin 1995, 128).

In addition, investments or projects Islamic banks finance under a profit-and-loss-sharing basis are also exposed to the risks associated with the principal-agent problem. This problem can be resolved if the principal can gather more information on the operations of the firm. One way of doing this is by monitoring. Monitoring, however, is costly in terms of both time and money. Islamic banks' encouragement and emphasis on profit-and-loss-based contracts that incur monitoring costs will further impose an adverse effect on their profitability compared to commercial banks, all else being equal.[44]

A negative externality, which arises from lack of adequate information about the behavior of entrepreneurs or the operations of firms in which an Islamic bank is an equity investor, is the possibility that entrepreneurs will waste or fraudulently misuse funds provided by the bank. Alternatively, the invested firm could suffer huge losses or go bankrupt. There is no assurance, even with the incurrence of high verification costs, that depositors or investors in Islamic banks would have sufficient information to see and understand how a bank is performing before it is too late.

Even *Shari'a* boards and large depositors can be misled, let alone small depositors. Several large Islamic financial institutions had deposited large amounts of money with BCCI (Bank of Credit and Commerce International) but were unable to see its collapse coming in 1991 (Grais and Pellegrini 2006, 8).

Bookkeeping of small and medium enterprises in many countries Islamic banks operate in are often elementary, which works against the use of profit-and-loss-sharing (PLS) modes of financing (*musharaka* and *mudaraba*). The problem Islamic banks have when funding small and medium enterprises on a profit-and-loss basis is further aggravated by the desire of entrepreneurs or firms to avoid the close monitoring implied by PLS partnerships (Visser 2009).

Moral hazard applies as much to religious or ethical organizations as to non-Islamic businesses. According to some scholars, stricter regulation indeed might be warranted because some crooks tend to seek cover in ethical or religious shelters (Warde 2005).

2. Risk of Shari'a Noncompliance

Rationalizing those areas of Islamic law that relate to commerce and other financial activities in order to create a legal framework for Islamic banking is not all that simple (Vogel and Hayes 1998). First, there is the provisional nature of much of Islamic jurisprudence (*fiqh*), which relies as much on the interpretive skills of individual Islamic jurists extrapolating from both primary and secondary sources (see chapter 7) as it does the principal tenets enshrined in *Shari'a* law (Vogel and Hayes 1998).

Divergences of opinion between the different schools of Islamic law (also covered in chapter 7) further complicate interpreting *Shari'a* law, as do different methodologies that may be called upon when elaborating the law. Since the emergence of contemporary Islamic financial markets a few decades ago, the institution of *fatwa*, which means a legal opinion issued by a qualified *mufti* (jurist-consultant) has been one of its key features (Hegazy 2005). Islamic financial institutions increasingly rely on *fatwas* as a source of regulation for the *Shari'a* aspect of their practice. There are inherent risks in relying on a *fatwa*-based regulatory system in today's Islamic financial markets.

This inherent risk in the *fatwas* issued by *Shari'a* scholars is not their willingness to take into account *maqasid al-Shari'a* (the objectives of *Shari'a*) but that they lack the exposure (experience in banking and financial markets) and/or knowledge of other related disciplines, such as economic analysis, psychology, sociology, political science, and management (Siddiqi 2007, 99–107).

What all this means is that, when it comes to modern financial activities, Islamic jurisprudence lacks certain consistency and predictability, unlike more codified systems of laws and edicts. Given the lack of standardization in *Shari'a* standards and rulings, Islamic banks and other nonbank financial institutions are susceptible to having their new financial products be ruled out as noncompliant with Islamic law. This risk exposure slows down product innovation, but more important, it could adversely impact their reputation.

Scholars in the Arab world considered their Malaysian counterparts to be a bit too lax in their religious interpretations and held that Islamic institutions, in their rush to grow, were cutting too many corners (Warde 2007).

Legal scholars, including those on *Shari'a* boards of Islamic banks, disagree on many key points. Institutions with sufficient authority to make universally accepted definitions do not yet govern Islamic finance. That is why the recent efforts to build regulatory frameworks at the Islamic Financial Standards Board (IFSB) and the Islamic International Rating Agency (IIRA) are such a significant step forward.

3. Less Profitability due to Higher Liquidity Balances

The constraints imposed by the *Shari'a* guidelines on Islamic banks to hold approximately 100 percent reserve requirements for current accounts (demand deposits for safekeeping and savings), which is mostly cash, means greater opportunity cost compared to that of commercial banks since they are not available to finance transactions with predetermined fixed returns, such as *murabaha* (markup financing) or *ijara* (leasing). Given this constraint, the funds accumulating in these accounts can be used to manage the banks' liquidity needs for short-term purposes only, which the bank is fully responsible for (Iqbal and Mirakhor 2007).

Furthermore, due to the prohibition of interest, Islamic banks are unable to invest these liquid funds in overnight current accounts for short durations in safe and liquid financial instruments. This limitation further worsens Islamic banks' competitive disadvantage.[45] Given that depositors of current accounts do not receive remuneration, Islamic banks provide a broad range of services to these customers, such as payment facilities, clearing mechanisms, bank drafts, bills of exchange, and traveler's checks at no charge (Algaoud and Lewis 2001, 47).

The upside of the higher liquidity balances and reserves is that Islamic banks have equity capital that can withstand liquidity or financial crises in contrast to commercial banks.

4. Lack of Good Governance, Institutional Capacity, and Human Capital

Another major obstacle Islamic banks face is that most Muslim countries lack the institutional infrastructure and legal framework required for the protection of property rights and the enforcement of contracts that are taken for granted in most countries where conventional finance dominates.

Chronic fiscal and monetary problems, lack of skilled human capital, and corruption further undermine Islamic countries' capacity to regulate and supervise the operations of Islamic banks. In many of these countries, fiscal deficits are financed through the banking system. To lower these costs of financing, the financial system is repressed by artificially maintaining limits on bank rates. This financial repression is a form of taxation, which provides governments with substantial revenue.

Efficient operation of system-wide banking in these countries is further severely constrained by distortions in the economy. There are several factors that impede the efficient operation of an Islamic financial system. These include pervasive government intervention and controls, inefficient and weak tax systems, and the lack of capital markets.

These distortions need to be eliminated to minimize waste and for the economy to efficiently allocate scarce resources. Their removal before or in conjunction with the adoption of Islamic banking can be expected to create the dynamics necessary for a sustainable and noninflationary economic growth.

5. Misperception and Confusion about Islamic Banking

Many people don't understand Islamic banking; this includes both Muslims and non-Muslims. The fact that

Shari'a boards, which oversee transactions in relation to Islamic law, often operate at the individual bank's level can lead to many interpretations of what is and what is not a suitable "Islamic" transaction. Although there have been many attempts to standardize *Shari'a* interpretations, there are still many differences among *Shari'a* scholars in their interpretations. Yet, despite efforts at explaining Islamic finance, some have complained of the opacity that makes it difficult to fully appreciate its risk exposure (Warde 2007).

Islamic financial institutions as they exist today are disadvantaged because they operate under what seems to be conflicting logics. Unlike secular systems, the legal rules of Islam incorporate both economic and religious logic.

The problems arising from confusion and misperceptions will not disappear until Islamic finance develops analytical models and theoretical foundations in economics and finance that distinguish it from conventional economics and finance. Without a solution to this challenge, Islamic finance is in danger of being marginalized as a small subset of the conventional financial system.

C. Conclusion

I have developed in this chapter the notion that Islamic banks' main advantage lies in being more stable compared to commercial banks, provided they are not labeled "Islamic" in name only. However, for Islamic banks to fully realize their potential, Muslim scholars and financial experts must overcome the constraining challenges I have enumerated in this chapter, if they aspire to present a viable alternative to the existing inherently unstable and dominant financial system.

Endnotes

28. Gold as a store of value allowed individuals the capacity to hold purchasing power over time.

29. For example, if a farmer harvested a lot of wheat in a season, the chances would be good that other farmers had a good harvest season too. If every farmer tried to sell at the same time, there would be too much wheat chasing too little gold, and pretty soon, you would have wheat deflation, or gold inflation, depending on your perspective.

30. Another solution was the creation of deposit insurance.

31. For more information on the concept of LLR, see J. C. Rochet, *Why Are There so Many Banking Crises?* (Princeton, NJ: University of Princeton, 2008).

32. For a detailed explanation of the money creation process, see J. Tobin (1965).

33. "Lender of last resort" was born out of a need to manage the innate instability of the fractional-reserve banking system; for a historical account perspective, see W. Bagehot, *Lombard Street: A Description of the Money Market* (London: H. S. King, 1873) and H. Thorton,, *An Enquiry into the Nature and Effects of the Paper Credit of Great Britain* (London: Hatchard, 1802).

34. If banks did not lend out their available funds after meeting their reserve requirements, depositors might have to pay banks to provide safekeeping services for their money.

35. During a liquidity crisis, firms and investors all attempt at the same time to sell illiquid financial assets so as to obtain funds to service their debts or roll over short-term borrowings. Most financial institutions, being in need of liquidity for their own operations, refuse to extend credit, causing more bankruptcies and triggering a deflationary cycle.

36. "SEC Temporarily Blocks Short Sales of Financial Stocks," *New York Times*, Business Section (September 20, 2008).

37. This is, as explained earlier, the commercial banks' ability to extend credit through small changes in the reserve ratios and the associated money-multiplying power.

38. Hyman P. Minsky, *Stabilizing an Unstable Economy* (Yale University Press, 1986).

39. Phillips (1995) extensively discusses the background and details of the Chicago proposal for banking reform. It should also be noted that Simons (1933) cites the Bank Charter Act of 1844 for the Bank of England (known as Peel's Act) as the original source of the Chicago Plan. This act separated the Bank of England into money issuing and lending departments and implemented the proposal of Ricardo's "Plan for the Establishment of a National Bank" (1851). Note: this footnote was obtained from V. Cibils, V. Garcia, and R. Maino, "Remedy for Banking Crisis: What Chicago and Islam Have in Common," *Islamic Economic Studies* (March 2004): 2–3.

40. See Davis and Lewis (1982); Lewis and Davis (1987), chapter 7, for an analysis of scale economies in banking.

41. This is similar to how venture capital firms finance new entrepreneurs or existing enterprises that need funding for new products or innovations.

42. Members of Japanese *keiretsu*—groups of allied firms organized around a main bank—typically owned substantial quantities of each other's shares, making management largely independent of the outside stockholders.

43. However, the results are more mixed in the case where the bank exercises more control (i.e., the bank has veto power over risky projects proposed by corporate management).

44. Since the quality and timeliness of financial data in most Islamic countries are poor, there will be greater need on the part of Islamic banks to undertake costly audits and other information-gathering activities.

45. According to a June 2009 report released by the International Islamic Rating Agency (IIRA) titled "Liquidity Assessment of Islamic Banks," at the end of 2007, the Islamic banks it evaluated were holding an average of 47 percent of their balance sheets in liquid assets.

The Origins and Evolution of Islamic Law and Finance

Of all the many religions, Islam is the only one today that requires banking and other financial activities to be carried out in a way that is compatible with its laws. Other religions, such as Judaism and Christianity, have similar ethical standards, but today the concept of interest goes largely unquestioned.[46]

Many countries prohibited "usury" by law for many centuries. In the Middle Ages, while Catholic Canon law forbade the use of interest, this did not apply to Jews. Whilst the Torah condemns interest, this was interpreted as meaning between Jews, and Jews became renowned as moneylenders, even helping to fund many national purses.

Modern conventional modes of banking date back to the Industrial Revolution of more than two and half centuries ago.[47] Up to that time, the merchants, moneylenders, and goldsmiths provided embryonic financial services.

A. Historic Origins of Islam to the Present

Prophet Mohammad was born in Mecca in what is now Saudi Arabia in AD 570 into a regionally prominent tribe known as Quraysh (Jackson-Moore 2009, 2). Following the death of his father and mother, Prophet Mohammad was brought up first by his grandfather Abdul-Muttalib and after his grandfather's death, by his uncle Abu Talib.

At the age of forty, while retreating to a lonely cave on Mount Hira for solitude and contemplation during the month of Ramadan, he was shaken to find himself in the presence of the angel Gabriel, who ordered him to recite[48] words. Angel Gabriel began to appear to the Prophet on a regular basis. Gradually, Prophet Mohammad gathered around him a small band of followers, but his tribe, Quraysh, became very hostile to him since he preached for people to abandon their worship of idols and instead worship only the one God.

Eventually, Quraysh persecuted Prophet Mohammad and his followers, and when the persecution became too severe, the Prophet and his followers left Mecca and migrated to Medina, where the inhabitants welcomed them. This was in AD 622, and the year of migration (*hijrah*) marks the first year of the Muslim calendar, which is represented by the letters "ah" (after *hijrah*).

Prophet Mohammad lived between the years AD 570 and 632, which is approximately some fifteen centuries ago. The major division in Islam would occur as a result of political differences over whether the leader of the Muslim community should always be a descendent of the family of Ali ibn Abu Talib (AD 595–660), the Prophet's cousin, or not. This gave birth to the Shi'a sect of Islam (this will be discussed in greater detail later in this chapter).

After the Prophet's death in AD 632, the leadership of the Muslim community passed to his great friend and companion, Abu Bakr, the first of the four "rightly guided" caliphs (successors of the Prophet) (Hallaq 1997). Over the next five hundred years, Islam continued to expand through sub-Saharan Africa and Asia Minor, and through the Moors to Southern Spain.

Bernard Lewis, author of *What Went Wrong? Western Impact & Middle Eastern Response* notes that Islamic power was at its peak from the ninth through to the thirteenth centuries. During this era, Islam represented "the greatest military power on earth—its armies, at the very same time, were invading Europe and Africa, India and China. It was the foremost economic power in the world [and] it had achieved the highest level so far in human history in the arts and sciences of civilizations."p.6.

The extraordinary enterprise represented by Muslim scholarship, science, religion, and commerce probably reached its highest level of achievement at the end of the fifteenth century; the reversal since that time has been quite remarkable (Lewis, D. L. 2008). From around the middle of the sixteenth century, Islamic learning began to be superseded by a dramatic growth of knowledge in the West.

Although, the fall of Constantinople to the Ottomans in 1453 prompted a mass exodus of Byzantine scholars to Rome and other European centers of learning (Runciman 1965), centuries earlier the flow of knowledge from intellectual and scientific centers extending from Baghdad to Andalusia created the very foundation of the Renaissance that changed European history.[49]

Later, many factors contributed to the decline and fall of the Islamic civilization. The invasion of the Crusaders, Iberians and the Mongols on Islamic lands between the eleventh and fifteenth centuries—especially the Crusade series of invasions that lasted from1095 to 1291—are considered to be the most significant factor in the demise of the Islamic civilization. The Crusaders occupied or dominated via piracy Muslim ports on the Eastern Mediterranean, destroyed agricultural infrastructure in the Levant displacing farming communities, and forced Muslims to spend vast resources on the military. Correspondingly, Mongols destroyed Muslim libraries, observatories, hospitals, and universities culminating in the destruction of Baghdad, the Abbasid capital (Hassan, A. Y. 2001). Ibn Khaldun's *Muqaddimah* ("Introduction")[50] written in 1377 points out that science was declining in Iraq, Al-Andalus (Spain), and the Magreb. The conflicts between Sunni and Shi'a Muslims further exacerbated the weakening of the Islamic empire. Political as well as economic factors were major causes that contributed to the decline as also stated in Ibn Khaldun's other book *Assabiyyah* ("Social Cohesion").

Muslim scholars and observers of the Islamic world wrote extensively about the economic problems that instigated its decline, such as corruption, favoritism, oppression, natural calamities, internal conflicts, foreign invasions, over spending on militarization, and higher taxes (Al-Omar, 2003). Besides, many Muslim observers advocated for socioeconomic reforms and appreciated at least some of the material products of Europe's transformation; such as shipbuilding techniques and new agricultural products and technology.

Vasco Da Gama's arrival off the Malabar Coast of India in 1498 marked the beginning of the end of long-standing Muslim domination of trade in the Indian Ocean and beyond. Little by little, Muslims began to lose out to economic, technological, and military advances of the West, and the Islamic world entered into a long, slow process of decline, drawn out over centuries, culminating in colonization by the West and the dividing up of the Ottoman Empire in the aftermath of the First World War (Hussain 1999, 11–23).

B. Sources of Islamic Law

Muslims' lives are ruled by the *Shari'a* (Islamic law). Literally, the word *Shari'a* can be translated as "the path that leads to the spring" (Ramadan 2004, 31). Figuratively, it means "a clear path to be followed and observed." Islamic religious law emanates from various sources.

By far the most important source is the *Holy Qur'an,* the collection of the revelations to Prophet Mohammad. The *Holy Qur'an* is obviously not purely a legal text; nevertheless, it does contain approximately five hundred injunctions of a legal nature (twenty of which are on economic issues) (Doi 1989, 38–39).

Table 7.1

The Sources and Techniques of Islamic Law

Primary Sources	*qur'an* (the book containing the message of Islam). Muslims believe that it is the word of God as conveyed to Prophet Mohammad. *sunna* (collection of the words or acts of the Prophet or the *ahadith* which Prophet Mohammad used to give for moral guidance on many issues).
Secondary Sources	*ijma'* (consensus) *qiyas* (analogy) *ijtihad* (expert interpretation)
Minor or Subsidiary Techniques	*istihsan* (juristic preference) *istislah* (public interest) *urf* (custom)
Some Principles	*darura* (necessity)

The *Qur'an* and the *Sunna* are the primary sources of Islamic law. They are thought to contain God's infallible and immutable will, or *Shari'a* in a narrow sense.

However, the *Qur'an* and the *Sunna* are silent on many issues that contemporary Muslims are facing. Furthermore, the *Qur'an* and the *Sunna* leave room for different interpretations. Muslims, therefore, often resort to secondary sources of law[51]. *Shari'a*, in a wide sense, includes all Islamic legislation. In so far as this is based on secondary sources, it is not necessarily valid for all times and all places.

It was Imam al-Shafii in the early ninth century (the founder of the Shafii school of law, see following section) who "authoritatively insisted on human reason as the final judge on matters not regulated by the *Qur'an*" (Hallaq 1997, 21). Imam al-Shafii stated that there are two secondary sources of law: *ijma'*, or consensus; and *qiyas*, or analogy. Together with the primary sources, they are the four principal *usul al-fiqh*, or fundamentals of jurisprudence (see table 7.1 above).

- *Ijma'* (consensus)—the informed consensus of the community of scholars was established, not for matters of faith or fundamental observances, which were agreed upon, but on the application of *Shari'a* to worldly affairs. This is a source of importance for Islamic finance because models of Islamic banking are not mentioned in either the *Qur'an* or in the hadith, the primary sources that govern the system. Consequently, the development of Islamic banking has been based to a large degree on the consensus of modern Muslim scholars and jurisprudents at both national and international levels. Hence decisions made in this manner are *ijma'*, the collective judgments of learned Muslim scholars, the *ulama.*

- *Qiyas* (analogical deduction)—additional sources of law are *qiyas* (analogy from established law).
- *Ijtihad* (formation of law by the individual's struggle for proper understanding)—using reason and judgment to determine a course of action in keeping with the spirit of the *Holy Qur'an* and *hadith* is called *ijtihad.*
- *Istihsan* (juristic preference)—this points to exceptions that a jurist can make to a strict or literal legal interpretation (Esposito 2003, 152). *Istihsan* can be applied to *qiyas*, or any other method, and does not provide a definite answer.
- *Istislah* (literally, "seeking the good" (Ramadan 2004, 38), or taking the public interest, *maslaha*, into account. Jurists have differing opinions over the scope of *istihsan* or *maslaha* as a source of law.
- *Urf* (customary practice)—this is recognized, within limits, by the Hanafi and Maliki Schools but rejected by the Shafi'i School. According to the Hanafi School, for example, *urf* or custom may prevail over *qiyas* but never over a *nass*, a text of the *Qur'an* or *Sunna*. The paramountcy of *nass* is in fact the common limitation of all the minor techniques as well as *ijma'* and *qiyas*. *Ijtihad* in general is believed to be permitted only in matters not covered by clear and definite *nass* or text of the *Qur'an* or *Sunna*.

- *Darura* (necessity)—this may be seen as being derived from *qiyas* or analogy to a principle contained in verses of the *Qur'an*, such as the ones permitting a Muslim to eat forbidden food, such as pork, or do an impermissible thing if that is the only way to preserve his or her life. The key question here is, of course, what constitutes a legitimate necessity of the degree justifying deviation from or relaxation of the strict rules of *shari'a*?

C. Islamic Schools of Thought

Unlike Christianity, classical Islam had no priestly hierarchy and no central religious authority to promulgate official doctrine; truth needed no authorization. The nearest to clergy in Islam are the jurists known as the *ulama* (from *alim*, meaning a jurist or scholar), who differ in their roles and gradation.

The most important sectarian division in Islam is the one that separates Sunni and Shi'a believers, which arose in AD 661 on the question of the rightful leadership of the community. Shi'ism, which has various subsects, is predominantly in Iran, and has a significant number of followers in Iraq, India, and many of the Gulf states. There are considerable doctrinal differences between the Shi'a and the four Sunni Schools of Islamic jurisprudence, in terms of who is permitted to interpret *Shari'a* law.

Sunni legal doctrine has four main schools, each with its own system of theory and applications of law, although each recognizes the legitimacy of all of the others. The four orthodox schools are:

- The *Hanafi* School—this is the oldest one. It derives its name from Abu Hanifa, a Persian who taught in Iraq and died in AD 767. It is the most flexible of the four schools, emphasizing private interpretation, *ray*'; juristic preference, *istihsan*; and reasoning by analogy, *qiyas*. *Ijma'*, consensus, is also accepted. This is the prevailing school in India and the Middle East.
- The *Maliki* School—this school was founded by Malik ibn Anas, who died in AD 795 in Medina. It accords *qiyas* (analogy) a larger place than the other schools; Malik seems to have given priority to *qiyas* over *ahaad (ahadith* with a weak chain of transmitters (Al-Mukhtar Al Salami 1999, 22)). Nonetheless, the Malikis strongly rely on the *hadith* and also on *ijma'* (consensus) of the scholars of Medina, where Prophet Mohammad lived after he had fled Mecca. The Moors and Arabs who ruled Spain were followers of the Maliki School. Today, it is found mostly in North, West, and Central Africa.
- The *Shafi'i* School—its founder was Mohammad ibn Idris al Shafi'i, an Arab who died in AD 820 in Egypt. He was a pupil of Imam Malik and is thought by some to be the most distinguished of all jurists. He was famed for his modernization and balanced judgment. He rejected the personal view of scholars (*ijtihad* in the form of *ray*'), juristic preference (*istihsan*), and considerations of public welfare (*istislah*), but fully accepted consensus (*ijma'*). Followers of the Shafi'i School today are found

predominately in Southeast Asia (Malaysia, Indonesia), Yemen, Egypt, and Somalia.

- The *Hanbali* School—this school was founded by disciples of Ahmad ibn Hanbal, who died in AD 855 in Baghdad. The Hanbali base themselves exclusively on the *Qur'an* and the *Sunna*, and the only *ijma'* that is accepted by this group is the consensus of the companions of the Prophet, among whom are the rightly guided caliphs. The Hanbali School today is predominant in Saudi Arabia. The most famous Hanbali scholar is ibn Taymiyya (1263–1328), who "emphasized the literal truth of the *Qur'an* and rejected independent reasoning, in line with his rejection of Aristotelian logic" (Visser 2009).

Ibn Taymiyya's writings influenced Mohammad ibn Abdul Wahhab, an eighteenth-century Sunni Muslim scholar, who founded the puritan Wahhabi movement of Saudi Arabia. He advocated a process of purifying Islam from what he considered innovation (*bidah*) by following a strict interpretation of Islamic jurisprudence based only on the *Qur'an*, *ahadith*, and the understandings of the companions of the Prophet (*sahaabah*). It has developed considerable influence in the Muslim world through the funding of mosques, schools and other means of transmission by wealthy individuals or groups in Saudi Arabia and other Gulf states.

There is a tendency for non-Muslims and those with rudimentary understanding of Islam to confuse what the term "Islamic law" entails. To clarify, the English term "Islamic law" conceals an important distinction between

Shari'a and *fiqh*. *Shari'a* is totally divine. Allah is the One who dictates the laws, which were revealed to Prophet Mohammad (Auda, 2008). *Fiqh,* on the other hand, is a human endeavor to understand *Shari'a* laws. Therefore, Muslims must obey *Shari'a*. But note, *Fiqh* cannot be enforced on all Muslims. Followers of any School of *Fiqh* are only subject to follow its *fatwas*. From the beginning, starting with Prophet Adam, *Shari'a* changed based on the needs of the community. Allah revealed different *Shari'as* to people throughout the history of mankind. However, the *Shari'a* of Prophet Mohammad sealed all *Shari'a* laws, therefore it is final.

The situation is further complicated by the different positions taken by the various schools of thought. For example, one might consider the varying perspectives of the different schools with regard to *bay' al-salam* (forward-purchasing contracts). The term refers to a contracted sale whereby the seller undertakes to supply specific goods to the buyer at a future date in exchange for an advanced payment up front. According to the Hanafi School, it is necessary that the commodity that is being sold remains available in the marketplace from the very day that the contract is initiated right up until the date of actual delivery.

If the commodity is not available in the marketplace at the time of the contract, *bay' al-salam* cannot be effected in respect to that commodity, even though it may be confidently expected that the commodity *will* be available in the marketplace on the agreed delivery date. The other three schools of thought—Shafi'i, Maliki, and Hanbali—differ on this and are of the opinion that the availability of the commodity at the time of the contract is not a condition for the validity of *bay' al-salam*. According to them, what is necessary is that it should be available at the time of delivery.

Another example of differences among the various schools of law is the case of when fruit can be sold. The Shafi'i and Hanbali jurists categorically prohibited the sale of unripe fruits; the Malikis and some of the Hanafis allowed "the sale of fruits...which ripen in succession during one harvest, if such sale accompanies the sale of what has already ripened" (Saleh 1986).

These are only two examples, but suffice to say, there can be considerable divergence between what is and is not permissible under Islamic law, depending on which school of thought or law is consulted. Such inconsistencies are not in themselves conceived as some kind of failure on the part of Islamic jurisprudence, but rather as a reflection of the fallibility of man. Ultimately, *fiqh* rulings are taken as truly and certainly God's law only when they are agreed upon *unanimously* by all Islamic scholars of a particular era. The latter agreement is called *ijma'* or consensus (Vogel and Hayes 1998, 34–35).

Malaysia, which is on the forefront in the development of Islamic financial products and follows the Shafi'i School of thought, introduced *bay' al-'inah* (a transaction in which somebody sells goods for cash and then buys it back from the same person at a higher price in exchange for deferred payment). However, the other three Islamic schools of law or thought consider this transaction as *hila* (ruse or legal artifice) to get around the prohibition of *riba* (interest) (Warde 2007).

Another unique financial product offered to investors in Malaysia is *bay' al-dayn* (the trading of debt in the secondary market) under the concept of *sukuk al-ijara* (certificates of leasing)—only documents evidencing debt arising from bona fide commercial transactions can be traded. Outside of Malaysia, most scholars consider debt trading to be noncompliant with *Shari'a* law (Warde 2007).

D. Revival of Islamic Finance

From the very early stages of Islamic history, Muslims were able to establish a system without interest for mobilizing resources to finance productive activities and consumer needs. The system to finance business transactions was based mostly on the profit-and-loss-sharing (PLS) modes of *mudaraba* (passive partnership) and *musharaka* (active partnership). Deferred trading and *qard hasan* (interest free loans) were also used to finance consumers' as well as businesses' transactions.

The system worked very effectively during the early days of Islamic civilization and for centuries thereafter. The Islamic modes of financing (*mudaraba* and *musharaka*) were able to mobilize the necessary financial resources at the beginning of Islamic civilization for the financing of long-distance trade, manufacturing, and agriculture.

Given the factors that I stated earlier were responsible for the decline of Islamic civilization, the Muslim world lost its technological and economic vitality. Therefore, conventional institutions displaced most Islamic institutions, including the Islamic system of financial intermediation. However, the independence of Muslim countries has led to the revival of Islam, and there is a strong longing to gradually reinstate most of the lost institutions, the Islamic financial system being one of them.

In the early 1960s, there was enough demand for *Shari'a*-complaint banking that it culminated in the creation of the *Mit Ghamr* Local Savings Bank in Egypt in 1963, founded by a noted social activist Ahmad-al-Najjar. It is modeled on Germany's *Sparkessen* (savings bank), employing profit-sharing techniques for financing rural small businesses. The establishment of Dubai Islamic Bank in 1975 is considered to be one of the earliest private initiatives in the United Arab Emirates. The 1970s witnessed the rise in the price of oil leading to the accumulation of oil revenues in several oil-rich Muslim countries, especially in the Middle East.

This oil revenue from the 1970s, also known as "petro-dollars," offered strong incentives for creating suitable investment outlets for Muslims wanting to comply with *Shari'a*, interest-free, or Islamic banking, which was a concept that by the early 1970s had found a strong business case to be explored further. Both domestic and international bankers, including some of the leading conventional banks, exploited this business opportunity.

Deregulation in the 1980s and 1990s in the United States and many other countries proved to be a boon for Islamic finance, as it fostered the creation of tailor-made Islamic products. Until then, financial institutions could only sell a narrow range of financial products. With the lifting of constraints on the products that "financial engineers" could devise to suit every need—religious or otherwise—countless new Islamic products could be created.

In recent years, the growth of the Islamic sector has greatly accelerated. This trend is being driven by a combination of factors. The most obvious one is the impact of surging oil prices and the related economic boom in the Gulf region. Excess liquidity has raised the demand for a wider range of financial products. Related factors include what could be broadly described as the "September 11 effect"—a combination of rising religious and nationalist sentiment since the launch of the "War on Terror." This increased religiosity translated into greater demand for Islamic financial products.

Also, unlike during the oil boom of the 1970s, more of the financial revenues are staying within the Islamic world. Another aspect of the new environment is the growing convergence of the Arab and Malaysian models of Islamic finance, which became an essential building block in the rationalization and harmonization effort.[52]

A crucial development was the freezing of the assets of Middle Eastern individuals and the crackdown on Islamic financial institutions and charities, which led many Muslim investors to take a significant chunk of their assets out of the United States. Home markets could not absorb all those withdrawals (estimated at about two hundred billion dollars), and the quest for a new diversification strategy led more or less naturally to Malaysia, a Muslim country that had achieved an impressive level of economic development. Other forms of political and economic development also intensified. Malaysia started working closely with Arab regulators, especially those of Bahrain and the United Arab Emirates, on matters of Islamic finance.

Endnotes

46. For a comparison of the attitude of Muslims and Christians toward interest, see chapter 8 of L. M. Algaoud and M. Lewis, *Islamic Banking* (Northampton, MA: Edward Elgar, 2001).

47. According to Niall Ferguson (2008), there was an explosion of financial innovation after the publication of *The Wealth of Nations* in 1776 with the variety of different banks that proliferated in Europe and North America.

48. The Prophet did not know how to read and write, so he memorized all revelations by reciting them aloud.

49. The Renaissance was a cultural movement that profoundly affected European intellectual life in the early modern period and it was founded upon the medieval sciences of Islam, which were themselves built upon the classical traditions lost to the west during the Germanic destruction of the Roman Empire. Beginning in Italy and spreading to the rest of Europe by the sixteenth century, its influence affected literature, philosophy, art, politics, science, religion, and other aspects of intellectual inquiry (Lewis, D., 2008 and Kennedy, 2007), in addition Italy's city-states were major maritime economic centers controlling trade at the Eastern Mediterranean and Black sea till mid-to-late the15[th] century.

50. Ibn Khaldun, *The Muqaddimah: An Introduction to History*, abridged and edited by N. J. Dawood, (Princeton University Press, 1967).

51. For example, Muslims have relied on *ijma'*, *qiyas* or *ijtihad* to distinguish between what is prohibited or permitted in modern times such brokerage, insurance (Al-Qaradawi, 2006) or the usage of banknotes.

52. Ibrahim Warde, "Islamic Finance after September 11: Toward Arab-Malaysian Integration" (Seattle, WA: National Bureau of Asian Research, 2007).

Regression and Data

Generally, banks in most conventional-finance countries are classified into three main categories: commercial, savings, and investment banks.[53] However, there is a fourth category, Islamic banks, though they are rare or nonexistent in most Western countries.

Conventional banks generally accept deposits and make consumer, commercial, and real estate loans. Within the commercial banks category, for example, in the United States, there are three types of banks: community, regional, and money center banks. Community banks generally have assets under US$1 billion and specialize in retail or consumer banking.

Regional banks' assets are generally over US$1 billion, and they engage in a more complete array of wholesale commercial banking activities encompassing consumer and residential lending and investment activities. However, some of the very biggest banks often have the distinct title *money center banks*. These banks are characterized by their heavy reliance on non-deposit or borrowed sources of funds. Savings banks are usually mutually owned banks that specialize in residential mortgages funded by deposits. Classified under this category are credit unions. Investment banks generally help corporations or governments raise capital through the capital markets by underwriting debt and equity securities. They also provide services that assist the trading of securities in the secondary markets (brokerage services and/or market making) (Saunders and Cornett 2003).

The bank data in my sample were obtained from BankScope, which is one of the most widely used and commercially available databases for analyzing banks. Under BankScope, banks are classified as commercial, savings, investment, or Islamic banks.

A. Data and Methodology

1. Measuring Bank Stability

The primary dependent variable I will use in measuring individual bank risk is the z-score. The popularity of the z-score measure stems from the fact that it is inversely related to the probability of a bank's insolvency (i.e., the probability the value of its assets will become lower than the value of the debt).

The z-score is calculated as:

$$z = (\kappa + \mu)/\sigma,$$

where κ is equity capital plus reserves as percent of assets, μ is average return as a percent of assets, and σ is standard deviation of return on assets as a proxy for return volatility.

The z-score corresponds to a lower upper bound of insolvency risk—a higher z-score therefore implies a lower probability of insolvency risk.[54] Estimation of the z-score depends critically on the volatility of returns (Boyd and Runkle 1993).

Furthermore, empirical evidence shows that volatility of return on assets based on accounting data is lower than those based on stock prices (Boyd and Runkle 1993; Greenwalt and Sinkey 1988). However, since most Islamic banks are not listed and traded on stock markets, I will be using a z-score that is based on accounting data. Despite this fact, the predictive power of the z-score and distance to default models (used to assess future levels of credit risk) has been established in numerous research projects and in the academic literature (Boyd and Runkle 1993; Merton 1974).

I perform basic statistical tests for the z-scores as a preliminary step in my analysis, and then I compare the z-scores of Islamic and conventional banks. Given that the size of banks is an important factor in the literature on their financial stability, I subdivide the banks in my sample into large and small banks based on their total assets regardless of whether they are Islamic or conventional.

For both the descriptive and regression analysis, I use four banks' asset sizes cutoff thresholds to classify banks in the data sample into large and small banks. Studies use these various cutoff thresholds to test the results for robustness. The cutoff thresholds I use in my samples are US$750, US$1 billion, US$1.5 billion, and US$2 billion (cutoff below US$750 million will produce relatively fewer small banks). Even though these cutoff thresholds might seem arbitrary, they have been used in many studies (see Mercieca, Schaaeck, and Wolfe 2007; Boyd and Runkle 1993; and Cihak and Hesse 2008).

In recent years, two important lines of literature on the *Theory of the Banking Firm* have been developed. Both predict relationships between the size of banking firms and their performance. One substantial batch of literature deals with deposit insurance and the effect that it has on bank decisions. A fundamental finding is that the U.S.

system of deposit insurance produces an incentive for insured banking firms to take more risk (Keeley 1990). Theoretically, in fact, this distortion pushes them to corner solutions, taking as much risk as they can (for example, through the use of leverage). If regulatory treatment were the same for insured banks of all sizes, this theory would predict no relationship between size and performance.

In practice, though, regulatory treatment of banking firms has not been symmetric by size. Large bank failures during 2008 were more feared than small bank failures, since the former are viewed as more likely to result in macroeconomic externalities. Under the policy of "too big to fail," all liabilities of very large banks—whether formally insured or not—have been de facto guaranteed (Rowley and Smith 2009).

The other literature deals with the economic role of banking firms (generally, financial intermediaries) in environments in which agents are asymmetrically informed. This modern intermediation theory predicts that large intermediary firms will be less likely to fail than small ones because they are considered to be more cost-efficient. Importantly, modern intermediation theory predicts efficiency gains related to size, whereas deposit theory predicts size-related subsidies and distortions.

However, empirical evidence does not indicate a clearly differentiable competitive advantage due to efficiency (as predicted by modern intermediation theory) or one due to a high subsidy rate (as predicted by deposit insurance theory) (Boyd and Runkle 1993). Findings from the Boyd and Runkle study suggest an inverse relationship between size and the volatility of asset returns, consistent with the predictions of modern intermediation theory (Boyd and

Runkle 1993). Furthermore, they found no evidence that large banking firms are less likely to fail than small ones.

In my descriptive statistics analysis, I perform a pairwise comparison of the z-scores as a measure of financial stability, as well as three other accounting ratios that measure liquidity, cost efficiency, and income diversification between Islamic and conventional banks.

In examining income diversification, I can see whether there is a benefit to income diversification when banks shift their activities into noninterest-income services. The literature briefly says that diversification in banking can be viewed as three-dimensional:

i. across financial products and services,

ii. through geographic expansion, and

iii. through a combination of geographic and business line diversification.

Studies of cross-functional mergers provide mixed results.

Cubb-Othone and Murgia (2000) investigated mergers and acquisitions (M&A) in European banking and found significant positive abnormal returns associated with product diversification of banks into insurance. However, they also found M&A with securities firms and foreign institutions did not achieve any gain. Sinkey and Nash (1993) examined conventional banks specializing in credit card lending that generated higher and more volatile returns and report a higher probability of insolvency than banks with traditional product mixes.

2. Regression Analysis

The objective of the regression is to test whether Islamic banks in general are more or less stable than conventional banks by using z-scores (the dependent variable) as a function for a number of variables. I ran two types of regressions. The first and most important uses a general class of panel models that controls for many variables. The second runs a pooled ordinary least squares (OLS) regression with cluster-robust standard error that clusters on the individual bank level.

The general class panel model controlling many variables is of the following form:

$$Z_{i,t} = \alpha + \beta B_{i,t-1} + \gamma I_{i,t-1} + \sum \delta_s T_s + \sum \phi_s T_s I_{t-1} + \sum \varphi_s B_{i,t-1} T_s + \sum \lambda_t D_t + \varepsilon_{i,t}$$

where $Z_{i,t}$ is the z-score for bank i at time t; $B_{i,t-1}$ is a vector of bank-specific variables; I_{t-1} contain time-varying industry-specific variables; T_s and $T_s I_{t-1}$ are the type of banks and the interaction between the type and some of the industry specific variables; D_t is a dummy variable; and $\varepsilon_{i,t}$ is the residual.

To distinguish the impact of bank type on the z-score, I include a dummy variable that takes the value of 1, if the bank in question is an Islamic bank, and 0 otherwise (i.e., if it is a conventional bank). For example, if Islamic banks were relatively less stable than conventional banks, the dummy variable would have a negative sign in the regression and would be statistically significant in explaining z-scores.

At the country level, my objective is to examine the impact Islamic banks have on other banks and thus the null hypothesis that the presence of Islamic banks makes no difference to systemic financial stability against the alternate hypothesis that it may increase or decrease systemic financial stability. To accomplish this, I have calculated the market share of Islamic banks by assets for each year for Bahrain and Malaysia and determined its interaction with Islamic and conventional banks' dummy variables. A negative sign for the interaction of the Islamic banks' market share and the Islamic dummy variable would indicate that a higher share of Islamic banks negatively affect financial stability (i.e., reduce their z-scores).

The regression also includes a number of other control variables at the individual bank level that controls for differences in asset size, asset composition (loans over assets), and cost efficiency (cost-income ratio). Furthermore, to control for differences in the structure of the bank's income, I calculated a measure of income diversity that follows Laeven and Levine (2005).[55] This variable captures the degree to which banks diversify from traditional or typical lending activities (those generating net interest income) to other activities. For Islamic banks, net interest income is generally defined as the sum of the positive and negative income flows associated with the profit-and-loss-sharing (PLS) arrangements. To further capture the differences of Islamic banks in their business orientation, I relate the income diversity variable with the Islamic bank dummy variable. Controlling for these variables is important because there are identifiable and significant differences between Islamic banks and conventional banks.

All bank-specific variables and the Islamic bank's market share and its interaction with the Islamic and conventional bank dummies are lagged to capture the possible past effects of these variables on the bank's individual risk.

The regression analysis starts with the ordinary least squares (OLS) technique. Given that the sample includes outliers, I used a robust estimation technique as an important estimation method. This method, through an iterative process, assigns lower weights to observations with large residuals, making the estimation less sensitive to outliers.

Finally, to assess the robustness of the results with regard to the selected sample further, I estimated the same regressions for different bank sizes. More specifically, I estimated the regressions separately for subsamples of large banks (depending on the cutoff, those with total assets of more than US$0.75, US$1, US$1.5 or US$2 billion) and small banks (all others).

The second model is a pooled OLS regression with cluster-robust standard errors on the individual bank level and is of the following form:

$$Z_{i,t} = a + bB_{i,t-1} + e_{i,t}$$

where $z_{i,t}$ is the z-score for bank i at time t; $B_{i,t-1}$ is a vector of bank-specific variables; and $e_{i,t}$ is the residual.

For both the preliminary descriptive statistics and the regressions, I present results first for the full period of the data (1996–2010) and then for a subperiod of the last five years (2006–2010). There are three reasons to look at the subperiod. First, a considerable number of Islamic banks entered the sample well after 2006 (more particularly in Malaysia) and also the share of Islamic banks in the banking system increased as well. Thus, the second subperiod has many more banks and less missing data than the first. Therefore, the inference for this sample is more robust. Third, it is my expectation in the cases of Bahrain and Malaysia that the relatively late entry of Islamic banks will work against their relative stability during the early phase of their existence.

3. Case Study of Bank Failures

To supplement the regression analysis, I will do an analysis of actual bank failures and/or banks with serious financial distress for both Bahrain and Malaysia that occurred during the recent global financial crisis of 2007 to 2009 and the East Asian financial crisis of 1997. Examination of these cases will provide additional information that will or will not support the assertion that Islamic banks are financially more stable than conventional banks.

4. Data

The data on individual banks was obtained from the BankScope database, as I stated earlier. The period under consideration is from 1996 to 2010 (fifteen years). Table 8.1 shows the number and type of banks used in the descriptive statistics and regression analysis for Bahrain and Malaysia in the sample sets versus banks registered with or licensed by the central banks.

Table 8.1

Number of Banks in the Sample Sets Versus Total Registered Banks

Country	Banks per Sample			Banks per Central Bank			Percent Used in Sample		
	Conventional	Islamic	Total	Conventional	Islamic	Total	Conventional	Islamic	Total
Bahrain	15	20	35	15	20	35	100%	100%	100%
Malaysia	22	17	39	24	17	41	95%	100%	95%
Total	37	37	74	39	37	76	95%	100%	97%

Wherever possible, I chose consolidated bank statements in BankScope's data. The distribution for the type of consolidation is approximately evenly divided between consolidated and unconsolidated for both Bahrain and Malaysia. The unavailability of consolidated data limits their usefulness for econometric analysis. Therefore, I used consolidated data when available; otherwise, I used an unconsolidated data.

Endnotes

53. Note: The activity of these three categories could be available under the structure of certain banks, such as the universal banks in Germany and Japan (see chapter 7 for a definition of universal banks) or the big money center banks in the United States (such as Bank of America, Citibank, or Chase JP Morgan) because of the repeal of the Glass-Steagall Act in 1999. However, most banks in Islamic countries are divided among these three categories.

54. A popular version of the z-score based on stock price data to estimate the volatility in the economic capital of the bank is the distance to default risk. The distance to default is based on methodology developed by Merton, "The Pricing of Corporate Debt: The Risk Structure of Interest Rates" (1974).

55. The income diversity measure is defined as 1 - absolute value *[(Total operating income - Non-operating income)/Total operating income)].* Higher values mean higher diversification.

Analytical History and Regression of Bahrain

A. Analytical History of Bahrain

The Kingdom of Bahrain, which literally means "Kingdom of the Two Seas," is a constitutional monarchy located in the Persian Gulf between the Qatar Peninsula and Saudi Arabia. The two main islands are Bahrain (the largest) and Al Muharraq; they are linked to each other and Saudi Arabia by a causeway. The capital and chief port is Al Manamah. The country has a modern communications and transportation infrastructure, a reliable regulatory structure, and a cosmopolitan outlook. In 2006, the United States and Bahrain implemented the first free trade agreement between the United States and a Persian Gulf state.

In 2010, Bahrain's population stood at 1.234 million, out of which more than 666,172 (54 percent) were non-nationals.[56] According to the 2001 census, 81.2 percent of Bahrain's population were Muslim, 9 percent were Christians, and 9.8 percent practiced Hinduism and other religions. The majority of Muslims are Shiites.

1. Economy

Bahrain has a free market economy, with no restrictions on capital movements, foreign exchange, foreign trade, or foreign investment. The kingdom has a leading position in the region as an open, free, transparent, and welcoming environment for investors. The economy has been based on oil, and oil revenues have financed modernization projects, particularly in health and education (IMF 2006). Bahrain's total nominal GDP was estimated in 2010 at US$29.82 billion and GDP per capita of US$40,400.[57]

Bahrain was not only the first oil producer in the region, but also the first to experience a decline in production. As a result, the process of economic diversification away from hydrocarbons has a longer history in the kingdom than in some of its GCC neighbors. However, oil and related activities still make up a large portion of the country's economy. Petroleum production and processing accounts for about 60 percent of export receipts, 60 percent of government revenue, and 30 percent of GDP.

The Kingdom of Bahrain was hit hard in 2009, recording negative year-on-year (y-o-y) growth rates in all sectors. The global financial crisis brought an end to the rapid economic growth that the GCC region had been witnessing, with Bahrain being no exception. The impact came mainly through the sharp fall in oil prices and the tightening of credit conditions. Economic activity slowed sharply, reflecting difficulties in the financial services sector and flat production of hydrocarbons. Other important sectors, such as aluminum and petrochemicals, also suffered with their outputs down 2.7 percent and 2.6 percent respectively. The real estate sector also came to a halt, because of the lack of liquidity and credit from banks and a fall in investor confidence.

The US$3 billion Financial Harbor project in Al-Manamah—one of several large-scale construction projects in Al-Manamah—when completed, is expected to be the centerpiece of its diversified economy. According to the Heritage Foundation's Index of Economic Freedom, Bahrain's freedom score of 76.3 makes its economy the thirteenth freest on the 2010 index and "its overall score is 1.5 points higher than last year, with improvements in trade freedom, investment freedom, labor freedom, and freedom from corruption."

Bahrain has one of the most diversified economies in the GCC, in part because its financial sector developed strongly, serving both the domestic economy and the economies of its neighbors, and contributes importantly to its GDP and employment.

In February and March 2011, Bahrain experienced a period of civil unrest inspired in part by recent revolutions in Egypt and Tunisia and in part by local dissatisfaction with government policies. Bahraini security forces moved quickly to restore order. Bahrain hosted military forces from Saudi Arabia, United Arab Emirates, and Kuwait under the aegis of the GCC Peninsula Shield Force to secure critical infrastructure while Bahraini security forces contained the unrest. An ongoing national dialogue seeks to address political grievances between political societies, civil society groups, and the government to prevent further instances of unrest.

2. Financial Sector Structure

Despite the small size of Bahrain's economy, the financial sector is well diversified and includes a full variety of institutions. It consists of a wide range of conventional and Islamic financial institutions and markets, including retail and wholesale banks, insurance companies, finance companies, investment advisors, moneychangers, insurance brokers, securities brokers, and mutual funds. It is dominated by banks, which are classified as retail or wholesale banks. There is also a stock exchange, listing and trading both conventional and Islamic instruments.

Bahrain is a regional financial center, which, until recently, was in competition with Dubai for dominance. However, since Dubai's serious financial crisis during 2009, Bahrain has clearly been established as the regional financial center. Bahrain is actively promoting Islamic finance through a *Shari'a*-compatible regulatory framework and the establishment of a variety of supporting national and international institutions. Conventional financial institutions now offer a comprehensive set of services in commerce in compliance with *Shari'a* law, including banking services and insurance (*takaful*), and the market for government and corporate Islamic securities (*sukuk*) has developed.

The financial sector is the largest single employer in Bahrain. Overall, the sector contributes 27 percent of Bahrain's gross domestic product (GDP), making it one of the key drivers of economic growth in the country. The financial sector is the largest single employer in Bahrain, with Bahrainis representing over 80 percent of the workforce. The financial sector is regulated and supervised by the Central Bank of Bahrain (CBB) (formerly Bahrain Monetary Agency).

3. Banking
Bahrain's banking institutions are made up of three categories: conventional banks, investment banks, and

Islamic banks. The conventional banks in turn consist of retail and wholesale banks. The retail and wholesale banks are further classified into those that are locally incorporated and those incorporated overseas. The Islamic banks are similarly classified into retail and wholesale banks, which in turn are also divided into those locally incorporated versus foreign incorporated.

My data sample of conventional banks consists of locally incorporated conventional banks whether retail or wholesale. The Islamic banks in my data sample similarly consist only of those that are locally incorporated. I chose locally incorporated banks because there are no restrictions on these with regard to the type of currency transactions that can be undertaken. Overseas-incorporated banks are limited to activities in foreign currencies. In other words, they are not allowed to execute transactions in Bahraini dinars.

According to the central bank of Bahrain, at the end of 2010, the total assets of the entire banking system added up to US$222 billion. Also at this time, there were 140 licensed financial institutions, thirty-two of which were retail banks and the remaining seventy-eight wholesale banks.

Before the recent appearance of Islamic banks in Bahrain in the last two decades, the traditional conventional banks in Bahrain had achieved a reputation as being among the most well managed and efficient banks in the Middle East. Moreover, these banks are known for their conservative approach to excessive risk-taking through debt leveraging and the maintenance of high levels of capital and reserves. This unique culture of the Bahraini banking system evolved through a combination of historical business and banking sophistication as well as the influence from their exposure to British colonialism.

Central Bank of Bahrain

Before the creation of the Central Bank of Bahrain (CBB) on September 7, 2006, the Bahrain Monetary Agency (BMA) had been responsible for carrying out central banking and regulatory functions since its establishment in 1973 (shortly after Bahrain secured full independence from Great Britain). Under the BMA, there were three types of banks: full commercial banks (FCBs), offshore banking units (OBUs), and banks with investment bank licensees (IBLs). Each category included both commercial and Islamic banks, as explained earlier in the chapter. The key differences between the three banking categories lay in their ability to offer residents services in Bahraini dinar (BD).

Responsibilities of the CBB include implementation of the kingdom's monetary and foreign exchange policies, management of reserves, debt and currency issuance, and overseeing the payments and settlement systems. It is also the sole regulator of Bahrain's financial sector, covering the full range of banking, insurance, investment funds, and capital market activities. CBB is recognized as the leader in monetary authority in the Arab world in terms of regulation, innovation, and operational efficiency, whose regulation has created a business-friendly environment by international standards.[58]

Currently under the CBB authority, Bahrain's banking system consists of both conventional and Islamic banks and is the largest component of the financial system accounting for over 85 percent of total financial assets (Bahrain 2011). As of September 30, 2011, the conventional segment includes nineteen retail banks, sixty-nine wholesale banks, and two specialized banks, as well as thirty-six representative offices of overseas banks (Bahrain 2011). The Islamic segment, offering a host of *Shari'a*-compliant products and services had six retail banks and eighteen wholesale banks.

The value of total assets in the banking system plunged during the last quarter of 2002 because of substantial withdrawals in the offshore banking units (OBU) due to major uncertainties regarding ramifications from the United States' preparation to invade Iraq[59] (see figure 9.2).

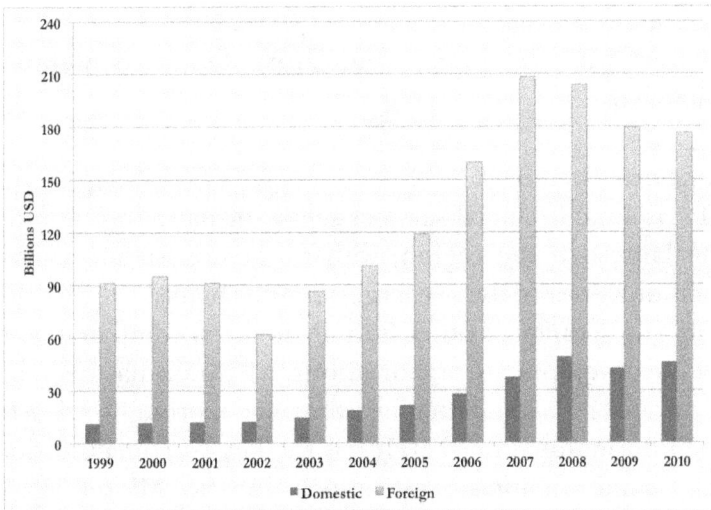

Figure 9.1 Asset Ownership of Bahrain's Entire Banking System

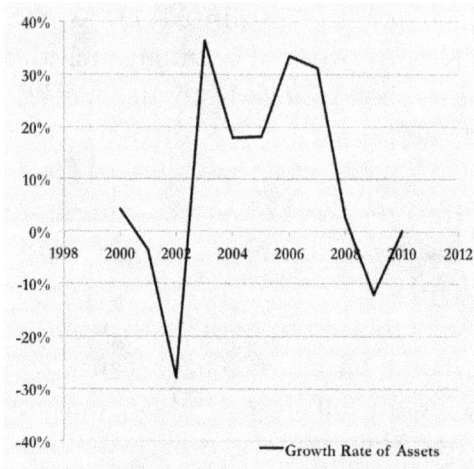

Figure 9.2 Asset Growth of Bahrain's Entire Banking System
Source: CBB—Economic Indicators Report, September 2009, No. 25

4. Islamic Finance

The Islamic financial services sector of Bahrain is among the largest in the region, with twenty-six Islamic banks, including four of the five largest Islamic banks in the world, and a wide range of other Islamic financial companies and sector development organizations.[60] Bahrain has been an innovator in Islamic finance ever since it brought *sukuk* to the international market. It has the largest concentration of Islamic financial institutions in the Middle East, including commercial, investment, and leasing companies; insurance companies; and mutual funds.

The growth of Islamic banking has been substantial, with total assets jumping from US$1.9 billion in 2000 to US$26.3 billion by June 2009.[61] On average, assets have been growing at least 15 percent per annum in the last decade. Figures 9.3 and 9.4 show ownership of assets and liabilities (between locals and foreigners) and the asset growth respectively. The market share of Islamic banks correspondingly increased from 1.6 percent of total banking assets in 1999 to 11.1 percent in June 2009 (figure 9.5 for the period 1999 to 2008). In GDP terms, the consolidated balance sheet of Islamic banks (in billions USD) was 10.1 times that of GDP in December 2010.[62]

Bahrain is a host to a number of organizations central to the development of Islamic finance, including the Accounting and Auditing for Islamic Financial Institutions (AAOIFI) organization, the International Islamic Financial Market (IIFM), the International Islamic Rating Agency (IIFA), and the Liquidity Management Center (LMC).

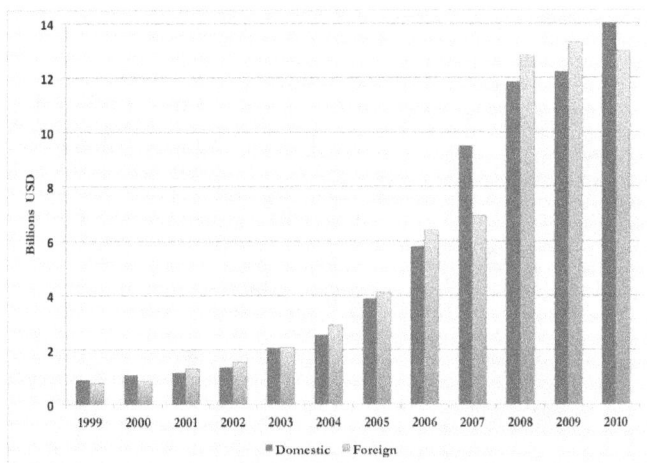

Figure 9.3 Asset Ownership of Bahrain's Islamic Banks (Consolidated Balance Sheets)

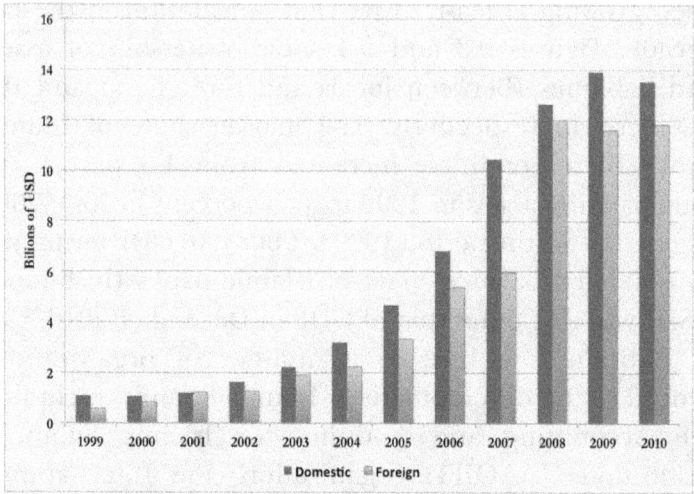

Figure 9.4 Liabilities Ownership Composition of Bahrain's Islamic Banks (Consolidated Balance Sheets)

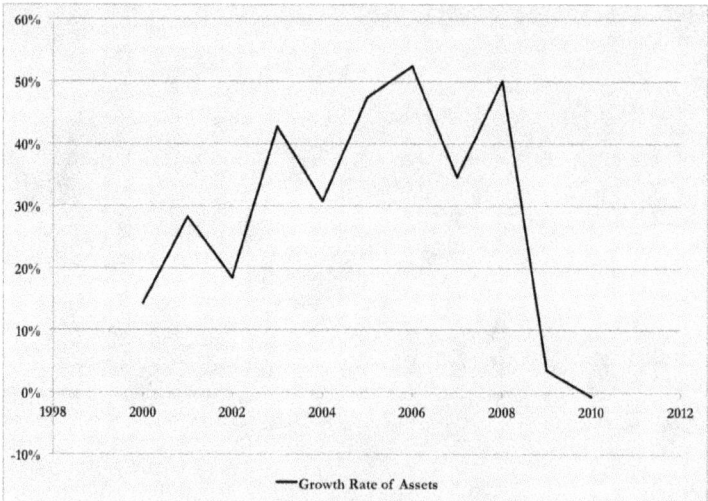

Figure 9.5 Asset Growth Rates of Bahrain's Islamic Banks

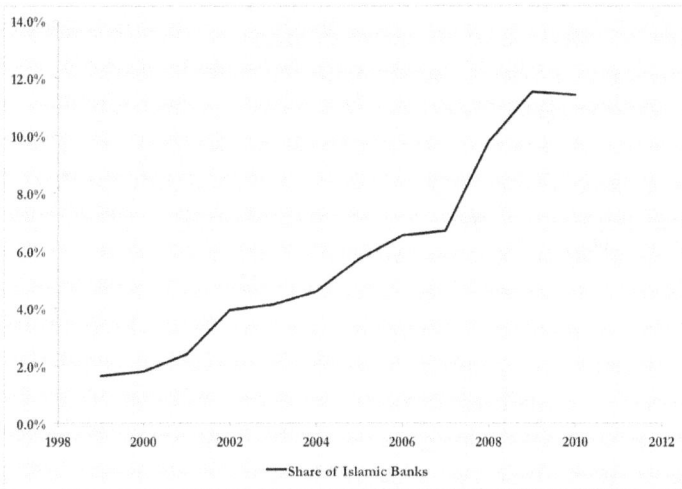

Figure 9.6 Share of Islamic Banks in Bahrain's Banking System

Note: The source for all the above charts is *Statistical Bulletin–December 2010*, published by Central Bank of Bahrain (CBB).

B. Data

Table 9.1 shows a summary overview of the input data from BankScope used for the descriptive statistics and regression analysis based on the balance sheets in 2010 for various banks' asset sizes cutoff thresholds in classifying banks as large or small. For lower level thresholds (US$750 million and US$1 billion) the numbers of large Islamic and conventional banks are about equal; however, the number of small conventional banks is approximately half that of large conventional banks. In the case of Islamic banks, the number of large and small banks are the roughly the same. However, for the higher cutoff thresholds (US$1.5 and 2 billion), the proportion of small and large banks for Islamic and conventional banks varies as shown in the table.

Table 9.1

Summary of Data Input for the Various Banks' Asset Sizes Cutoff Thresholds

Cutoff Threshold for Banks' Asset Sizes		Conventional Banks	Islamic Banks	All Banks
US $750 million				
	Number of Banks	*17*	*22*	*39*
	Large Banks	11	10	21
	Small Banks	6	12	18
	Number of Observations	*168*	*137*	*305*
	Large Banks	117	66	183
	Small Banks	551	71	122
US $1 billion				
	Number of Banks	*17*	*22*	*39*
	Large Banks	11	10	21
	Small Banks	6	12	18
	Number of Banks	*168*	*137*	*305*
	Large Banks	117	66	183
	Small Banks	51	71	122
US $1.5 billion				
	Number of Banks	*17*	*22*	*39*
	Large Banks	8	5	13
	Small Banks	9	17	26
	Observations	*168*	*137*	*305*
	Large Banks	105	39	144
	Small Banks	63	98	161
US $2 billion				
	Observations	*17*	*22*	*39*
	Large Banks	6	5	11
	Small Banks	11	17	28
	Observations	*168*	*137*	*305*
	Large Banks	84	39	123
	Small Banks	84	98	182

For closer examination of one of the bank asset size cutoff thresholds, I selected the US$1 billion category (table 9.2); approximately two-thirds of the data is based on consolidated bank financial statements for all banks taken together as a group.

Table 9.2

Overview— US$1 Billion Banks Asset Sizes Cutoff Threshold

	Conventional Banks			Islamic Banks			All Banks
	Consolidated	Unconsolidated	Subtotal	Consolidated	Unconsolidated	Subtotal	
All Banks							
Number of Banks	10	7	17	16	6	22	39
Retail Banks	3	5	8	6	2	8	16
Wholesale Banks	7	2	9	10	4	14	23
Number of Observations	110	58	168	103	34	137	305
Retail Banks	30	49	79	41	12	53	132
Wholesale Banks	80	9	89	62	22	84	173
Large Banks							
Number of Banks	7	4	11	9	1	10	21
Retail Banks	3	3	6	5	1	6	12
Wholesale Banks	4	1	5	4	0	4	9
Number of Observations	87	30	117	61	5	66	183
Retail Banks	30	26	56	27	5	32	88
Wholesale Banks	57	4	61	34	0	34	95
Small Banks							
Number of Banks	3	3	6	7	5	12	17
Retail Banks	0	2	2	1	1	2	4
Wholesale Banks	3	1	4	6	4	10	14
Number of Observations	23	28	51	42	29	71	122
Retail Banks	0	23	23	14	7	21	44
Wholesale Banks	23	5	28	28	22	50	78

Source: Calculations based on BankScope data.

Note: Large (small) banks are defined as having assets larger (smaller) than US$1 billion.

As I stated in chapter 8, I would have opted to use consolidated statements for all financial institutions if they had been available. Using the cutoff threshold of one billion USD in total assets, the sample for Bahrain consisted of seventeen small conventional and Islamic banks and twenty-one large conventional and Islamic banks. Of the thirty-nine financial institutions in the sample, sixteen are retail banks and the rest are wholesale banks.

C. Results of the Descriptive Statistics

Hypothesis Test:
Test whether the difference in mean variables (i.e., *z-score, z-score excluding outliers, loans/assets, cost/income,* and *income diversity*) between Islamic banks and conventional banks is due to random chance. This hypothesis test will be applied to all banks taken together, all large banks taken together, and all small banks taken together.

Result 1
A preliminary look at the z-scores across the sample for the various bank asset sizes cutoff thresholds for the full sample (1996–2010) is shown in table 9.3. The differences in mean z-scores between conventional banks and Islamic

banks are 29.02 versus 11.05 respectively (taking all banks together as a group) and are statistically significant at the 1 percent level (95 percent confidence interval) for all bank asset sizes cutoff thresholds. The higher z-score values of conventional banks mean they are financially more stable in comparison to Islamic banks. The results for the z-score excluding outliers show statistical significance similar to those of the z-score measure for all the different banks' asset sizes cutoff thresholds.

The loan-to-assets ratio is not statistically significant for all the different banks asset sizes cutoff thresholds, taking all banks together as a group. The cost-to-income ratio is statistically significant at the 1 percent level with a 95 percent confidence interval for the entire banks' asset sizes threshold.

Result 2

Performing an analysis similar to that of the data input in the previous section, I closely examine the descriptive statistics of the US$1 billion bank asset sizes cutoff threshold (see table 9.4).

The z-score distribution ranges between a minimum of 0.11 to a maximum of 30.86, with a mean of 5.35 and a standard deviation of 6.26 for all banks taken together as a group. Furthermore, the z-score distribution comparison between conventional and Islamic banks is graphically illustrated by the two histograms in figures 9.7 and 9.8.

Table 9.3

Summary Statistics for Various Banks' Assets Sizes Cutoff Thresholds, 1996–2010

Cut-off for Bank Asset Size: US $750 million

Financial Variable	Conventional Banks	Islamic Banks
Z-Score	*29.02*	*11.05****
Large Banks	30.20	11.31***
Small Banks	26.67	10.80***
Z-Score Excl. Outliers	*25.48*	*11.14****
Large Banks	24.59	11.50***
Small Banks	27.24	10.80***
Loans / Assets	*35.17*	*36.39*
Large Banks	36.16	39.03
Small Banks	32.91	33.01
Cost / Income	*53.98*	*72.08****
Large Banks	45.10	55.76***
Small Banks	74.99	87.88
Income Diversity	*-0.05*	*-0.22*
Large Banks	0.08	0.11
Small Banks	-0.32	-0.54

Cut-off for Bank Asset Size: US $1 billion

Financial Variable	Conventional Banks	Islamic Banks
Z-Score	*29.02*	*11.05****
Large Banks	30.20	11.31***
Small Banks	26.67	10.57***
Z-Score Excl. Outliers	*25.48*	*11.14****
Large Banks	24.59	11.50***
Small Banks	27.24	10.80***
Loans / Assets	*35.17*	*36.39*
Large Banks	36.16	39.03
Small Banks	32.91	33.01
Cost / Income	*53.98*	*72.08****
Large Banks	45.10	55.76***
Small Banks	74.99	87.88
Income Diversity	*-0.05*	*-0.22*
Large Banks	0.08	0.11
Small Banks	-0.32	-0.54

	US $1.5 billion		US $2 billion	
Z-Score	29.02	11.05***	29.02	11.05***
Large Banks	23.19	9.03***	24.50	9.03***
Small Banks	37.35	11.85***	34.53	11.85***
Z-Score Excl. Outliers	25.48	11.35***	25.48	11.14***
Large Banks	23.19	9.03***	24.50	9.03***
Small Banks	28.98	11.98***	26.75	11.98***
Loans / Assets	35.17	36.39	35.17	36.39
Large Banks	36.25	36.24	39.75	36.24
Small Banks	33.41	36.47	30.80	36.47
Cost / Income	53.98	72.08***	53.98	72.08***
Large Banks	46.71	63.42***	46.24	63.42***
Small Banks	66.36	75.68	61.81	75.68
Income Diversity	-0.05	-0.22	-0.05	-0.22
Large Banks	0.06	0.19	0.03	0.19
Small Banks	-0.21	-0.42	-0.13	-0.42

Source: Calculations based on BankScope data.

Note: The difference between the value of conventional and Islamic banks at the 95 percent confidence interval is significant at 10 percent (*); at 5 percent (**); and at 1 percent (***).

Table 9.4

Summary Statistics by Bank Category—US$1 Billion Cut-off Threshold, 1996–2010

	Small Banks		Large Banks		All Banks	
	Conventional	Islamic	Conventional	Islamic	Conventional	Islamic
Z-score	26.67	10.57***	30.20	11.31***	29.02	11.05***
Retail Banks	21.43	16.57	48.84	9.56***	40.86	12.34***
Wholesale Banks	30.97	8.38***	7.51	12.96	16.39	10.23
Z-score Excl. Outliers	27.24	10.80***	24.59	11.50***	25.48	11.14***
Retail Banks	22.49	16.57	39.42	9.56***	34.46	12.34***
Wholesale Banks	30.97	8.38***	7.51	13.51*	16.39	10.37
Loans/Assets	32.91	33.01	36.16	39.03	35.17	36.39
Retail Banks	49.86	37.01***	46.28	41.18	47.33	39.42***
Wholesale Banks	17.90	30.01	25.86	37.19	23.30	33.95**
Cost/Income Ratio	74.99	87.88	45.10	55.76***	53.98	72.08***
Retail Banks	48.11	53.34	45.04	57.65***	45.93	55.91***
Wholesale Banks	98.76	104.76	45.16	53.87	61.37	83.44
Income Diversity	-0.32	-0.54	0.08	0.11	-0.05	-0.22
Retail Banks	0.12	-2.00	0.14	0.28**	0.13	-0.51
Wholesale Banks	-0.68	0.03	0.02	-0.10	-0.23	-0.02
Assets in Billions USD	872.26	456.67	8,447.82	1,710.82	6,147.77	1,060.86
Retail Banks	624.57	1,018.56	5,252.45	2,055.87	3,905.09	1,644.86
Wholesale Banks	1,075.71	220.67	11,380.37	1,386.06	8,138.46	692.37

Source: Calculations based on BankScope data.
Note: The difference between the value of conventional and Islamic banks at the 95 percent confidence interval is significant at 10 percent (*); at 5 percent (**); and at 1 percent (***).

It clearly shows conventional banks have higher z-score distribution variability compared to Islamic banks.

Table 9.4 further shows that conventional banks, as a group, have a higher z-scores (29.02 versus 11.05) compared to Islamic banks, and this difference is statistically significant at the 1 percent level for a 95 percent confidence level. The overall higher z-score comparative advantage of conventional banks over Islamic banks extends to both large and small banks, each taken together as a group, and is statistically significant at the 1 percent level. However, within the small banks as a group, the advantage of conventional banks stems from wholesale banks and is significant at the 1 percent level. In contrast, the higher z-score superiority of large conventional banks as a group over large Islamic banks is due to large retail banks and is statistically significant at the 1 percent level.

The other variables of table 9.4 show Islamic banks taken as a group have, on average, higher loan-to-asset ratios, reflecting the fact that Islamic banks, due to the prohibition of investing in fixed-income securities (whether government or corporate), would have large loan portfolios in comparison to conventional banks. However, this ratio is not statistically significant for banks taken together as group. Conventional banks, as a group, had on average lower cost-to-income ratios, and this was statistically significant at the 1 percent level for a 95 percent confidence level. For this ratio, lower value is more favorable, as it implies a higher degree of operational efficiency as well as overall lower overhead or other costs. The conventional banks' overall lower cost advantage emanates from large retail banks. Finally, the income diversity difference between conventional and Islamic banks is not statistically significant—indicating that the difference in the mean value for all banks taken together as a group is not different from random chance.

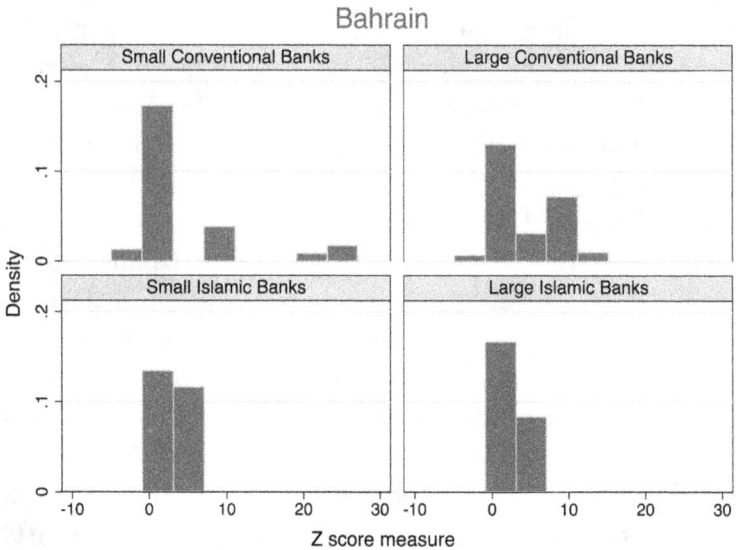

Figure 9.7 Z-score Distribution by Type of Bank and Asset Size

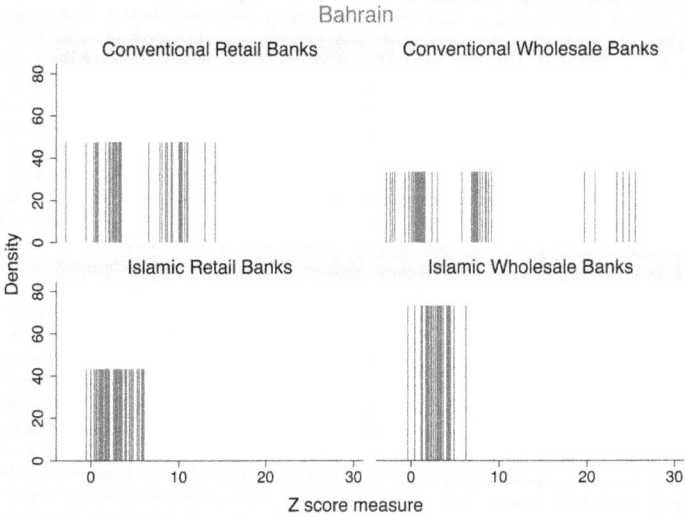

Figure 9.8 Distribution of Z-score by Bank Type and Category

Table 9.5 shows the summary statistics for the subperiod (2006–2010) for the various banks' asset sizes cutoff thresholds.

Table 9.5

Summary Statistics for Various Cutoffs of Bank Asset Sizes, 2006–2010

	Cutoff for Bank Asset Size: US$750 Million		Cutoff for Bank Asset Size: USD 1 Billion	
	Conventional Banks	Islamic Banks	Conventional Banks	Islamic Banks
Z-score	*30.48*	*9.74****	*30.48*	*9.74****
Large Banks	37.04	12.42***	37.04	12.42***
Small Banks	12.35	7.23***	12.35	7.23***
Z-score Exclud. Outliers	*21.39*	*9.86****	*21.39*	*9.86****
Large Banks	24.89	12.74***	24.89	12.74***
Small Banks	12.35	7.23***	12.35	7.23***
Loans / Assets	*33.58*	*33.58*	*33.58*	*33.85*
Large Banks	38.68	35.39	38.68	35.39
Small Banks	16.99	31.43	16.99	31.43
Cost / Income	*61.86*	*84.03****	*61.86*	*84.03****
Large Banks	40.79	57.51***	40.79	57.51***
Small Banks	133.52	110.54	133.52	110.54
Income Diversity	*-0.23*	*-0.46*	*-0.23*	*-0.46*
Large Banks	0.12	0.05	0.12	0.05
Small Banks	-1.21	-0.91	-1.21	-0.91

	US$1.5 Billion		USD 2 Billion	
Z-score	**30.48**	**9.74*****	**30.48**	**9.74*****
Large Banks	21.35	7.49***	24.09	7.49***
Small Banks	41.49	10.52***	36.11	10.52***
Z-score Exclud. Outliers	**21.39**	**9.86*****	**21.39**	**9.86*****
Large Banks	21.35	7.49***	24.09	7.49***
Small Banks	21.44	10.69***	18.78	10.69***
Loans / Assets	**33.58**	**33.85**	**33.58**	**33.85**
Large Banks	39.64	33.11	41.78	33.11
Small Banks	24.92	34.19	27.10	34.19
Cost / Income	**61.86**	**84.03*****	**61.86**	**84.03*****
Large Banks	43.75	65.44***	40.60	65.44***
Small Banks	88.02	91.08	78.53	91.08
Income Diversity	**-0.23**	**-0.46**	**-0.23**	**-0.46**
Large Banks	0.07	0.12	0.09	0.12
Small Banks	-0.60	-0.70	-0.44	-0.70

Source: Calculations based on BankScope data.

Note: The difference between the value of conventional and Islamic banks at the 95 percent confidence interval is significant at 10 percent (*); at 5 percent (**); and at 1 percent (***).

Again, parallel to table 9.3, the z-score and the z-score excluding outliers are statistically significant at the 1 percent level for all banks' asset sizes cutoff thresholds. The results for the rest of the ratios follow a pattern similar to that of the full period sample as explained earlier.

Table 9.6

Supports for Summary Statistics for the US$1 Billion Cutoff Threshold, 2006–2010

	Small Banks		Large Banks		All Banks	
	Conventional	Islamic	Conventional	Islamic	Conventional	Islamic
ROAA (Return on Avg. Assests)	1.31	1.61	1.67	3.79***	1.56	2.66***
Retail Banks	1.01	3.52**	1.44	3.17***	1.31	3.31***
Wholesale Banks	1.56	0.81	1.89	4.37	1.79	2.25
Equity / Assets	29.37	71.65***	17.04	36.25***	20.78	54.60***
Retail Banks	19.18	48.53***	13.37	28.32***	15.06	36.33***
Wholesale Banks	37.74	81.36***	20.40	43.71***	25.86	66.12***
Total Non-Earnings Assets/Assets	0.08	0.14***	0.06	0.14***	0.07	0.14***
Retail Banks	0.07	0.09	0.06	0.13***	0.06	0.11***
Wholesale Banks	0.10	0.16**	0.06	0.15***	0.07	0.16***
Cash and Due from Banks/Assets	0.06	0.03***	0.03	0.04	0.04	0.03
Retail Banks	0.06	0.03	0.04	0.06	0.05	0.05
Wholesale Banks	0.06	0.24***	0.02	0.02	0.03	0.02**
Std. Deviation of ROAA	3.80	11.42***	1.78	6.34***	2.39	8.97***
Retail Banks	2.55	2.91	0.59	3.73***	1.16	3.40***
Wholesale Banks	4.84	14.99***	2.87	8.79***	3.49	12.48***

Source: Author's Calculations based on BankScope data

Note: The difference between the value of conventional and Islamic banks at the 95 percent confidence interval is significant at 10 percent (*); at 5 percent (**); and at 1 percent (***).

The variables on table 9.6 consist of the components required for the calculation of the z-score[63] for the subperiod for the US$1 billion assets size cutoff threshold. In this category, taking all banks together as a group, conventional banks are deemed to be financially more stable than Islamic banks because the return on their average assets is less volatile (Standard Deviation of ROAA 2.39 versus 8.97) and is statistically significant at the 1 percent level. This advantage also holds at the 1 percent level of statistical significance for all small and large banks taken together as a group for conventional banks. The calculation for the z-score is highly sensitive to this variable. Supporting summary statistics for the US$1 billion cutoff threshold for the full sample and subperiod is shown in tables I (a) and I (b) respectively in appendix A.

D. Regression Results and Analysis

To separate the financial stability impact of the Islamic nature of a bank from the impact of other bank-level characteristics, I turn to regression analysis, following the methodology described in chapter 8. I ran several specifications for the various banks asset sizes cutoff thresholds. The regression results for these various thresholds for bank sizes were more or less similar. Therefore, in light of this fact, I present in detail the analysis for the US$1 billion cutoff threshold, which is parallel to the approach I used for the analysis of the input data and descriptive statistics.

The results of the regression for the US$1 billion bank asset sizes cutoff threshold for the full period sample (1996–2010) and subperiod (2006–2010) are shown in tables 9.8 and 9.9 respectively at the end of this chapter. Regression results for the rest of the banks' asset sizes cutoff thresholds are shown in tables II to IV in appendix A.

The regression for the full sample period confirms the result from the simple comparison of z-scores, which states conventional banks tend to be more stable than Islamic banks. The sign of the Islamic dummy variable in table 9.8 is negative[64] for all specifications of the regression but is statistically significant at the 1 percent level at the 95 percent confidence interval for specifications (1) to (6). So, for all banks taken together as a group (1–3) and all the large banks taken together as a group, the results indicate conventional banks are more stable than Islamic banks. For small banks, specifications (7–9), even though the sign of the Islamic dummy variable is negative, they are statistically insignificant.

As to the control variables, they generally have the expected signs. In particular, banks with lower loan-to-asset ratios tend to have higher z-scores (see tables 9.3 and 9.4), which is the case for conventional banks (the reverse holds for Islamic banks). This slope coefficient is consistently positive for all specifications (1–9) and is statistically significant at the 1 percent level. Similarly, lower cost-to-income ratios have a consistently positive link to the z-scores; the sign is consistent except for large banks.

In general, Islamic banks large or small tend to have higher income diversity than conventional banks. This suggests that greater income diversity tends to decrease z-scores, indicating that a move from lending-based operations to other sources of income might not improve stability for those banks. The impact of the Herfindahl index is consistently positive for specifications and statistically insignificant for all sizes. So, the overall effect of the Herfindahl index is less clear.

The regression for the sub-period 2006 to 2010 seems to indicate that Islamic banks' performance improved in comparison to conventional banks taken together as a group, given their increase in market share during this period in Bahrain's banking system (even though their share is still at a relatively lower level). This effect is supported by the inconclusive result for the sign of the Islamic dummy as shown in table 9.9 where it is positive for specifications (7) through (9) and is only statistically significant at the 1 percent level for specifications (1) and (4) and, more important, is statistically *in*significant for the rest of the specifications.

1. Regression with Cluster-Robust Standard Errors

Table 9.7 shows the output of the regression with cluster-robust standard errors on the individual bank level.

The regression's R-squared of 21 percent is approximately similar to the regression results for the full sample for the different banks' asset sizes cutoff thresholds (see table 9.8 and tables II (a), III (a), and IV(a) in appendix A). The negative value of the Islamic bank dummy variable is consistent with the regression in table 9.8 and is statistically significant at the 2 percent level. The cost-to-income ratio has the expected sign and is statistically significant at the 1 percent level for the 95 percent confidence interval. Regression results for the subperiod (2006–2010) and years 2008–2009 are similar to those of the full sample but statistically significant at the 6 and 9 percent levels respectively.

Table 9.7

Regression Results of the Cluster-Robust Standard Errors for 1996–2010

Linear Regression

Number of Observations	226
$F_{(6, 33)}$	2.43
Prob. > F	0.0465
R-Squared	0.2063
Root MSE	30.515

(Standard Error Adjusted for 34 Clusters in index)

Z-Score	Coefficient	Robust Std. Error	t	$p > |t|$	[95% Confidence]	Interval
Total Assets (*millions BHD*)	-0.0023957	0.0015906	-1.51	0.142	-0.0056317	0.0008404
Equity to Total Assets	0.1649476	0.1527791	1.08	0.288	-1.1458837	0.475779
Net Loans to Total Assets	0.4305665	0.2443767	1.76	0.087	-0.0666217	0.9277546
Total Cost to Income	-0.0544658	0.0204921	-2.66	0.012	-0.0961574	-0.0127743
Income Diversity	0.2256479	0.2745726	0.82	0.417	-0.3329743	0.7842701
Islamic Dummy Variable	-27.03824	11.03905	-2.45	0.020	-49.49735	-4.579132
Constant	20.61598	10.8015	1.91	0.065	-1.359827	42.591

2. *Cases of Bank Failures or Crises*

Bahrain's banking system for most of the sample period (1996–2010) is characterized by steady growth in general underpinned by high capital adequacy, low nonperforming assets, and plenty of liquidity. However, the global financial crisis during the 2007 to 2009 period made the operating environment for financial institutions more challenging.

The Bahraini financial sector has not experienced a systemic crisis. In the early days of the crisis, some banks suffered substantial losses because of their exposure to toxic mortgage-related securities.[65] These losses have not translated into generalized systemic problems, and the central bank took measures to address the specific difficulties of the banks under stress. Most of these difficulties are related to wholesale banks facing liquidity difficulties. Unlike in the United States, no major bank became functionally insolvent. The central bank's measure ensured that the impact of the global financial crisis was contained.

E. Overall Assessment

Conventional banks are financially sounder than Islamic banks based on the full sample period, as reflected in both the descriptive statistical and regression analyses. However, the results for the shorter subperiod (2006–2010) are somewhat mixed. All the descriptive statistics, as shown in tables 9.3, clearly indicate that conventional banks are relatively stronger financially than Islamic banks for each of the four asset sizes cutoff thresholds. Furthermore, the regression results in table 9.8 show conventional banks are stronger than Islamic banks and are statistically significant at the 1 percent level for specification (1) and statistically insignificant for specifications (2) and (3), taking all banks together as a group.

This outcome is in line with expectations, as I stated in chapter 8, because the increase in the share of Islamic banks as well as the practical expertise they gained in management and customer service closed the gap. More important, another reason for the increase in market share and possible improvement in the performance of Islamic banks for the shorter sample sub-period could be due to preferences and awareness.

In general, the potential advantage Islamic banks would have over conventional banks during periods of financial crises and/or economic downturn would have been due to ruling out the use of debt leveraging and maintenance of higher levels of capital. This potential advantage in the case of Islamic banks in Bahrain has been neutralized by the conservative approach of conventional banks due to minimal use of debt leveraging and the maintenance of higher levels of capital.

At the end of 2010, Bahraini banks, whether Islamic or conventional, because of their higher levels of capital—significantly higher than required by regulation—and higher liquidity positions coupled with their lack of use of debt leveraging were able to weather effects arising from the global financial crisis of 2007–2009.[66]

Table 9.8

Regression Results: Robust Estimation, 1996–2010

Estimated Variable	All Banks (1)	All Banks (2)	All Banks (3)	Large Banks (4)	Large Banks (5)	Large Banks (6)	Small Banks (7)	Small Banks (8)	Small Banks (9)
Islamic Bank Dummy	-19.88***	-16.90***	-16.90***	-32.13***	-29.66***	-29.66***	-8.755	-7.045	-7.045
P-value	(1.46e-07)	(0.00243)	(0.00243)	(1.62e-06)	(2.43e-06)	(2.43e-06)	(0.131)	(0.428)	(0.428)
Net Loans / Total Assets (t-1)	0.335***	0.309***	0.309***	0.0632	0.0222	0.0222	0.538***	0.394***	0.394***
P-value	(0.00185)	(0.00562)	(0.00562)	(0.673)	(0.886)	(0.886)	(0.000215)	(0.00533)	(0.00533)
Costs / Net Income (t-1)	-0.0463**	-0.0723***	-0.0723***	0.0103	0.0451	0.0451	-0.0195	-0.0120	-0.0120
P-value	(0.0339)	(0.00250)	(0.00250)	(0.905)	(0.684)	(0.684)	(0.291)	(0.674)	(0.674)
Total Assets (t-1)	0.00224***	-0.00225***	0.00225***	0.00319***	0.00327***	0.00327***	-0.00563	-0.00238	-0.00238
P-value	(0.000716)	(0.00103)	(0.00103)	(0.00102)	(0.000990)	(0.000990)	(0.135)	(0.414)	(0.414)
Income Diversity (t-1)	9.734	8.110	8.110	15.28	15.05	15.05	-1.112	-5.295	-5.295
P-value	(0.241)	(0.314)	(0.314)	(0.211)	(0.238)	(0.238)	(0.901)	(0.633)	(0.633)
Income Diversity* Islamic Bank Dummy (t-1)	-12.61	-10.51	-10.51	-15.70	-12.81	-12.81	5.079	5.560	5.560
P-value	(0.131)	(0.202)	(0.202)	(0.164)	(0.258)	(0.258)	(0.643)	(0.645)	(0.645)

	(1)	(2)	(3)	(4)	(5)	(6)	(7)	(8)	(9)
Herfindahl Index (t-1)	97.24	97.24		3.317	3.317		53.34	53.34	
P-value	(0.137)	(0.137)		(0.911)	(0.911)		(0.148)	(0.148)	
Share of Islamic Banks (t-1)	64.53	95.18		83.69	37.98		101.9	74.56*	
P-value	(0.473)	(0.142)		(0.239)	(0.332)		(0.101)	(0.0814)	
Share of Islamic Banks * Conventional Bank Dummy (t-1)		-30.65			45.71			27.38	
P-value		(0.622)			(0.486)			(0.585)	
Share of Islamic Banks * Islamic Bank Dummy (t-1)	30.65			-45.71			-27.38		
P-value	(0.622)			(0.486)			(0.585)		
Constant	-19.01	-19.01	9.756**	30.81***	30.81***	39.78***	3.136	3.136	23.41***
P-value	(0.332)	(0.332)	(0.0379)	(0.00771)	(0.00771)	(1.82e-09)	(0.799)	(0.799)	(9.01e-09)
Observations	75	75	75	126	126	126	201	201	201
Adjusted R-squared	0.230	0.230	0.181	0.252	0.252	0.238	0.192	0.192	0.183

ρ values in parentheses
* significant at 10 percent; ** significant at 5 percent; *** significant at 1 percent

Table 9.9

Regression Results: Robust Estimation, 2006–2010

Estimated Variable	All Banks (1)	All Banks (2)	All Banks (3)	Large Banks (4)	Large Banks (5)	Large Banks (6)	Small Banks (7)	Small Banks (8)	Small Banks (9)
Islamic Bank Dummy	-14.02****	-0.897	-0.897	-33.28***	-21.94	-21.94	0.968	10.55	10.55
P-value	(0.00906)	(0.954)	(0.954)	(0.000189)	(0.258)	(0.258)	(0.764)	(0.243)	(0.243)
Net Loans / Total Assets (t-1)	0.171	0.131	0.131	-0.307	-0.319	-0.319	0.0244	0.00142	0.00142
P-value	(0.261)	(0.393)	(0.393)	(0.119)	(0.119)	(0.119)	(0.727)	(0.984)	(0.984)
Costs / Net Income (t-1)	-0.0331	-0.0674*	-0.0674*	0.102	0.0446	0.0446	-0.00415	-0.0205	-0.0205
P-value	(0.242)	(0.0866)	(0.0866)	(0.422)	(0.761)	(0.761)	(0.739)	(0.364)	(0.364)
Total Assets (t-1)	-0.00130	-0.00129	-0.00129	-0.00309*	-0.00300*	-0.00300*	-0.00116	-0.000666	-0.000666
P-value	(0.277)	(0.266)	(0.266)	(0.0583)	(0.0581)	(0.0581)	(0.376)	(0.624)	(0.624)
Income Diversity (t-1)	64.27**	61.29**	61.29**	103.2***	101.0***	101.0***	19.44*	16.60	16.60
P-value	(0.0449)	(0.0498)	(0.0498)	(0.00524)	(0.00483)	(0.00483)	(0.0742)	(0.141)	(0.141)
Income Diversity * Islamic Bank Dummy	-67.18**	-63.60**	-63.60**	-97.82***	-96.06***	-96.06***	-24.85***	-20.19*	-20.19*

P-value	(0.0891)	(0.0891)	(0.0334)	(0.00421)	(0.00421)	(0.00399)	(0.0391)	(0.0391)	(0.0337)
Herfindahl Index (t-1)	210.9	210.9		257.2	257.2		380.1	380.1	
P-value	(0.327)	(0.327)		(0.672)	(0.672)		(0.466)	(0.466)	
Share of Islamic Banks (t-1)	141.3	79.87		222.1	159.8		262.7	184.5	
P-value	(0.174)	(0.367)		(0.379)	(0.527)		(0.243)	(0.394)	
Share of Islamic Banks * Conventional Bank Dummy (t-1)		61.45			62.25			78.19	
P-value		(0.241)			(0.566)			(0.367)	
Share of Islamic Banks * Islamic Bank Dummy (t-1)	-61.45			-62.25			-78.19		
P-value	(0.241)			(0.566)			(0.367)		
Constant	-44.19	-44.19	7.637*	-23.79	-23.79	48.30***	-73.88	-73.88	21.35**
P-value	(0.328)	(0.328)	(0.0977)	(0.844)	(0.844)	(3.17e-05)	(0.495)	(0.495)	(0.0102)
Observations	33	33	33	68	68	68	101	101	101
Adjusted R-squared	0.286	0.286	0.266	0.463	0.463	0.461	0.306	0.306	0.298

ρ values in parentheses

* significant at 10 percent; ** significant at 5 percent; *** significant at 1 percent

Endnotes

56. "290,000 Indians in Bahrain," *GulfDailyNews.com* (July 5, 2008) (retrieved June 27, 2010).

57. Source: *2011 CIA World Factbook.*

58. According to Heritage Foundation's Index of Economic Freedom in the last several years.

59. Source: Bahrain Monetary Authority (BMA) Annual Report 2003 (Foreword). Data available from the central bank of Bahrain does not break down assets between foreign and locally incorporated banks. As I stated in chapter 9, my analysis focuses only on locally incorporated commercial banks.

60. See the Oxford Analytical Report of December 2008.

61. Source: Web site of Bahrain Central Bank, www.cbb.gov.bh/cmsrule/index.jsp?action=article&ID=19 (accessed on February 5, 2010).

62. *Statistical Bulletin—December 2010,* p. 3, issued by the Bahrain Central Bank.

63. $z = (k+m)/s$, where k is equity capital plus reserves as a percent of assets; m is the average return as a percent of assets; and s is the standard deviation of return on assets as a proxy for return volatility.

64. The negative sign for the Islamic dummy variable means conventional banks are financially more stable than Islamic banks, and the reverse means Islamic banks are more stable than conventional banks.

65. Central Bank of Bahrain, "Financial Stability Report" (June 2009).

66. Central Bank of Bahrain, "Financial Stability Report" (December 2008).

Analytical History and Regression of Malaysia

A. Analytical History of Malaysia

The Federation of Malaysia, formed in 1963, originally consisted of Malaya, Singapore, Sarawak, and Sabah. Because of internal political tensions, Singapore left in 1965. Malaya is now known as Peninsular Malaysia, and the two other territories on the island of Borneo as East Malaysia. Prior to 1963, these territories were under British rule for varying periods from the eighteenth century. Malaya gained independence in 1957, Sarawak and Sabah (the latter known previously as British North Borneo) in 1963, and Singapore full independence in 1965.

As of 2010, Malaysia's population was estimated at 28.3 million with an ethnic makeup of approximately 54 percent Malay, 25 percent Chinese, 7.5 percent Indian, 11.8 percent Bumiputera, and 1.7 percent other. Nominal GDP and nominal per capita income (GNI) was estimated in 2010 at US$255.34 billion and US$8,126 respectively.[67] The country has an area of approximately 127,354 square miles.

1. Economy

Malaysia is generally regarded as one of the most successful non-Western countries to have achieved a relatively smooth transition to modern economic growth over the last century or so. Since the late nineteenth century, it has been a major supplier of primary products, such as tin, palm oil, timber, oil, liquefied natural gas, etc., to industrialized countries. As one of the three countries that control the Straits of Malacca, international trade plays a large role in its economy.

However, since the 1970s, the leading sector in development has been a range of export-oriented manufacturing industries, such as textiles, electrical and electronic goods, rubber products, etc. Also starting in the 1970s, government policy accorded a central role to the attraction of foreign capital and the transformation of the economy from one based on mining and agriculture to one based more on manufacturing and exports similar to the four Asian Tiger economies of South Korea, Taiwan, Hong Kong, and Singapore.

By 1990, the country had largely met the criteria for Newly Industrialized Country (NIC) status, in which 30 percent of exports consisted of manufactured goods. During the 1980s and 1990s, Malaysia consistently achieved more than 7 percent GDP growth annually along with low inflation (Kanagasingam 2005). Although the East Asian financial crisis of 1997–1998 slowed growth temporarily, the country's current economic plan, titled Vision 2020, aims to achieve "a fully developed industrialized economy" by that date. This will require an annual growth rate in real GDP of 7 percent.[68]

Malaysia has an economic freedom score of 64.8 in 2010, making its economy the fifty-ninth freest according to the Heritage Foundation's 2010 Index of Economic Freedom. It ranked ninth out of the forty-one countries in the Asia-Pacific region, with an overall score of above average in world and regional ranking. The country is also undertaking ongoing reforms to foster its overall entrepreneurial environment. The labor sector is relatively flexible with no mandated minimum wage. According to the 2010 Index of Economic Freedom report, "the top income and corporate income tax rates are moderate and have been reduced, and the overall tax burden is low as a percentage of GDP."

Malaysia's annual real GDP growth rates for the last five years were: 5.9 percent (2006); 6.3 percent (2007); 4.6 percent (2008); -1.7 percent (2009), and 7.2 percent (2010). The resilience of the Malaysian economy during the global financial crisis is in part due to valuable lessons learned from the 1997–1998 East Asian financial crisis that were applied in its economic management of the 2008–2009 global financial crisis. Another important factor is that Malaysian banks—whether conventional or Islamic—are well capitalized, conservatively managed, and had no measure of exposure to the U.S. subprime market.

After the sharp contraction in the first half of 2009, the Malaysian economy experienced a strong resumption of growth, recording an expansion of 7.2 percent for 2010. Growth was driven mainly by robust domestic demand and primarily by private sector activity.

The intensification of regional integration in East Asia has resulted in a broader trading base for Malaysia in terms of both markets and products. East Asia is currently Malaysia's main trading partner and a major consumer of both manufactured products and commodities. Although the advanced economies will remain an important source of financial demand, the East Asian market has become an increasingly important source of external demand for Malaysia.

Malaysia is a founding member of the ASEAN Free Trade Area, which was established in 1992 to promote trade among ASEAN members. Most tariffs among the first-generation member states were scrapped in 2007. The Malaysian government is currently negotiating free trade deals with Australia, New Zealand, the United States, Chile, and India.[69]

Although the federal government promotes private enterprise and ownership in the economy, the government, through five-year development plans, has heavily influenced the economic direction of the country since independence.

The view of the IMF is that the economic model that produced significant advances over three decades has lost the ability to drive the country forward. Old policies are under review, and the political leadership is making the case for a national transformation to free Malaysia from the middle-income trap where it is now stuck.

The Malaysian currency, the ringgit, was floating from the beginning of the 1970s until September 1998, when, due to the impact of the East Asian financial crisis in 1997–1998, the central bank imposed capital controls on the currency. As part of a series of capital controls, the currency was pegged between September 1998 to July 21, 2005, at MYR 3.8 to the dollar (Asian Strategy and Leadership Institute 2005). The central bank of Malaysia (Bank Negara Malaysia) after July 21, 2005, switched to managing float for the currency and began to relax the capital controls. The IMF, several years later, conducted an in-depth analysis of the effects of the imposition of capital controls by Malaysia during the 1997–1998 financial crisis and concluded that these controls neither yielded major benefits nor were costly (Johnson, Kochhar, Milton, and Tamirisa 2006).

2. Financial Sector Structure

Malaysia's financial markets are relatively deep by regional standards. Total assets of the financial sector (bank and nonbank) were about 350 percent of GDP in 2008.[70] Malaysia also has an offshore financial center in Labuan, where, as of the end of 2008, fifty-nine banks operated with assets totaling US$29 billion (about 4 percent of Malaysia's financial sector assets).[71] The Labuan Offshore Services Authority supervises Labuan-based institutions. The central bank can also conduct on-site inspections as necessary.

Malaysia has the second largest stock market capitalization and the largest bond market within the ASEAN countries. Although bank financing remains the predominant source of funding, the corporate sector has increasingly tapped the debt market. The country made significant progress in opening its financial sector with the exception of the brief period it imposed the foreign exchange controls during the East Asian financial crisis.

3. Banking

Before the beginning of the 1997 financial crisis, the Malaysian banking system consisted of four types of financial institutions: commercial banks (domestic and foreign), finance companies, merchant banks, and Islamic banks (domestic and foreign). The Malaysian financial system's assets and liabilities continue to be dominated by the commercial banking sector with total assets and liabilities of about US$200.3 billion or 3.05 times the national GDP at the end of 2004 (Sufian 2007).

Foreign commercial banks controlled over 90 percent of the banking market in 1957 when Malaysia gained its independence, but by 1997, they controlled only 16.7 percent of banking assets (Sufian 2007). This decline in the share of foreign commercial banks has been the result of a government policy geared toward domestic ownership coupled with the prohibition of foreign banks opening new branches. Domestic and foreign banks obtain most of their funding from demand deposits and engage in retail and corporate banking whether Islamic or conventional.

Even though finance companies are numerous, they are very small in size and provide mainly installment credit to consumers and small businesses, with funding provided from time and savings deposits. Merchant banks have a minor presence in the Malaysian economy.

4. Islamic Finance

Since the early 1980s, development of the Islamic financial industry and institutions has been one of the central objectives for Malaysian policy makers. The regulatory and tax systems have been developed to support the market-driven environment in which Islamic finance coexists with conventional finance. As a result, Malaysia now has robust Islamic and conventional financial systems that operate parallel to each other.

Islamic banking was introduced to Malaysia through the Islamic Banking Act (IBA) of 1983 and the simultaneous establishment of Bank Islam Malaysia Berhad (BIMB). The move was part of the Malaysian government's strategy to support Muslim Malays who were perceived to be losing out to the more commercially minded Chinese, even though Malays make up the majority of the country's population nationwide. However, in the capital Kuala Lumpur and the province Penang, it is the Chinese who dominate the business sector and who have played a leading role in the industrialization and economic growth of Malaysia (Davies, R. 2002).

Islamic finance has grown tremendously since it first emerged in the 1970s. Current global Islamic banking assets and assets under management have reached US$750 billion and are expected to hit US$1 trillion by 2010 (Bank Negara Malaysia 2010). At the end of 2007, Malaysia's Islamic banking assets reached US$65.6 billion with an average growth rate of 18 to 20 percent annually.[72] Assets of Islamic banks have doubled since 2000 and account for about 17 percent of total banking sector assets as of May 2009. At the end of 2007, *Shari'a*-compliant stocks accounted for about 88 percent of the stocks listed and 64 percent of total market capitalization of the Malaysian stock market (IMF 2009, 14).

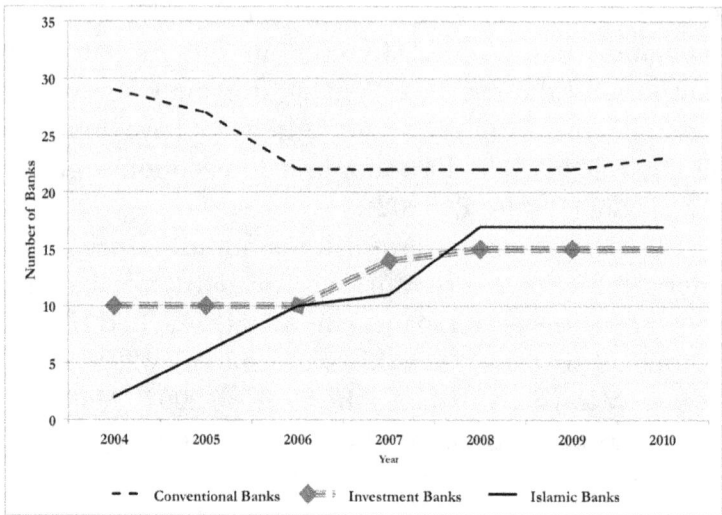

Figure 10.1 Recent Rise in the Number of Islamic Banks in Malaysia

Source: Financial Stability and Payment Systems Report 2010

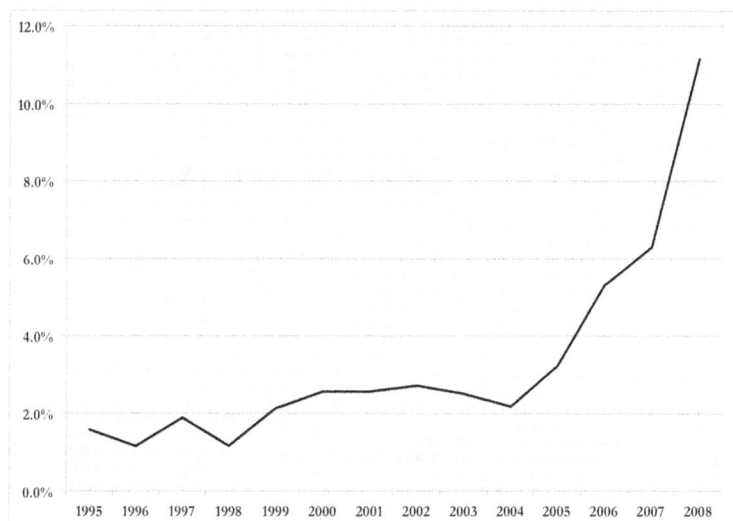

Figure 10.2 Growth of Islamic Banks' Assets in Malaysian Banking System

Source: Calculations based on BankScope data.

Note: Assets in the chart are those of fully licensed Islamic banks and do not include assets of commercial banks that have Islamic windows.

The central bank of Malaysia (Bank Negara Malaysia—BNM) played an important role in the effort to restructure and standardize the *Shari'a* interpretations among banks and *takaful* (insurance) companies by establishing the National Shari'a Advisory Council (NSAC) on May 1, 1997, as the highest *Shari'a* authority on Islamic banking and *takaful* in Malaysia. The council's goals are to act as the sole authoritative body to advise BNM on Islamic banking and *takaful* operations, to coordinate *Shari'a* issues with respect to Islamic banking and finance, and to analyze and evaluate new products and innovations.

Malaysia has achieved significant milestones in the development of its *takaful* (insurance) industry. With the enactment of the Takaful Act 1984, the first *takaful* company was established in 1985. Since then, Malaysia's *takaful* industry has been gaining momentum and increasingly is recognized as a significant contributor to Malaysia's overall Islamic financial system.

As of 2007, total assets of Malaysia's *takaful* industry amounted to US$2.8 billion, with market penetration of 7.2 percent.[73] *Takaful* assets and net contributions experienced strong growth with an average annual growth rate of 27 percent from 2003 to 2007.[74]

Guidelines pertaining to Islamic banking, issued by Bank Negara from time to time, are as good as legal requirements, because under the Bank Negara Ordinance, Malaysia's central bank is vested with some powers to regulate the market. In 2004, Bank Negara further opened the Islamic banking market by issuing three new licenses to major Islamic financial institutions in the Middle East in an effort to expedite the development of the Islamic banking sector.

Malaysia is taking initiatives and making progress in its efforts to become an international Islamic financial hub. To begin with, the country is the world's largest issuer of *sukuk* (Islamic bonds), which were estimated at RM155 billion or 59 percent of total outstanding bonds in Malaysia. Malaysian *sukuk* accounted for about 61 percent of the total outstanding global *sukuk* in 2008. However, the global financial crisis adversely impacted the *sukuk* market and reduced issuance of global *sukuk* by about half.[75] Figure 10.3 shows the breakdown of global *sukuk* by issuance currency.

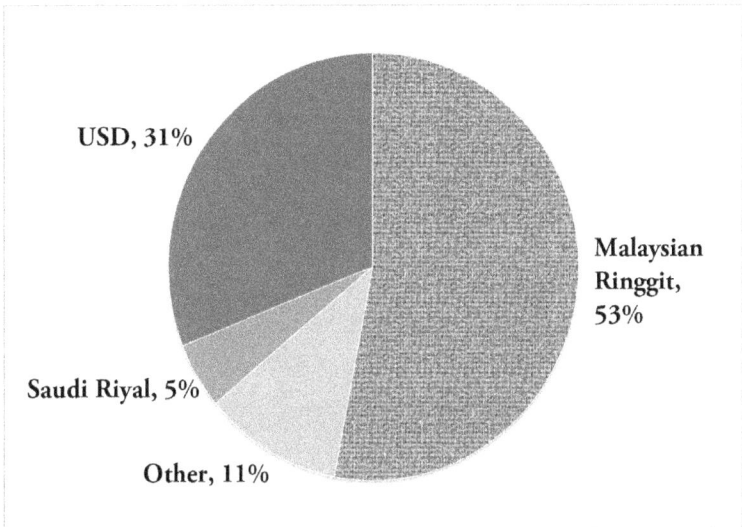

Figure 10.3 Currency Breakdown of Global *Sukuk* Market, 2008

Source: Moody's; Bloomberg L.P.; IFIS Zawya

B. Data

Table 10.1 provides a summary overview of the input data from BankScope used for the descriptive statistics and regression analysis based on the balance sheets in 2010 for various banks' asset sizes cutoff thresholds in classifying banks into large and small categories. For lower-level thresholds (US$750 million and US$1 billion), the number of large and small banks is approximately the same: 63 percent are large, and the remaining 37 percent are small. However, for the higher cutoff thresholds (US$1.5 and 2 billion), roughly one half are large banks and the other half are small banks.

Table 10.1

Summary of Data Input for the Various Banks' Asset Sizes
Threshold Cutoffs

Cutoff Threshold for Bank-Asset Sizes		Conventional Banks	Islamic Banks	All Banks
US$750 million	Number of Banks	40	16	56
	Large Banks	21	14	35
	Small Banks	19	2	21
	Number of Observations	374	71	445
	Large Banks	286	62	348
	Small Banks	88	9	97
US$1 billion	Number of Banks	40	16	56
	Large Banks	20	14	32
	Small Banks	20	2	23
	Number of Observations	374	71	445
	Large Banks	281	62	343
	Small Banks	93	9	102
US$1.5 billion	Number of Banks	40	16	56
	Large Banks	18	11	29
	Small Banks	22	5	27
	Number of Observations	374	71	445
	Large Banks	251	53	304
	Small Banks	123	18	141
US$2 billion	Number of Banks	40	16	56
	Large Banks	17	10	27
	Small Banks	23	6	29
	Number of Observations	374	71	445
	Large Banks	236	48	284
	Small Banks	138	23	161

To examine one of the banks' asset sizes cutoff
thresholds more closely, I selected the US$1 billion (table
10.2). Approximately 53 percent of the data is based
on consolidated bank statements, and the remaining
43 percent came from unconsolidated bank financial
statements. As noted in chapter 8, I would have opted for
using only consolidated data for all financial institutions

if it had been available. Using this two-size classification, the data sample for Malaysia consisted of twenty-three small conventional and Islamic banks and thirty-two large conventional and Islamic banks.[76]

Looking at it differently, forty of the total fifty-six banks (71 percent) are conventional banks of which twenty-six are locally owned while the remaining fourteen are foreign owned. Islamic banks account for sixteen banks or about 29 percent of the total number of banks in the data sample, eleven of which are locally owned.

C. Results of the Descriptive Statistics

Hypothesis Test:
Test whether the difference in mean variables (i.e., *z-score, z-score excluding outliers, loans/assets, cost/income,* and *income diversity*) between Islamic banks and conventional banks is due to random chance. This hypothesis test will be applied to all banks taken together, all large banks taken together, and all small banks taken together.

Table 10.2

Input Data Overview—US$1 Billion Banks' Asset Sizes Cutoff Thresholds

	Conventional Banks			Islamic Banks			Total
	Consolidated	Unconsolidated	Subtotal	Consolidated	Unconsolidated	Subtotal	
All Banks							
Number of Banks	**29**	**11**	**40**	**3**	**13**	**16**	**56**
Local Banks	20	6	26	2	9	11	37
Foreign Banks	9	5	14	1	4	5	19
Number of Observations	**298**	**76**	**374**	**16**	**55**	**71**	**445**
Local Banks	196	26	222	10	39	49	271
Foreign Banks	102	50	152	6	16	22	174
Large Banks							
Number of Banks	**17**	**3**	**20**	**3**	**11**	**14**	**34**
Local Banks	11	1	12	2	8	10	22
Foreign Banks	6	2	8	1	3	4	12
Number of Observations	**246**	**35**	**281**	**16**	**46**	**62**	**343**
Local Banks	156	5	161	10	35	45	206
Foreign Banks	90	30	120	6	11	17	137
Small Banks							
Number of Banks	**12**	**8**	**20**	**0**	**2**	**2**	**22**
Local Banks	9	5	14	0	1	1	15
Foreign Banks	3	3	6	0	1	1	7
Number of Observations	**52**	**41**	**93**	**0**	**9**	**9**	**102**
Local Banks	40	21	61	0	4	4	65
Foreign Banks	12	20	32	0	5	5	37

Result 1

A preliminary look at the z-scores across the sample for the various cutoff thresholds for bank sizes for the entire period (1996 to 2010) is shown below in table 10.3. The differences in the mean scores between Islamic and conventional banks are statistically significant at the 5 percent level for all banks' asset sizes cutoff thresholds except the US$2 billion, which is significant at the 1 percent level in favor of Islamic banks (at the 95 percent confidence interval).[77] Drilling down, the data shows the overall higher financial stability advantage of Islamic banks holds for large and small banks as well.

This outcome, unlike that of Bahrain in chapter 9, supports my thesis that Islamic banks are more likely to be stable than conventional banks. As noted earlier in the book, the conceptual underpinning for the expected higher stability for Islamic banks versus conventional banks, occurred in this case for Malaysia because of higher ratios for equity capital to total assets, total nonearning assets to total assets, and cash and due from banks to total assets (see table 10.9 and table I (a) at Appendix B). However, this favorable result has been offset by the conventional banks' higher return on average assets (ROAA), higher operational efficiency (lower cost/income), and lower return volatility (lower standard deviation for ROAA)—as also shown in table I (a) in appendix B. Nonetheless, these favorable variables to conventional banks are insufficient to offset the other variables that contributed for the higher z-score values of Islamic banks.[78]

Table 10.3

Summary Statistics for Banks' Asset Sizes Cutoff Thresholds, 1996–2010

Cutoff for Bank Asset Size	US$750 million		US$1 billion		
Variables	Conventional Banks	Islamic Banks	Variables	Conventional Banks	Islamic Banks
Z-score	*21.20*	*29.00***	*Z-score*	*21.20*	*29.00***
Large Banks	20.84	25.90**	Large Banks	20.44	25.90**
Small Banks	22.41	50.00***	Small Banks	23.53	50.00***
Z-score Exclud. Outliers	*20.83*	*26.07***	*Z-score Exclud. Outliers*	*20.83*	*26.07***
Large Banks	20.51	24.39***	Large Banks	20.11	24.39**
Small Banks	21.94	38.47**	Small Banks	23.14	38.47**
Loans / Assets	*54.50*	*50.55*	*Loans / Assets*	*54.50*	*50.55*
Large Banks	54.49	51.97	Large Banks	24.34	51.97
Small Banks	54.53	41.20*	Small Banks	54.99	41.20*
Cost / Income	*42.36*	*62.61****	*Cost / Income*	*42.36*	*62.61****
Large Banks	40.47	62.93***	Large Banks	40.54	62.93***
Small Banks	48.71	59.74	Small Banks	48.02	59.74
Income Diversity	*0.13*	*0.04*	*Income Diversity*	*0.13*	*0.04*
Large Banks	0.12	0.03	Large Banks	0.11	0.03
Small Banks	0.19	0.15	Small Banks	0.20	0.15

US$1.5 billion

Z-score	**21.20**	**28.00****
Large Banks	20.52	26.12***
Small Banks	22.60	37.32***
Z-score Exclud. Outliers	**20.83**	**26.07***
Large Banks	20.15	24.34
Small Banks	22.28	31.15**
Loans / Assets	**54.50**	**50.55***
Large Banks	56.28	51.50*
Small Banks	50.74	47.91
Cost / Income	**42.36**	**62.61*****
Large Banks	41.75	65.53***
Small Banks	43.63	53.84*
Income Diversity	**0.13**	**0.04**
Large Banks	0.10	0.03
Small Banks	0.20	0.12

US$2 billion

Z-score	**21.20**	**29.00*****
Large Banks	20.84	28.71***
Small Banks	21.81	29.59*
Z-score Exclud. Outliers	**20.83**	**26.07*****
Large Banks	20.45	26.85***
Small Banks	21.51	24.47
Loans / Assets	**54.50**	**50.55**
Large Banks	58.07	51.24
Small Banks	48.21	49.18
Cost / Income	**42.36**	**62.61*****
Large Banks	40.13	63.42***
Small Banks	46.25	60.73**
Income Diversity	**0.13**	**0.04**
Large Banks	0.19	0.17
Small Banks	0.03	-0.32

Source: Calculations based on BankScope data.

Note: The difference between the value of commercial and Islamic banks at the 95 percent confidence interval is significant at 10 percent (*); at 5 percent (**); and at 1 percent (***).

Drilling down further, table 10.9 shows that small local Islamic banks and large foreign Islamic banks were the drivers (statistically significant at the 1 percent level) for Islamic banks being deemed more stable than conventional banks. This conclusion holds as well for the z-score measure excluding the outliers, albeit with a lower level of significance.

The net-loans-to-total-assets ratio, a rough measure of liquidity, was statistically significant at the 10 percent level only for size cutoff threshold US$1.5, all banks taken together as a group. This higher ratio for conventional banks means they are slightly less liquid than Islamic banks. This finding is in line with my earlier analysis of the difference in characteristics between Islamic and conventional banks (chapter 4). Islamic banks carry more liquid assets in their balance sheets than conventional banks because of the constraint on Islamic banks of not being able to invest in safe and highly liquid short-term debt instruments, since Islamic law prohibits the receipt and payment of interest.

Conventional banks' lower cost-to-income ratios are statistically significant at the 1 percent level for all four banks' asset sizes cutoff thresholds. This finding is supported by several studies on the efficiency difference between Islamic and conventional banks in Malaysia (Rosly and Abu Bakar 2003; Moktar and Al Habshi 2006; Bader, Hassan, and Mohamad 2006). The income diversity ratio indicates that conventional banks in general have a more diversified loan portfolio than Islamic banks; however, the differences in the mean ratios are all statistically insignificant for all levels of banks' assets sizes cutoff thresholds.

Result 2

The summary statistics for the subperiod 2006 to 2010 for all the various banks' asset sizes cutoff thresholds is shown in table 10.4. The results of the z-score and the z-score excluding the outliers are by and large similar to those of the full sample period explained in result 1; however, the difference in mean scores between conventional and Islamic banking narrowed markedly—z-score 21.20 versus 29.00 obtained in result 1 against z-score 26.14 versus 27.51 for conventional versus Islamic banks—but still in favor of Islamic banks.

So, for this accounting measure of financial stability, the performance improvement of conventional banks taken together in comparison to Islamic banks is primarily due to a significant decrease in their standard deviation or the volatility of the return on average assets as well as improvement in equity to total assets, total nonearning assets to total assets, and cash due from banks to total assets ratios compared to the full sample period (see table I (b) in appendix B) despite an increase in the number and market share of Islamic banks during the 2006 to 2010 period. The increase in Islamic banks' market share in the banking system is mostly likely due to customer preferences.

Table 10.4

Summary Statistics for Banks' Asset Sizes Cutoff Thresholds, 2006–2010

Cutoff for Bank Asset Size	Variables	US$750 million		US$1 billion	
		Conventional Banks	Islamic Banks	Conventional Banks	Islamic Banks
	Z-score	*26.14*	*27.51***	*26.14*	*27.51***
	Large Banks	22.91	23.96**	21.91	23.96**
	Small Banks	74.56	50.00***	61.35	50.00***
	Z-score Exclud. Outliers	*24.37*	*26.18***	*24.37*	*26.18***
	Large Banks	22.04	24.43**	20.99	24.43**
	Small Banks	64.63	38.47**	54.74	38.47**
	Loans / Assets	*48.13*	*51.58*	*48.13*	*51.58*
	Large Banks	50.34	53.25	49.72	53.25
	Small Banks	19.14	41.20*	35.91	41.20**
	Cost / Income	*42.08*	*49.94****	*42.08*	*49.94****
	Large Banks	42.03	48.77***	42.32	48.77***
	Small Banks	42.76	59.74	40.25	59.74
	Income Diversity	*0.20*	*0.02*	*0.20*	*0.02*
	Large Banks	0.19	0.01	0.18	0.01
	Small Banks	0.37	0.15	0.38	0.15

US$1.5 Billion

	26.14	27.51**
Z-score		
Large Banks	22.23	23.83**
Small Banks	42.11	37.32***
Z-score Exclud. Outliers	24.37	26.18*
Large Banks	21.21	24.39**
Small Banks	37.73	31.15**
Loans / Assets	48.13	51.58*
Large Banks	51.51	52.99*
Small Banks	34.90	47.91
Cost / Income	42.08	49.94***
Large Banks	43.26	48.52***
Small Banks	37.46	53.84*
Income Diversity	0.20	0.02
Large Banks	0.17	0.00
Small Banks	0.32	0.12

US$2 Billion

	26.14	27.51***
Z-score		
Large Banks	22.73	26.40***
Small Banks	36.89	29.59
Z-score Exclud. Outliers	24.37	26.18***
Large Banks	21.65	27.08***
Small Banks	33.15	24.47
Loans / Assets	48.13	51.58***
Large Banks	54.12	52.90***
Small Banks	29.95	49.18
Cost / Income	42.08	49.94***
Large Banks	41.41	44.84***
Small Banks	44.10	60.73**
Income Diversity	0.20	0.02
Large Banks	0.22	0.16
Small Banks	0.14	-0.32

Source: Calculations based on BankScope data.

Note: The difference between the value of conventional and Islamic banks at the 95 percent confidence interval is significant at 10 percent (*); at 5 percent (**); and at 1 percent (***).

Result 3

To discern the difference in performance between conventional and Islamic banks during the global financial crisis of 2008–2009, I generated similar summary statistics as shown in table 10.5 in a format parallel to the 2006–2010 samples.

The z-score results show conventional banks with higher mean scores are more likely to be stable than Islamic banks given their stronger level of statistical significance. Consequently, in comparing this outcome to the results of the 2006–2010 sample, where overall, Islamic banks were deemed to be more stable, conventional banks performed better than Islamic banks during the two-year period of the global financial crisis. However, this interesting outcome does not hold in the case of the z-score measure excluding the outliers. So, it seems this points to a somewhat mixed result, which goes against the notion that Islamic banks perform better than conventional banks during periods of financial crisis.

The strength demonstrated by conventional banks is attributable mostly to higher levels of operational efficiency as demonstrated by the widening of the cost-income ratios between the periods of 2006–2010 and 2008–2009 (42.08 versus 49.94 and 41.23 versus 51.54 respectively).[79] Digging a little deeper, tables 10.4 and 10.5 show most of the improvement in the conventional banks' z-scores came from small banks.

Compared to the results of the sample subperiod (2006–10), the net-loans-to-total-assets ratio changed from 0.48 versus 0.52 (conventional banks versus Islamic banks) to 0.49 versus 0.55 (conventional banks versus Islamic banks) for all banks taken together as a group.

This means that during the global financial crisis, Islamic banks became slightly less liquid than conventional banks. However, this result is statistically significant only for the US$1.5 billion and US$2 billion thresholds at the 5 and 1 percent levels respectively.

Table 10.5

Summary Statistics for Banks' Asset Sizes Cutoff Thresholds, 2008–2009

Cutoff for Bank Asset Size US$750 million			Cutoff for Bank Asset Size US$1 billion		
Variables	Conventional Banks	Islamic Banks	Variables	Conventional Banks	Islamic Banks
Z-score	*26.58*	*24.86***	*Z-score*	*26.58*	*24.86***
Large Banks	22.77	23.24**	Large Banks	21.97	23.24**
Small Banks	79.92	35.76***	Small Banks	63.48	35.76***
Z-score Exclud. Outliers	*24.14*	*24.86***	*Z-score Exclud. Outliers*	*24.14*	*24.86***
Large Banks	22.77	23.24**	Large Banks	21.97	23.24**
Small Banks	52.83	35.76**	Small Banks	45.82	35.76**
Loans / Assets	*48.53*	*54.56*	*Loans / Assets*	*48.53*	*54.56*
Large Banks	50.55	56.07	Large Banks	49.78	56.07
Small Banks	20.18	44.38*	Small Banks	38.56	44.38*
Cost / Income	*41.23*	*51.54****	*Cost / Income*	*41.23*	*51.54****
Large Banks	41.10	50.76***	Large Banks	41.19	50.76***
Small Banks	43.09	58.62	Small Banks	41.50	58.62
Income Diversity	*0.26*	*0.12*	*Income Diversity*	*0.26*	*0.12*
Large Banks	0.27	0.10	Large Banks	0.26	0.10
Small Banks	0.16	0.31	Small Banks	0.24	0.31

	US$1.5 billion		US$2 billion	
Z-score	*26.58*	*24.86**	*26.58*	*24.86***
Large Banks	22.35	22.61**	22.80	24.89***
Small Banks	43.51	29.57***	38.27	24.80
Z-score Exclud. Outliers	*24.14*	*24.86**	*24.14*	*24.86***
Large Banks	22.35	22.61*	22.80	24.89***
Small Banks	32.18	29.57**	28.68	24.80
Loans / Assets	*48.53*	*54.56**	*48.53*	*54.56***
Large Banks	51.15	57.49*	53.74	56.91***
Small Banks	38.03	48.42	32.43	50.86
Cost / Income	*41.23*	*51.54***	*41.23*	*51.54***
Large Banks	42.33	50.80***	41.46	44.31***
Small Banks	36.84	53.29*	40.51	64.04**
Income Diversity	*0.26*	*0.12*	*0.26*	*0.12*
Large Banks	0.26	0.14	0.22	0.17
Small Banks	0.28	0.05	0.40	0.02

Source: Calculations based on BankScope data.

Note: The difference between the value of conventional and Islamic banks at the 95 percent confidence interval is significant at 10 percent (*); at 5 percent (**); and at 1 percent (***).

Result 4

Parallel to the data input analysis segment above, I closely examine the summary descriptive statistics of the US$1 billion banks' asset sizes cutoff threshold and point out where they illustrate the difference in performance between foreign and locally owned banks within conventional and Islamic banks for the full sample period 1996–2010 and the subperiods 2006–2010 and 2008–2009 as shown in table 10.9 at the end of this chapter.

Overall, the z-scores and z-scores excluding outliers for all three-sample periods are parallel and similar to those of results 1–3. The additional insight this analysis provides is that the improved performance of conventional banks during the global financial crisis is attributable exclusively to large foreign banks. Table 10.9 also clearly shows that taken together as a group, for the full sample, smaller Islamic banks are financially more stable than smaller conventional banks, since the differences in their mean z-scores are statistically significant at the 1 percent level. More specifically, this financial strength is attributable to the higher equity to total assets of domestic small Islamic banks in comparison to domestic small conventional banks.

For all banks taken together, total net loans to total assets for the full and subperiod samples are not statistically significant. However, results show overall large domestic Islamic banks have higher mean values that are significant at the 1 percent level. This means that in general, large Islamic banks have loan portfolios that are slightly less liquid than the loan portfolios of commercial banks.[80]

The cost-to-income ratio (*efficiency* measure) shows that conventional banks by and large are more efficient than

Islamic banks (42.36 conventional versus 62.61 Islamic) for the full sample period and that is statistically significant at the 1 percent level for all banks taken together (this holds also for the two sample subperiods).

The reversal of the z-score measure during the 2008–2009 global financial crisis—as was true of all four banks' asset cutoff thresholds (Result 3)—Islamic banks' poor performance was the result of a combination of a deterioration in efficiency and equity capital compared to the five-year period sample (2006–2010).

Figures 10.4 and 10.5 show the z-score distribution by bank type and asset size as well as by bank type and ownership for conventional and Islamic banks respectively for the full sample period (1996–2010).

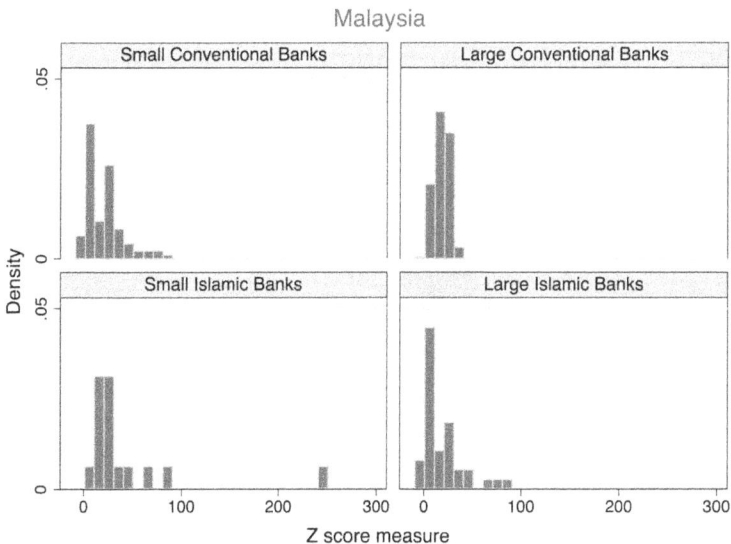

Figure 10.4 Z-score Distribution by Bank Type and Size

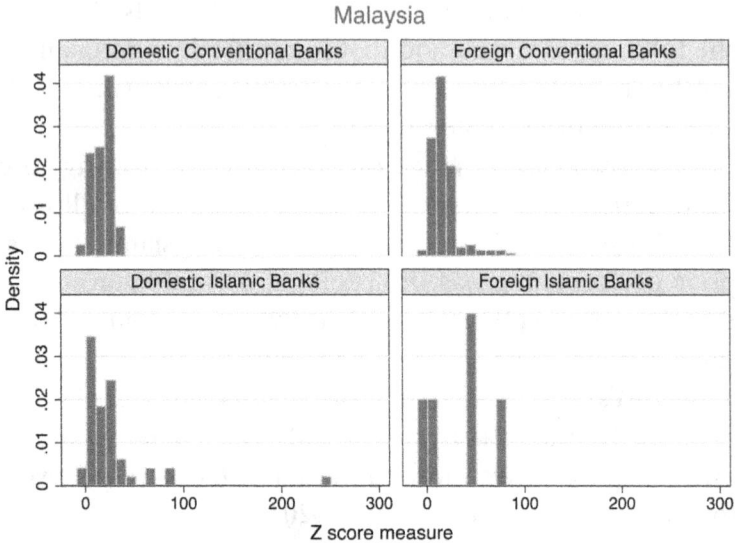

Figure 10.5 Z-score Distribution by Bank Type and Ownership

D. Regression Results and Analysis

To separate the financial stability impact of the Islamic nature of a bank from the impact of other bank-level characteristics, I turned to regression analysis, following the methodology described in chapter 8. I ran several specifications for the various banks' asset sizes cutoff thresholds. The regression results for the various size cutoff thresholds were more or less similar. Therefore, in light of this fact, I present the analysis of the regression for the US$1 billion cutoff threshold parallel with the analysis of the data input and summary descriptive statistics.

The results of the regressions for the full sample (1996–2010), subperiod (2006–2010), and the years 2008–2009 are shown in tables 10.10, 10.11, and 10.12 respectively at the end of this chapter. The regression results for the rest of the other banks' asset sizes cutoff thresholds are shown in tables II through IV in appendix B.

For the full sample period (table 10.10), the regression results indicate that Islamic banks, taken together as a group, are more stable than conventional banks, and this is statistically significant at the 5 percent level for a 95 percent confidence interval for specifications (2) and (3) and significant at the 10 percent level for specification (1). This result extends over both large and small Islamic banks and is statistically significant at the 1 percent level for all specifications except (4). The sign of the Islamic bank dummy variable for specifications of these findings is positive.

This finding for the full sample period (1996–2010) is similar to the simple comparison of the mean z-scores, which indicates that the differences in the mean z-scores between conventional and Islamic banks taken together are statistically different than a random occurrence as shown in table 10.9.

The result of the (2006–2010) sample regression (table 10.11) differs from that of the full sample in that none of the specifications are statistically significant. Similarly, the regression result of the period of the global financial crisis (2008–2009) (table 10.12) shows that none of the specifications are statistically significant.

As to the control variables, they generally have the expected signs. More precisely, banks with higher loan-to-asset ratios tend to have lower z-scores and negative coefficients. In the case of the full sample, this variable is statistically significant for large bank specifications (4)– (9) and for small bank specifications (7)–(9). Similarly, higher cost-to-income ratios have a consistently negative link to the z-scores; the sign is consistently significant except in all regressions for small banks.

Z-scores tend to increase with bank size for small banks, but decrease with size for large banks. Conventional banks tend to have greater income diversity than Islamic banks, suggesting that a move from lending-based operations to other sources of income might improve the stability of these banks.

1. Regression with Cluster-Robust Standard Errors

Tables 10.6, 10.7, and 10.8 show the output of the regression with cluster-robust standard errors on the individual bank level for the full sample period, subperiod 2006–2010, and the years 2008–2009 respectively.

For the full sample period (1996–2010)—table 10.6—the Islamic bank dummy variable is positive; however, it is not statistically significant. This finding differs from the results of the descriptive statistics (table 10.3) and regression results (table 10.11). Equity to total assets and total cost to income are statistically significant at the 1 and 5 percent levels respectively. Total assets are significant at the 10 percent level. The regression explains approximately 21 percent of the change in the z-score variable, which is quite significant.

In the cluster-robust regression for the 2006–2010 period (table 10.7), the Islamic bank dummy variable has a negative sign and is not statistically significant; however, this outcome is in agreement with the regression results of table 10.11 but differs from that of the descriptive statistics in table 10.4. Equity to assets and net loans to total assets are statistically significant at the 1 and 10 percent levels respectively. The regression explains about 20 percent of the changes in the z-score variable.

Table 10.6

Regression Results of the Cluster-Robust Standard Errors for 1996–2010

Linear Regression					Number of Observations	379
					F (6, 50)	5.94
					Prob. > F	0.0001
					R-Squared	0.2091
					Root MSE	13.721
					(Standard Error Adjusted for 34 Clusters in index)	
Z-Score	Coefficient	Robust Std. Error	t	$p > \lvert t \rvert$	[95% Confidence	Interval]
Total Assets (*millions* MYR)	0.0000361	0.0000202	1.78	0.080	-4.53E-06	0.0000768
Equity to Total Assets	1.331142	0.3790787	3.51	0.001	0.5697396	2.092543
Net Loans to Total Assets	0.1073204	0.0859774	1.25	0.218	-0.0653704	0.2800112
Total Cost to Income	-0.0274172	0.0128709	-2.13	0.038	-0.0532692	-0.0015652
Income Diversity	0.7691134	0.5888474	1.31	0.197	-0.4136215	1.951848
Islamic Dummy Variable	7.746819	5.207141	1.49	0.143	-2.71203	18.20567
Constant	1.6672	6.070159	1.49	0.785	-10.52507	13.85947

Table 10.7

Regression Results of the Cluster-Robust Standard Errors for 2006–2010

Linear Regression					Number of observations	123
					$F_{(6, 36)}$	8.64
					Prob. > F	0.0000
					R-Squared	0.1992
					Root MSE	19.593

(Standard Error Adjusted for 34 Clusters in index)

Z-Score	Coefficient	Robust Std. Error	t	$p > |t|$	[95% Confidence	Interval]
Total Assets (*millions MYR*)	-0.0000259	0.0000546	-0.47	0.638	-0.0001367	0.0000848
Equity to Total Assets	1.582294	0.3884645	4.07	0.000	0.7944517	2.370137
Net Loans to Total Assets	0.2225103	0.1245209	1.79	0.082	-0.0300297	0.4750504
Total Cost to Income	0.0270379	0.125437	0.22	0.831	-0.2273601	0.2814358
Income Diversity	3.063631	2.107999	1.45	0.155	-1.211447	7.338708
Islamic Dummy Variable	-0.1606564	8.310331	-0.02	0.985	-17.01479	16.69348
Constant	-1.577846	10.88384	-0.14	0.886	-23.6513	20.49561

The regression result for 2008–2009 is shown in table 10.8. The Islamic bank dummy variable, though positive, is not statistically significant. Equity to total assets is the only variable that is statistically significant and is significant at the 1 percent level. The regression explains about 28 percent of the changes in the z-score variable, which is quite significant.

Table 10.8

Regression Results of the Cluster-Robust Standard Errors for 2008–2009

Linear Regression				Number of Observations		35
				F (6, 34)		2.43
				Prob. > F		0.0000
				R-Squared		0.2826
				Root MSE		18.348

(Standard Error Adjusted for 34 Clusters in index)

Z-Score	Coefficient	Robust Std. Error	t	$p > |t|$	[95% Confidence	Interval]
Total Assets (*millions MYR*)	-0.0000168	0.0000577	-0.29	0.773	-0.0001341	0.0001005
Equity to Total Assets	1.360408	0.3896028	3.49	0.001	0.56864	2.152176
Net Loans to Total Assets	0.2054451	0.14146	1.45	0.156	-0.0820361	0.4999264
Total Cost to Income	-0.1544471	0.1140175	-1.35	0.184	-0.3861586	0.0772643
Income Diversity	3.214868	11.28555	0.28	0.777	-19.72013	26.14987
Islamic Dummy Variable	3.144616	8.044743	0.39	0.698	-13.20427	19.4935
Constant	6.506987	11.26298	0.58	0.567	-16.38214	29.39611

2. Cases of Bank Failures or Crises

1997–98 East Asian Financial Crisis
Before the onset of the East Asian financial crisis in 1997–98, Malaysia's macroeconomic performance was good. Growth was about 8 percent a year, driven in part by higher savings. Prudential financial policies had kept inflation low at about 3 percent, and there was a history of fiscal surpluses.

Beginning with the emergence of the financial crisis in Thailand in mid-1997, Malaysia experienced increased turbulence in its financial markets. Market concerns about the economic vulnerabilities in Malaysia were reflected in a sharp fall of the ringgit and the stock market on the order of 40 percent and 50 percent respectively by the end of 1997.

The Malaysian authorities responded to market pressures initially through intervention in the foreign exchange market, accompanied by an increase in interest rates, and subsequently allowing the ringgit to depreciate. There was substantial outflow of capital thereafter. The authorities then imposed capital controls in September 1998 and pegged the ringgit to the dollar (Malaysa 1998). A package of measures to strengthen the financial sector was also introduced at the same time.

During this period of the financial crisis, there was only one Islamic bank, so most of the banks that were adversely affected were conventional banks. There were no clear cases of bank failures; however, Malaysia established an institutional framework to strengthen and rehabilitate the conventional banking system by using public funds to acquire nonperforming loans and recapitalize conventional banks. This framework involved

debt restructuring for some conventional banks as an
alternative to filing for bankruptcy.

2007–2009 Global Financial Crisis
The recent global financial crisis (2007–2009) had no
major systemic impact on the Malaysian financial system.
The government and the Bank Negara Malaysia took
preemptive and precautionary measures to preserve
confidence and maintain the stability of the financial
system.

The impact of the global financial turmoil on the
domestic financial sector was well contained given the
limited direct or indirect exposure to affected assets
that were linked to the global financial turmoil. The
level of capitalization of the banking system was high
during 2008, and the Malaysian economy registered a
growth rate of 4.6 percent. The economy was supported
by strong performance in the services sector, expansion
in trade and tourism, and robust external demand
from non-U.S. markets as well as higher exports of
resource-based products, which benefited from rising
commodity prices (Malaysia 2009). The central bank
eased monetary policy and supplied liquidity to the
financial system.

However, the adverse impact of the global financial
crisis was reflected in the domestic financial markets in
the form of higher asset price volatility and lower trading
liquidity. In the domestic equity market (The Kuala
Lumpur Composite Index—KLCI), market capitalization
contracted almost 40 percent. Volatility in the KLCI
remained high during 2008 because of heightened risk
aversion and uncertainty. Exports of electronic equipment
also declined during 2008.

E. Overall Assessment

The result of the mean pairwise comparison of the descriptive statistics for the z-score and z-score excluding outliers indicate Islamic banks are deemed more stable than conventional banks since their values are higher and statistically significant. This is in large measure due to the higher equity capital and reserves of Islamic banks in comparison to conventional banks. On the other hand, other variables, such as operational efficiency (cost/income), return on average assets (ROAA), and the volatility of return on average assets are robustly favorable to conventional banks for all samples (1996–2010, 2006–2010, and 2008–2009).

The results of the general panel regression for the full sample are stronger and similar to those of the descriptive statistics; they are also in favor of Islamic banks. Evidence on the shorter sub-periods is inconclusive in the 2006–2010 case and insignificant during the period of the global financial crisis. Finally, the regression results from the cluster-robust standard errors all indicate there is no statistically notable indication whether Islamic banks are more stable than the conventional banks across all sample periods.

Furthermore, the data robustly shows that conventional banks are operationally more efficient than Islamic banks with lower levels of the cost-to-income ratio and the volatility of average return on assets (see table 10.9 and tables I (a), (b), and (c) in appendix B). In general, the results also indicate that Islamic banks have slightly more liquid loans in their portfolio than conventional banks.

Overall, the data shows a common trend that holds for the descriptive statistics of Bahrain and Malaysia. First, conventional banks in both countries were established before the Islamic banks, which entered relatively recently, and as a result, they had a competitive advantage in efficiency and a steady return on average assets. Second, Islamic banks have higher levels of equity capital and reserves. Bank capital is a buffer against losses. Low bank capital creates serious systemic risk particularly during periods of financial and liquidity crisis. Due to the recent entrance of Islamic banks in the banking industry in both Bahrain and Malaysia, the major challenge they face is to overcome the comparative competitive advantage conventional banks enjoy in operational efficiency and earnings stability.

Table 10.9

Summary Statistics US$1 Billion Cutoff Threshold: 1996–2010, 2006–2010, and 2008–2009

	SMALL BANKS						LARGE BANKS						ALL BANKS					
	1996–2010		2006–2010		2008–2009		1996–2010		2006–2010		2008–2009		1996–2010		2006–2010		2008–2009	
	CB	IB	CB	IB	CB	IB	CB	IB	CB	IB	CB	IB	CB	IB	CB	IB	CB	IB
Z-Score	**23.53**	**50.00*****	**61.35**	**50.00*****	**63.48**	**35.76*****	**20.44**	**25.90*****	**21.91**	**23.96*****	**21.97**	**23.24****	**21.20**	**29.00*****	**26.14**	**27.51*****	**26.58**	**24.86*****
Domestic Banks	13.58	46.84***	0.00	46.84***	0.00	45.12***	22.49	24.55	25.54	24.62	25.44	22.50	20.07	26.41***	25.54	26.59***	25.44	24.66**
Foreign Banks	42.78	52.54	61.35	52.54	63.48	26.40	17.70	29.39***	16.47	22.28***	16.77	25.01***	22.85	34.65***	26.83	29.49***	27.89	25.29***
Z-Score Excl. Outliers	**23.14**	**38.47****	**54.74**	**38.47****	**45.82**	**35.76*****	**20.11**	**24.39****	**20.99**	**24.43****	**21.97**	**23.24****	**20.83**	**26.07*****	**24.37**	**26.18*****	**24.14**	**24.86*****
Domestic Banks	14.41	46.84***	0.00	46.84***	0.00	45.12***	21.92	25.17	24.06	25.29	25.44	22.50	19.95	27.02***	24.06	27.25***	25.44	24.66**
Foreign Banks	39.74	3010.00	54.74	30.10	45.82	26.40	17.70	22.28**	16.47	22.28**	16.77	25.01**	22.11	23.85	24.72	23.85	22.58	25.29
Loans / Assets	**54.99**	**51.97**	**35.91**	**41.20****	**38.56**	**44.38****	**24.34**	**51.97**	**49.72**	**53.25**	**49.78**	**56.07**	**54.50**	**50.55**	**48.13**	**51.58**	**48.53**	**54.56**
Domestic Banks	61.73	71.32*	0.00	71.32*	0.00	65.68*	61.73	51.66***	58.84	53.43***	58.61	56.40***	61.73	53.34***	58.84	55.06***	58.61	57.29***
Foreign Banks	42.98	17.11**	35.91	17.11**	38.56	23.08**	44.43	52.80	36.04	52.80	36.52	55.29	44.12	44.30	36.01	44.30	37.01	48.84
Cost / Income	**48.02**	**59.74**	**40.25**	**59.74**	**41.50**	**58.62**	**40.54**	**62.93*****	**42.32**	**48.77*****	**41.19**	**50.76*****	**42.36**	**62.61*****	**42.08**	**49.94*****	**41.23**	**51.54*****
Domestic Banks	51.05	46.72	0.00	46.72	0.00	46.26	41.46	62.70**	43.38	43.77**	43.29	44.83**	44.00	61.22***	43.38	44.07	43.29	44.97**
Foreign Banks	42.51	85.77***	40.25	85.77***	41.50	83.33***	39.31	63.52***	40.72	61.63***	38.08	64.84***	39.99	66.14***	40.61	64.64***	38.87	66.90***
Income Diversity	**0.20**	**0.15**	**0.38**	**0.15**	**0.24**	**0.31**	**0.11**	**0.03**	**0.18**	**0.01**	**0.26**	**0.10**	**0.13**	**0.04**	**0.20**	**0.02**	**0.26**	**0.12**
Domestic Banks	0.16	0.20	0.00	0.20	0.00	0.31	0.16	0.19	0.16	0.20	0.16	0.16	0.16	0.19	0.16	0.20	0.16	0.18

Table 10.9 (Continued)

	SMALL BANKS						LARGE BANKS						ALL BANKS					
	1996–2010		2006–2010		2008–2009		1996–2010		2006–2010		2008–2009		1996–2010		2006–2010		2008–2009	
	CB	IB	CB	IB	CB	IB	CB	IB	CB	IB	CB	IB	CB	IB	CB	IB	CB	IB
Foreign Banks	0.27	0.00	0.38	0.00	0.24	0.00	0.04	-0.32	0.20	-.42	0.42	-.01	0.09	-0.29	0.25	-0.38	0.39	-.01
ROAA	**0.69**	**-.29***	**1.07**	**-0.29***	**0.99**	**-0.03***	**1.18**	**-0.07*****	**1.11**	**-0.04*****	**1.15**	**0.62*****	**1.06**	**-0.09*****	**1.10**	**-0.07*****	**1.13**	**0.54*****
Domestic Banks	0.45	0.39	0.00	0.39	0.00	0.40	0.92	0.56**	0.99	0.65**	1.04	0.82**	0.79	0.55	0.99	0.63	1.04	0.78
Foreign Banks	1.15	-.84***	1.07	-0.84***	0.99	-0.45***	1.54	-1.70***	1.28	-1.81***	1.32	0.14***	1.46	-1.50***	1.23	-1.58***	1.24	0.02***
Equity / Assets	**11.67**	**22.70*****	**23.55**	**22.70*****	**21.82**	**11.83*****	**9.45**	**14.08*****	**8.72**	**13.25*****	**8.96**	**9.39*****	**10.00**	**15.17*****	**10.43**	**14.52*****	**10.39**	**9.71*****
Domestic Banks	7.99	7.27	0.00	7.27	0.00	6.86	7.79	11.68***	7.35	11.84***	7.39	8.13***	7.84	11.32***	7.35	11.44***	7.39	8.01***
Foreign Banks	18.70	35.05**	23.55	35.05**	21.82	16.80***	11.68	20.41***	10.77	0.31	11.31	12.39***	13.16	23.74***	13.90	21.28***	13.81	13.27***
Total Nonearning Assets / Assets	**0.24**	**0.41****	**0.51**	**0.41****	**0.52**	**0.50***	**0.22**	**.30*****	**0.25**	**0.29*****	**0.25**	**0.29*****	**0.23**	**0.32*****	**0.28**	**.30*****	**0.28**	**0.32*****
Domestic Banks	0.16	0.23**	0.00	0.23**	0.00	0.28***	0.18	0.28***	0.20	0.28***	0.21	0.26***	0.17	0.28***	0.20	0.27***	0.21	0.26***
Foreign Banks	0.41	0.55	0.51	0.55	0.52	0.71	0.28	0.35	0.33	0.31	0.32	0.36	0.31	.40*	0.37	0.37*	0.37	0.43*
Cash and Due from Banks / Assets	**0.22**	**0.39****	**0.50**	**0.39****	**0.52**	**0.48****	**0.20**	**0.27*****	**0.23**	**0.25*****	**0.22**	**0.27*****	**0.20**	**0.28*****	**0.26**	**0.27*****	**0.26**	**0.29*****
Domestic Banks	0.13	0.21***	0.00	0.21***	0.00	0.27***	0.16	0.25***	0.18	0.24***	0.19	0.25***	0.15	0.25***	0.18	0.24***	0.19	0.25***
Foreign Banks	0.40	0.54	0.50	0.54	0.52	0.69	0.25	0.31	0.29	0.28	0.28	0.31	0.28	0.37*	0.34	**0.34***	0.34	0.39*

Std. Dev. ROAA	1.09	0.45**	0.46	0.45**	0.42**	0.69	1.71***	0.67	1.78***	0.79	1.58***	0.79	1.55***	0.65	1.60***	0.65	1.43***
Domestic Banks	1.39	0.17**	0.00	0.17**	0.17**	0.57	0.98***	0.55	1.01***	0.79	0.94***	0.79	0.91	0.55	0.93	0.55	0.87
Foreign Banks	0.53	0.67***	0.46	0.67***	0.67***	0.86	3.59***	0.86	3.78***	0.79	3.11***	0.79	2.92***	0.76	3.04***	0.76	2.62***

Legend:

CB = Conventional Bank; IB = Islamic Bank; DB = Domestic Bank; FB = Foreign Bank

$z = (\varkappa + \mu)/\sigma$, where z = z-score; $\varkappa$ = equity capital and reserves as a percent of assets; μ = average return as a percent of assets; and σ = standard deviation of average return as a percent of assets.

$\varkappa$ = equity/assets + reserves/assets = equity/assets + (Total Nonearning Assets/Assets + Due from Central Banks/Assets + Due from Other Banks/Assets)

μ = ROAA; σ = Std. Dev. ROAA

Source: Calculations based on BankScope data.

Note: The difference between the values of conventional and Islamic banks at the 95 percent confidence interval is significant at 10 percent (*); at 5 percent (**); and at 1 percent (***).

Table 10.10

Regression Results: Robust Estimation for the Full Sample: 1996–2010

Estimated Variable	All Banks (1)	All Banks (2)	All Banks (3)	Large Banks (4)	Large Banks (5)	Large Banks (6)	Small Banks (7)	Small Banks (8)	Small Banks (9)
Islamic Bank Dummy	7.252*	20.66**	20.66**	5.867	22.47***	22.47***	42.77***	21.83***	21.83***
P-value	(0.0523)	(0.0194)	(0.0194)	(0.125)	(0.00977)	(0.00977)	(0)	(0.00227)	(0.00227)
Net Loans / Total Assets (t-1)	-0.0279	0.0206	0.0206	0.116***	0.148***	0.148***	-0.537***	-0.385***	-0.385***
P-value	(0.574)	(0.697)	(0.697)	(4.30e-05)	(0.000132)	(0.000132)	(5.28e-08)	(2.08e-06)	(2.08e-06)
Costs / Net Income (t-1)	-0.0443**	0.0518***	0.0518***	-0.0255*	-0.0396**	-0.0396**	-0.0640	-0.0486	-0.0486
P-value	(0.0125)	(0.00354)	(0.00354)	(0.0673)	(0.0124)	(0.0124)	(0.149)	(0.286)	(0.286)
Total Assets (t-1)	5.97e-06	-1.62e-05	-1.62e-05	1.07e-05	-4.89e-07	-4.89e-07	-0.000225	0.000287***	0.000287***
P-value	(0.587)	(0.380)	(0.380)	(0.381)	(0.981)	(0.981)	(0.172)	(0.00719)	(0.00719)
Income Diversity (t-1)	0.517	0.547	0.547	0.268	0.214	0.214	21.87***	16.27***	16.27***
P-value	(0.207)	(0.176)	(0.176)	(0.420)	(0.515)	(0.515)	(0.00351)	(0.00819)	(0.00819)
Income Diversity * Islamic Bank Dummy	3.089	3.092	3.092	0.684	0.177	0.177	-51.47***	-91.59***	-91.59***

	(1)	(2)	(3)	(4)	(5)	(6)	(7)	(8)	(9)
P-value	(0.800)	(0.787)	(0.787)	(0.947)	(0.984)	(0.984)	(0.000175)	(0)	(0)
Herfindahl Index (t-1)		259.4**	259.4**		86.01	86.01		827.8**	827.8**
P-value		(0.0129)	(0.0129)		(0.361)	(0.361)		(0.0164)	(0.0164)
Share of Islamic Banks (t-1)		-120.8	76.15*		-165.1*	45.14		364.2***	189.6***
P-value		(0.221)	(0.0591)		(0.0869)	(0.290)		(4.22e-06)	(3.19e-05)
Share of Islamic Banks * Conventional Bank Dummy (t-1)		197.0*			210.3**			-174.6**	
P-value		(0.0612)			(0.0460)			(0.0266)	
Share of Islamic Banks * Islamic Bank Dummy (t-1)			-197.0*			-210.3**			174.6**
P-value			(0.0612)			(0.0460)			(0.0266)
Constant	23.85***	-4.664	-4.664	14.33***	4.115	4.115	53.03***	-34.52	-34.52
P-value	(0)	(0.668)	(0.668)	(0)	(0.689)	(0.689)	(0)	(0.291)	(0.291)
Observations	327	327	327	258	258	258	69	69	69
Adjusted R-squared	0.014	0.040	0.040	0.029	0.042	0.042	0.479	0.572	0.572

p values in parentheses

* significant at 10 percent; ** significant at 5 percent; *** significant at 1 percent.

Table 10.11

Regression Results: Robust Estimation for Subperiod: 2006–2010

Estimated Variable	All Banks (1)	All Banks (2)	All Banks (3)	Large Banks (4)	Large Banks (5)	Large Banks (6)	Small Banks (7)	Small Banks (8)	Small Banks (9)
Islamic Bank Dummy	-2.078	14.18	14.18	-0.0660	17.87	17.87	-20.57		
P-value	(0.742)	(0.215)	(0.215)	(0.992)	(0.106)	(0.106)	(0.419)		
Net Loans / Total Assets (t-1)	0.0564	0.0770	0.0770	0.156**	0.198**	0.198**	-0.283*		
P-value	(0.586)	(0.467)	(0.467)	(0.0450)	(0.0177)	(0.0177)	(0.0822)		
Costs / Net Income (t-1)	-0.0267**	-0.0366**	-0.0366**	-0.0134	-0.0239	-0.0239	-0.274		
P-value	(0.0298)	(0.0294)	(0.0294)	(0.148)	(0.107)	(0.107)	(0.810)		
Total Assets (t-1)	-5.58e-05*	-6.00e-05*	-6.00e-05*	-3.14e-05	-3.71e-05	-3.71e-05	0.0105		
P-value	(0.0977)	(0.0842)	(0.0842)	(0.369)	(0.315)	(0.315)	(0.315)		
Income Diversity (t-1)	-16.12	-15.08	-15.08	-10.38	-7.892	-7.892	-31.83		
P-value	(0.150)	(0.169)	(0.169)	(0.289)	(0.379)	(0.379)	(0.136)		
Income Diversity * Islamic Bank Dummy	20.50	19.44	19.44	12.12	9.054	9.054	-67.06		
P-value	(0.228)	(0.235)	(0.235)	(0.419)	(0.499)	(0.499)	(0.315)		
Herfindahl Index (t-1)	178.0	178.0	178.0	261.2	261.2	261.2			

P-value		(0.805)	(0.805)		(0.713)	(0.713)	
Share of Islamic Banks (t-1)		-119.3	79.72		-124.9	82.83	
P-value		(0.407)	(0.338)		(0.372)	(0.290)	
Share of Islamic Banks * Conventional Bank Dummy (t-1)		199.0			207.8*		
P-value		(0.105)			(0.0938)		
Share of Islamic Banks * Islamic Bank Dummy (t-1)			-199.0			-207.8*	
P-value			(0.105)			(0.0938)	
Constant	28.00***	5.418	5.418	17.70***	-14.19	-14.19	56.19
P-value	(0.000476)	(0.941)	(0.941)	(0.00104)	(0.842)	(0.842)	(0.152)
Observations	109	109	109	99	99	99	10
Adjusted R-squared	0.007	0.002	0.002	0.004	0.000	0.000	0.605

p values in parentheses

* significant at 10 percent; ** significant at 5 percent; *** significant at 1 percent

Table 10.12

Regression Results: Robust Estimation for Year 2008–2009

Estimated Variable	All Banks (1)	All Banks (2)	All Banks (3)	Large Banks (4)	Large Banks (5)	Large Banks (6)	Small Banks (7)	Small Banks (8)	Small Banks (9)
Islamic Bank Dummy	-3.144	15.80	15.80	-1.848	23.26	23.26			
P-value	(0.730)	(0.559)	(0.559)	(0.844)	(0.374)	(0.374)			
Net Loans / Total Assets (t-1)	0.141	0.137	0.137	0.234**	0.240**	0.240**			
P-value	(0.322)	(0.351)	(0.351)	(0.0190)	(0.0140)	(0.0140)			
Costs / Net Income (t-1)	-0.168*	-0.167*	-0.167*	-0.126	-0.131	-0.131			
P-value	(0.0622)	(0.0688)	(0.0688)	(0.197)	(0.191)	(0.191)			
Total Assets (t-1)	-6.54e-05	-6.54e-05	-6.54e-05	-4.42e-05	-4.40e-05	-4.40e-05			
P-value	(0.147)	(0.154)	(0.154)	(0.342)	(0.354)	(0.354)			
Income Diversity (t-1)	-6.940	-7.558	-7.558	-1.934	-1.648	-1.648			
P-value	(0.685)	(0.661)	(0.661)	(0.908)	(0.913)	(0.913)			
Income Diversity * Islamic Bank Dummy	12.84	4.799	4.799	7.683	-5.795	-5.795			
P-value	(0.609)	(0.864)	(0.864)	(0.752)	(0.806)	(0.806)			
Herfindahl Index (t-1)	0	0	0	0	0	0			

P-value					
Share of Islamic Banks (t-1)		-146.1	28.28		-215.4	4.645
P-value		*(0.477)*	*(0.815)*		*(0.270)*	*(0.968)*
Share of Islamic Banks * Conventional Bank Dummy (t-1)		174.4			220.0	
P-value		*(0.466)*			*(0.334)*	
Share of Islamic Banks * Islamic Bank Dummy (t-1)			-174.4			-220.0
P-value			*(0.466)*			*(0.334)*
Constant	29.39**	27.11*	27.11*	18.72*	18.12	18.12
P-value	*(0.0235)*	*(0.0849)*	*B*	*(0.0573)*	*(0.217)*	*(0.217)*
Observations	61	61	61	55	55	55
Adjusted R-squared	-0.025	-0.057	-0.057	-0.032	-0.065	-0.065

ρ values in parentheses

* significant at 10 percent; ** significant at 5 percent; *** significant at 1 percent

242   ISLAMIC BANKING: STEADY IN SHAKY TIMES?

Endnotes

67. IMF's *World Economic Outlook Report 2010.*

68. *Far Eastern Economic Review* (November 6, 2003).

69. Rupa Damodaran, "Malaysia to Take a Proactive Approach to FTAs," *Business Times* (April 12, 2008).

70. IMF report on Malaysia titled "Staff Report for the 2009 Article IV Consultation" (July 1, 2009).

71. See footnote 64.

72. Bank Negara Malaysia: Annual Banking Statistics 2007.

73. Bank Negara Malaysia: Annual Banking Statistics 2007.

74. MIF Monthly 2008 Supplement Series published by Malaysia—The International Islamic Financial Center, Takaful Industry in Malaysia: Performance and Key Developments.

75. Source: Moody's; Bloomberg LP.

76. Banks with assets over US$1 billion at the end of the year 2008 are classified as large banks and the rest as small banks.

77. Note: Banks with higher mean z-score values are considered to be financially more stable.

78. $z = (k+m)/s$, where z is the z-score measure; k is equity capital reserves (nonearning assets and cash due from banks) as a percent of assets; m is average return as a percent of assets; and s is the standard deviation of return on assets as a proxy for return volatility. In this case, the numerator and, more particularly, equity capital and reserves weighed more for Islamic banks in the calculation of the z-score measure than those variables in the formula that favored conventional banks.

79. Remember, the lower the cost-to-income ratio, the more efficient a bank is considered to be.

80. Net loans / total assets is a measure that reflects how deep any bank's investments are tied up in loans. The liquidation of assets when needed cannot be instant unless assets were diversified among other investment alternatives. Thus, the lower the ratio, the less exposed a bank would be to liquidity risk.

Implications of Regression and Basic Statistics Results

For Bahrain, the empirical evidence does *not* support the main thesis of the book —conceptually, Islamic banks are deemed to be more stable than conventional banks[81]— however, in the case of Malaysia the results support the thesis, but only for the full sample period (1996–2010). The results are robust for all the descriptive statistics as well as all the general panel regressions from the full samples for the different asset size thresholds (US$0.75, 1, 1.5 and 2 billion).

For the sub-period sample (2006–2010), the results are robust in the descriptive statistics and clustering regression but weak in the general panel regressions so that Bahrain's conventional banks are deemed more stable than Islamic banks. With regard to Malaysia's, the descriptive statistics bolster the results of the full sample; however, the regression results are inconclusive.

Finally, the findings during the global financial crisis period of (2008–2009) are mixed. For Bahrain, the result is robust in the case of the descriptive statistics but is not different from random chance for all the regressions. In the case of Malaysia, all the empirical evidence robustly indicates that the performance of Islamic banks is not different than that of conventional banks. In the following sections, I will briefly comment on several key factors that uniquely affected the performance of Islamic banks in comparison to conventional banks.

Late Entrance of Islamic Banks
In Bahrain's case, the results for the full sample period (1996–2010) for both the descriptive statistics and regressions worked against the relative stability of Islamic banks since most fully fledged and independent Islamic banks came into existence during the 2000s (see figures 9.5 and 9.6). However, in the case of Malaysia, even though the number of Islamic banks increased significantly during the period from 2005 to 2010 (see figures 10.1 and 10.2),[82] this increase did not really improve the performance of Islamic banks.

Lower Profitability, Higher Earnings Volatility, and Lower Efficiency
The higher and statistically significant z-scores in favor of conventional banks as well as the negative and statistically significant values for the Islamic bank dummy variables in the general panel regressions of Bahrain support the idea that conventional banks are more stable than Islamic banks. With regard to Malaysia, the higher degree of financial stability for Islamic banks is limited only for the full sample period, unlike Bahrain.

So, for Bahrain, the higher degree of stability favoring conventional banks across the board for the different sample periods is attributable to higher profitability (higher ROAA), lower earnings volatility (lower standard deviations of ROAA), and the higher operational efficiency of conventional banks in comparison to Islamic banks (see tables 9.3, 9.4, and tables I (a)–I (b) of appendix A).

Other empirical evidence (Benaissa, Jopart, Maddux, Tanrikulu, and Whelan 2007) indicates that Islamic banks, with a few exceptions, generally have lower profitability than conventional banks because of their smaller size, limited financial products, lower-quality service to customers, and inefficient management of their cost base.

Shari'a norms undoubtedly impose costly procedures on Islamic banks. First, there is the expense of having to ask a *Shari'a* board for a *fatwa* each time a new product is launched. Next, Islamic banks may be expected to face higher monitoring costs than conventional banks. Furthermore, more separate contracts are required under *Shari'a* law than under conventional legal systems. This leads to higher costs. Other operating costs are also likely to be higher as well in comparison to those of conventional banks. For example, in the case of the prevalent *murabaha* (cost plus or markup) finance, an Islamic bank is required to purchase a good and resell it to its client, which is more labor intensive than a comparable single loan transaction by a conventional bank and requires additional expense on insurance and storage.

Liquidity Management

The profitability of Islamic banks is adversely affected by the ban on *riba* (interest), which makes liquidity management difficult, as it precludes Islamic banks from operating in the money market. Investing short-term in safe and highly liquid government treasury fixed-income securities or in time deposits and certificates of deposit is prohibited. Even floating-rate notes, although not offering a fixed interest rate, are not considered *Shari'a* compatible. One mitigating solution available to Islamic banks is to invest liquid funds in the London Metal Exchange, which ensures that the investments are backed by real assets.[83]

Conservative Approach of Bahraini and Malaysian Conventional Banks

The sophisticated banking tradition and practice of Bahraini conventional banks is legendary—particularly, their conservative approach to debt leveraging and maintenance of high levels of capital and reserves. The practices of Malaysian conventional banks are similar to those in Bahrain, although slightly weaker. Given this reality, the conceptual comparative advantage Islamic banks are expected to enjoy, which should have emanated from constraints in debt financing and maintenance of higher levels of capital (as a buffer), has been blunted or neutralized by the conservative approach of the Bahraini and Malaysian conventional banks. Furthermore, overall safety of the banking industry in both countries has been reinforced by the prudent and balanced regulatory supervision of the governments in Bahrain and Malaysia.

In contrast, as the recent global financial crisis of 2007 to 2009 clearly demonstrated, the consequences when banks engage in excessive debt leveraging coupled with opaque and complex innovative financial instruments through securitization can be enormous.[84] This recent crisis also unambiguously exposed the likely bad consequences when regulators fail to prudently supervise banks. Not implementing necessary regulations can lead markets to fail—and fail frequently as described in chapters 3 and 4. There are many reasons for these failures, but two are particularly germane to the recent global financial crisis – namely the agency problem and securitization.

Agency Problem
In today's world, scores of people are handling and making decisions on behalf of others—and externalities are increasingly important. The agency problem in the investment process manifests itself through pension funds and other institutions. Those who make the investment decisions—and assess corporate performance—do so not on their own behalf but on behalf of those who entrusted their funds to their care. All along the "agency" chain, concern about performance has been translated into a focus on *short-term returns.* The drive for short-term results led banks to focus on how to generate more fees—and, in some cases, on how to circumvent accounting and financial regulations.

Securitization
The most attractive financial products field in the years leading up to the collapse in Wall Street—mortgage-backed securities—provide a good example of the risks generated by new innovations, for they severed the relationship between lender and borrower.[85] In contrast, strict compliance with the principles of Islamic finance would not have permitted this to occur since debt financing is limited only to activities for real transactions.

Endnotes

81. See chapter 5 for an explanation of this assertion.

82. Malaysian commercial banks had Islamic windows during most of the 1990s. It is very difficult to discern activities related to Islamic windows in the financial statements of commercial banks. However, early in the 2000s the government encouraged Islamic banks to be operated and licensed as independent and fully separate entities from their parent entities.

83. Euromoney, *Islamic Banks Tap a Rich New Business* (December 2001).

84. Millions of homeowners have lost their homes, and millions have seen the equity in their homes disappear; whole communities have been devastated; taxpayers had to pick up the tab for the losses of the banks; and workers have lost their jobs. The costs have been borne not only in the United States but also around the world, by billions who reaped no gains from the reckless behavior of banks.

85. Reliability on rating agencies (as another source of protection for investors) was further undermined by their dependence on the fees that were paid by the banks whose securities they were supposed to rate objectively.

Conclusion

Based on the historical analysis of the banking system in Bahrain as well as a careful review of the empirical findings, it seems clear that Islamic banks do not yet appear to pose a direct challenge to the financial stability advantage conventional banks hold now. However, in the case of Malaysia, even though the overall evidence points to that Islamic banks are deemed more stable than conventional banks, it would be wrong to conclude if this advantage is sustainable.

Given that Islamic banks are still in their infancy in both Bahrain and Malaysia, there are encouraging signs that they are improving their performance and bolstering their relative financial stability. Recent empirical studies (Cihak and Hesse 2008; Benaissa, Jopart, Maddux, Tanrikulu, and Whelan 2007) have also noted the recent trend of the increased financial stability of Islamic banks in the Gulf States and Malaysia.

For Islamic banks to successfully narrow the advantage conventional banks enjoy due to the expertise in management or provision of quality customer services learned over the longer period they were in business, Islamic banks will have to make significant improvements in several key areas.

Growth and Profitability

Although Islamic banks have been a growing section of financial markets worldwide, a closer look reveals that the penetration and growth of Islamic banking, as well as profitability levels compared with conventional peers, vary significantly across countries. Despite asset growth, competitive market pressure and major harmonization and regulatory challenges have to be resolved if Islamic banks are to grow even faster and improve their profitability. In this context, overall competitiveness with conventional banks is critical to be deemed as successful.

What drives the profit and growth performance of the Islamic banking sector? Clearly, the managers of Islamic financial institutions, through the decisions they make, influence the profit and growth performance of their institutions. The disappointing profitability record can be attributed to three main factors.

The first factor is lack of size; in spite of tremendous growth, most Islamic banks remain relatively small and have not yet managed to generate market-acceptable returns on average assets.

The second factor relates to the business model. While Islamic banks in general have been successful in capturing deposits, they have been less successful on the financing side. The institutions have, thus far, focused largely on the thinner margin corporate financing business rather than the lucrative retail business, or they have invested in lower-yielding instruments.

Finally, and most important, Islamic banks are still not at par with their conventional peers in either managing their business for optimal profitability through good service or tightly managing their cost base.

A recent survey[86] among retail customers of Islamic banks has shown that the majority of these customers are captive customers, that is, those who have chosen the bank not because of its products or service, but simply for its *Shari'a* compliance. The survey also shows that the overall levels of satisfaction with service and convenience are low. Islamic banks will have to improve their offering to capture customers beyond the captive base, including those who mainly seek performance and convenience and are indifferent to the *Shari'a* compliance.

Regulation

The framework that regulators choose for the industry can have a positive or negative impact on the Islamic banks' credibility, ability to compete, and financial performance. Many different regulatory models exist around the world, and each of them presents both advantages and drawbacks. None of them emerges as a clear winner.

In general, the guideline that regulators should adopt is to foster a healthy competition between conventional and Islamic banks. This does not mean treating them equally (especially given the asset-backed transaction nature of Islamic banks), but it does mean removing all possible barriers to competition.

Thus, regulators are faced with significant problems. Should Islamic banks be held to different standards than conventional banks? Both the United Kingdom and United States' regulators have said that Islamic institutions should comply fully with regulations designed primarily for conventional banks.

The evolution of Islamic banking regulations, which vary substantially from country to country, may be a main reason for the wide variation observed in growth performance and the structure of these markets. In response to market globalization, attempts to harmonize the regulatory framework have increased. It is very hard to say at this point if any specific model will emerge, as there is still a lot of work and thinking to be done surrounding the various models if they are to be developed fully and if convergence to global standards is to be achieved. Recent innovations in regulation and attempts at harmonization are starting to create some consistency in regulatory frameworks and approaches across countries. While we are still far from the level of harmonization that can be seen in the conventional sector, nevertheless, these efforts are encouraging and should be intensified.

Innovation and Financial Products

Obviously, there is a demand for Islamic financial products; otherwise, there would be no Islamic financial institutions, at least in countries where people are free to choose between Islamic and conventional banks. Product innovation within *Shari'a* guidelines is perhaps the key element governing the future of Islamic banking and finance.

Islamic banks have now reached the stage—and this assertion is supported by a number of surveys—where the "religious value" alone is not enough. They operate in a market in which many conventional banks themselves have Islamic "windows," and factors such as the quality of the service, the availability and reliability of electronic networks, and the return paid on investment accounts have become the major conditioning factors. In such a market, it is increasingly likely that the preferences of depositors, rather than the preferences of the banks, will shape the

Islamic investment portfolios of banks. How innovatively and effectively the industry responds to this challenge will determine if the products and services they offer will meet the needs of their customers.

The Promise of Profit-and-Loss Sharing
When Islamic banks first started to become players in the market, the belief was that their financing should be provided through *musharaka* (equity partnerships) and *mudaraba* (trustee financing) agreements. They should be partners with their clients and share the risks of their business ventures. Quite quickly, the banks discovered that the risks in this business model were huge and that they did not have the necessary skills to determine the likely success of their clients' new businesses.

Not only was the problem linked to their own adverse selection of projects but also to the asymmetric availability of information. They quickly looked to other ways of providing asset-based financing, most often through *murabaha* (cost-plus-financing) or *ijara* (leasing) contracts, which bear similarities to those of traditional banking in that the goods themselves can serve as collateral and there is a relatively certain rate of profit, albeit with some attendant risk.

Nowadays, there is much diversity in the banks' Islamic investment portfolios, with some Islamic banks establishing systems for evaluation and monitoring under *musharaka* partnership financing and others engaging in direct real investments and long-term investments. This monitoring effort is not necessarily a weakness of the system. Clearly, many conventional banks over-relied on the protection afforded by collateral, which proved to be illusory during the downturn in housing prices that triggered the global financial crisis of 2007 to 2009 and the East Asian financial crisis of 1997 to mention just a couple.

Direction of Shari'a Setting and Compliance

Islamic banking depends fundamentally on the interpretation and application of *Shari'a* law to previously unknown problems. Because there is no single answer to how Islamic law should be interpreted and applied, there is currently a wide variation, domestically and internationally, in the ways in which different Islamic banks operate. Not only are there clearly several schools of thought on *Shari'a* interpretation, but also interpretations vary within each school among the leading scholars. How the Islamic industry handles this challenge will have an important impact on whether the industry will thrive and succeed in the future.

Future Scenarios

The future prospects of Islamic banking will depend upon how the industry responds to the challenges it faces. The best scenario Islamic banks can aim for would occur if the industry orchestrated strategies that promoted competitive, dynamic, and sustainable Islamic financial products in order to respond to the requirements of local economies and the international market, via innovation and customer-focused quality service.

Developing new Islamic financial products in compliance with *Shari'a* is challenging. Failure to provide a full range and the right quality of products will lead to difficulties in retaining current customers and attracting new ones and will more likely lead to the realization of the worst-case scenario.

The prospects of the best scenario are likely to be realized if Islamic institutions also promote knowledge and awareness of their products among their employees by employing internal marketing strategies. This awareness is an important tool as Islamic banks strive to develop close relationships with individuals and business clients. They might thereby gain a competitive advantage based on superior customer relationships and at the same time gain insights, through customer collaboration and feedback, into new customers' needs and wants. Failure to implement these strategies will most likely result in a stagnant industry that faces the risk of being overtaken by conventional banks with Islamic windows.

Another important factor that will determine whether the best- or worst-case scenario for Islamic banking will be realized is how the industry resolves the problem of the wide variation between Islamic banks and scholars in the interpretation of *Shari'a* laws.

Finally, the best scenario is likely to occur if Islamic banks succeed in recruiting and retaining a qualified and skilled workforce well versed in both *Shari'a* and modern financial management, which is indispensable for innovation. Widening the product range calls for substantial and continuous investment in research and development. In this context, an industry-sponsored research and training institute, such as the Islamic Banking and Finance Institute of Malaysia (IBFIM), will help in meeting the challenge from conventional banks in offering innovative Islamic financial products.

Tomorrow's successful marketers of Islamic financial products will be those who identify and anticipate the evolving needs of Muslim consumers and pioneer product innovation and improvements to meet those needs. They should also be able to address non-Muslim financing needs. It is difficult to say now whether Islamic banks will succeed in meeting best-case scenario requirements.

Endnotes

86. 2005 Islamic banking customer survey; McKinsey Analysis.

Bahrain

Table I (a)—Support for Summary Statistics for the Full Sample Period 1996–2010 for the Four Banks' Asset Sizes Cutoff Thresholds

Cut-off for Bank-Asset Size	Financial Variable	Conventional Banks	Islamic Banks	Cut-off for Bank-Asset Size	Financial Variable	Conventional Banks	Islamic Banks
USD 750 Million	ROAA	1.56	2.66***	USD 1 Billion	ROAA	1.56	2.66***
	Large Banks	1.67	3.79***		Large Banks	1.67	3.79***
	Small Banks	1.31	1.61		Small Banks	1.31	1.61
	Equity / Assets	20.78	54.60***		Equity / Assets	20.78	54.60***
	Large Banks	17.04	36.25***		Large Banks	17.04	36.25***
	Small Banks	29.37	71.65***		Small Banks	29.37	71.65***
	Total Non-Earning Assets / Assets	0.07	0.14***		Total Non-Earning Assets / Assets	0.07	0.14***
	Large Banks	0.06	0.14***		Large Banks	0.06	0.14***
	Small Banks	0.08	0.14***		Small Banks	0.08	0.14***
	Cash and Due from Banks / Income	0.04	0.03		Cash and Due from Banks / Income	0.04	0.03
	Large Banks	0.03	0.04		Large Banks	0.03	0.04
	Small Banks	0.06	0.03***		Small Banks	0.06	0.03***
	Standard Deviation of ROA	2.39	8.97***		Standard Deviation of ROA	2.39	8.97***
	Large Banks	1.78	6.34***		Large Banks	1.78	6.34***
	Small Banks	3.80	11.42***		Small Banks	3.80	11.42***

	USD 1.5 Billion		USD 2 Billion	
ROAA	*1.56*	*2.66****	*1.56*	*2.66****
Large Banks	1.60	3.83***	1.30	3.83***
Small Banks	1.50	2.20	1.82	2.20
Equity / Assets	*20.78*	*54.60****	*20.78*	*54.60****
Large Banks	15.58	33.58***	13.05	33.58***
Small Banks	29.45	62.96***	28.51	62.96***
Total Non-Earning Assets / Assets	*0.07*	*0.14****	*0.07*	*0.14****
Large Banks	0.06	0.16***	0.06	0.16***
Small Banks	0.09	0.13***	0.08	0.13***
Cash and Due from Banks / Income	*0.04*	*0.03****	*0.04*	*0.03****
Large Banks	0.03	0.05***	0.03	0.05***
Small Banks	0.06	0.02***	0.06	0.02***
Standard Deviation of ROA	*2.39*	*8.97****	*2.39*	*8.97****
Large Banks	1.82	4.80***	1.60	4.80***
Small Banks	3.34	10.63***	3.19	10.63***

* significant at 10 percent; ** significant at 5 percent; *** significant at 1 percent

Table I (b)—Support Summary Statistics for the Sample Period 2006–2010 for the Four Asset Sizes Cutoff Thresholds

Cut-off for Bank-Asset Size	Financial Variable	Conventional Banks	Islamic Banks	Cut-off for Bank-Asset Size	Financial Variable	Conventional Banks	Islamic Banks
USD 750 Million				USD 1 Billion			
	ROAA	*1.00*	*0.04****		*ROAA*	*1.00*	*0.04****
	Large Banks	1.35	1.53***		Large Banks	1.35	1.53***
	Small Banks	-0.10	-1.35		Small Banks	-0.10	-1.35
	Equity / Assets	*24.95*	*53.85****		*Equity / Assets*	*24.95*	*53.85****
	Large Banks	18.33	29.29***		Large Banks	18.33	29.29***
	Small Banks	45.18	76.81***		Small Banks	45.18	76.81***
	Total Non-Earning Assets / Assets	*0.09*	*0.15****		*Total Non-Earning Assets / Assets*	*0.09*	*0.15****
	Large Banks	0.08	0.14***		Large Banks	0.08	0.14***
	Small Banks	0.13	0.15***		Small Banks	0.13	0.15***
	Cash and Due from Banks / Income	*0.06*	*0.04*		*Cash and Due from Banks / Income*	*0.06*	*0.04*
	Large Banks	0.05	0.05		Large Banks	0.05	0.05
	Small Banks	0.09	0.02***		Small Banks	0.09	0.02***
	Standard Deviation of ROA	*2.51*	*9.43****		*Standard Deviation of ROA*	*2.51*	*9.43****
	Large Banks	1.74	5.30***		Large Banks	1.74	5.30***
	Small Banks	4.89	13.30***		Small Banks	4.89	13.30***

USD 1.5 Billion

ROAA	*1.00*	*0.04****
Large Banks	1.08	1.87***
Small Banks	0.89	-0.60
Equity / Assets	*24.95*	*53.85****
Large Banks	14.90	24.47***
Small Banks	38.80	64.09***
Total Non-Earning Assets / Assets	*0.09*	*0.15****
Large Banks	0.08	0.17***
Small Banks	0.12	0.14***
Cash and Due from Banks / Income	*0.06*	*0.04****
Large Banks	0.04	0.07***
Small Banks	0.09	0.02***
Standard Deviation of ROA	2.51	9.43***
Large Banks	1.85	4.35***
Small Banks	3.42	11.20***

USD 2 Billion

ROAA	*1.00*	*0.04****
Large Banks	0.66	1.87***
Small Banks	1.25	-0.60
Equity / Assets	*24.95*	*53.85****
Large Banks	13.14	24.47***
Small Banks	34.03	64.09***
Total Non-Earning Assets / Assets	*0.09*	*0.15****
Large Banks	0.08	0.17***
Small Banks	0.11	0.14***
Cash and Due from Banks / Income	*0.06*	*0.04****
Large Banks	0.04	0.07***
Small Banks	0.08	0.02***
Standard Deviation of ROA	2.51	9.43***
Large Banks	1.59	4.35***
Small Banks	3.22	11.20***

ρ values in parentheses
* significant at 10 percent; ** significant at 5 percent; *** significant at 1 percent

Regressions for Bank Sizes at the US\$2 Billion Cutoff Threshold (Banks with total assets over this threshold are classified as big banks and the rest are considered small banks.)

Table II (a)—Regression Results for the Full Sample: Robust Estimation, 1996–2010

Estimated Variable	All Banks (1)	All Banks (2)	All Banks (3)	Large Banks (4)	Large Banks (5)	Large Banks (6)	Small Banks (7)	Small Banks (8)	Small Banks (9)
Islamic Bank Dummy	-19.88***	-16.90***	-16.90***	-24.64***	-27.45***	-27.45***	-8.717	1.480	1.480
P-value	(1.46e-07)	(0.00243)	(0.00243)	(9.59e-08)	(2.49e-06)	(2.49e-06)	(0.213)	(0.893)	(0.893)
Net Loans / Total Assets (t-1)	0.335***	0.309***	0.309***	0.323***	0.321***	0.321***	0.431**	0.396**	0.396**
P-value	(0.00185)	(0.00562)	(0.00562)	(0.00239)	(0.00402)	(0.00402)	(0.0151)	(0.0373)	(0.0373)
Costs / Net Income (t-1)	-0.0463**	-0.0723***	-0.0723***	-0.173**	-0.144**	-0.144**	0.0176	-0.0280	-0.0280
P-value	(0.0339)	(0.00250)	(0.00250)	(0.0120)	(0.0394)	(0.0394)	(0.676)	(0.446)	(0.446)
Total Assets (t-1)	-0.00224***	-0.00225***	-0.00225***	0.00283***	0.00298***	0.00298***	0.000410	-0.000627	-0.000627
P-value	(0.000716)	(0.00103)	(0.00103)	(4.41e-07)	(2.33e-07)	(2.33e-07)	(0.938)	(0.857)	(0.857)
Income Diversity (t-1)	9.734	8.110	8.110	1.397	1.932	1.932	46.60	42.09	42.09
P-value	(0.241)	(0.314)	(0.314)	(0.635)	(0.559)	(0.559)	(0.124)	(0.135)	(0.135)
Income Diversity * Islamic Bank Dummy	-12.61	-10.51	-10.51	-10.72**	-9.713**	-9.713**	-46.40	-40.21	-40.21

P-value	(0.131)	(0.202)	(0.202)	(0.0156)	(0.0314)	(0.0314)	(0.140)	(0.151)	(0.151)
Herfindahl Index (t-1)		53.34	53.34		-16.27	-16.27		127.8*	127.8*
P-value		(0.148)	(0.148)		(0.524)	(0.524)		(0.0518)	(0.0518)
Share of Islamic Banks (t-1)		74.56*	101.9		4.185	-1.408		155.1**	221.9**
P-value		(0.0814)	(0.101)		(0.881)	(0.975)		(0.0373)	(0.0300)
Share of Islamic Banks * Conventional Bank Dummy (t-1)		27.38			-5.594			66.80	
P-value		(0.585)			(0.881)			(0.399)	
Share of Islamic Banks * Islamic Bank Dummy (t-1)			-27.38			5.594			-66.80
P-value			(0.585)			(0.881)			(0.399)
Constant	23.41***	3.136	3.136	35.92***	38.83***	38.83***	6.842	-43.06*	-43.06*
P-value	(9.01e-09)	(0.799)	(0.799)	(0)	(5.84e-05)	(5.84e-05)	(0.525)	(0.0804)	(0.0804)
Observations	201	201	201	98	98	98	103	103	103
Adjusted R-squared	0.183	0.192	0.192	0.421	0.409	0.409	0.168	0.215	0.215

p values in parentheses

* significant at 10 percent; ** significant at 5 percent; *** significant at 1 percent

Table II (b)—Regression Results for Sample Subgroup: Robust Estimation, 2006–2010

Estimated Variable	All Banks (1)	All Banks (2)	All Banks (3)	Large Banks (4)	Large Banks (5)	Large Banks (6)	Small Banks (7)	Small Banks (8)	Small Banks (9)
Islamic Bank Dummy	-14.02***	-0.897	-0.897	-20.98**	-20.81	-20.81	-3.162	29.14	29.14
P-value	(0.00906)	(0.954)	(0.954)	(0.0199)	(0.191)	(0.191)	(0.725)	(0.316)	(0.316)
Net Loans / Total Assets (t-1)	0.171	0.131	0.131	0.221	0.221	0.221	0.138	0.129	0.129
P-value	(0.261)	(0.393)	(0.393)	(0.147)	(0.173)	(0.173)	(0.531)	(0.543)	(0.543)
Costs / Net Income (t-1)	-0.0331	0.0674*	0.0674*	-0.190*	-0.194*	-0.194*	0.00789	-0.0531	-0.0531
P-value	(0.242)	(0.0866)	(0.0866)	(0.0661)	(0.0980)	(0.0980)	(0.849)	(0.317)	(0.317)
Total Assets (t-1)	-0.00130	-0.00129	-0.00129	-0.00182	-0.00181	-0.00181	0.00257	0.00281	0.00281
P-value	(0.277)	(0.266)	(0.266)	(0.108)	(0.143)	(0.143)	(0.643)	(0.614)	(0.614)
Income Diversity (t-1)	64.27**	61.29**	61.29**	2.581	2.676	2.676	88.84**	81.52**	81.52**
P-value	(0.0449)	(0.0498)	(0.0498)	(0.874)	(0.875)	(0.875)	(0.0235)	(0.0282)	(0.0282)
Income Diversity * Islamic Bank Dummy	-67.18**	-63.60**	-63.60**	-12.01	-12.20	-12.20	-101.9**	-90.70**	-90.70**

P-value	(0.0337)	(0.0391)	(0.0391)	(0.448)	(0.459)	(0.459)	(0.0143)	(0.0204)	(0.0204)
Herfindahl Index (t-1)		380.1	380.1		41.08	41.08		393.5	393.5
P-value		(0.466)	(0.466)		(0.925)	(0.925)		(0.646)	(0.646)
Share of Islamic Banks (t-1)		184.5	262.7		15.62	15.62		218.9	402.4
P-value		(0.394)	(0.243)		(0.929)	(0.931)		(0.531)	(0.269)
Share of Islamic Banks * Conventional Bank Dummy (t-1)		78.19	-78.19		-0.00598			183.6	
P-value		(0.367)	(0.367)		(1.000)			(0.237)	
Share of Islamic Banks * Islamic Bank Dummy (t-1)						0.00598			-183.6
P-value						(1.000)			(0.237)
Constant	21.35**	-73.88	-73.88	36.16***	27.81	27.81	10.15	-111.5	-111.5
P-value	(0.0102)	(0.495)	(0.495)	(0.000868)	(0.759)	(0.759)	(0.461)	(0.531)	(0.531)
Observations	101	101	101	44	44	44	57	57	57
Adjusted R-squared	0.298	0.306	0.306	0.355	0.298	0.298	0.344	0.379	0.379

P values in parentheses

* significant at 10 percent; ** significant at 5 percent; *** significant at 1 percent

Regressions for Bank Sizes at the US$1.5 Billion Cutoff threshold (Banks with total assets over this threshold are classified as big banks and the rest are considered small banks.)

Table III (a)—Regression Results for the Full Sample: Robust Estimation, 1996–2010

Estimated Variable	All Banks (1)	All Banks (2)	All Banks (3)	Large Banks (4)	Large Banks (5)	Large Banks (6)	Small Banks (7)	Small Banks (8)	Small Banks (9)
Islamic Bank Dummy	-19.88***	-16.90***	-16.90***	-20.45***	-21.85***	-21.85***	-11.03	-1.500	-1.500
P-value	(1.46e-07)	(0.00243)	(0.00243)	(4.54e-06)	(0.000276)	(0.000276)	(0.143)	(0.888)	(0.888)
Net Loans / Total Assets (t-1)	0.335***	0.309***	0.309***	0.154	0.180	0.180	0.562***	0.567**	0.567**
P-value	(0.00185)	(0.00562)	(0.00562)	(0.180)	(0.126)	(0.126)	(0.00354)	(0.0102)	(0.0102)
Costs / Net Income (t-1)	-0.0463**	-0.0723***	-0.0723***	-0.187**	-0.202**	-0.202**	0.0290	-0.0276	-0.0276
P-value	(0.0339)	(0.00250)	(0.00250)	(0.0432)	(0.0356)	(0.0356)	(0.503)	(0.503)	(0.503)
Total Assets (t-1)	-0.00224***	-0.00225***	-0.00225***	-0.00211***	-0.00205***	-0.00205***	0.00289	0.000771	0.000771
P-value	(0.000716)	(0.00103)	(0.00103)	(0.000263)	(0.000442)	(0.000442)	(0.587)	(0.854)	(0.854)
Income Diversity (t-1)	9.734	8.110	8.110	1.832	1.489	1.489	48.40	40.67	40.67
P-value	(0.241)	(0.314)	(0.314)	(0.560)	(0.616)	(0.616)	(0.112)	(0.127)	(0.127)
Income Diversity * Islamic Bank Dummy	-12.61	-10.51	-10.51	-10.75**	-11.04**	-11.04**	-46.52	-35.45	-35.45

P-value	(0.185)	(0.185)	(0.144)	(0.0308)	(0.0308)	(0.0387)	(0.202)	(0.202)	(0.131)
Herfindahl Index (t-1)	108.2	108.2		3.422	3.422		53.34	53.34	
P-value	(0.100)	(0.100)		(0.897)	(0.897)		(0.148)	(0.148)	
Share of Islamic Banks (t-1)	237.9**	157.1**		-11.95	9.241		101.9	74.56*	
P-value	(0.0207)	(0.0429)		(0.794)	(0.732)		(0.101)	(0.0814)	
Share of Islamic Banks * Conventional Bank Dummy (t-1)		80.81			-21.19			27.38	
P-value		(0.317)			(0.574)			(0.585)	
Share of Islamic Banks * Islamic Bank Dummy (t-1)	-80.81			21.19			-27.38		
P-value	(0.317)			(0.574)			(0.585)		
Constant	-42.22*	-42.22*	3.971	37.08***	37.08***	37.48***	3.136	3.136	23.41***
P-value	(0.0762)	(0.0762)	(0.713)	(0.000713)	(0.000713)	(1.66e-08)	(0.799)	(0.799)	(9.01e-09)
Observations	98	98	98	103	103	103	201	201	201
Adjusted R-squared	0.267	0.267	0.220	0.266	0.266	0.286	0.192	0.192	0.183

p values in parentheses
significant at 10 percent; ** significant at 5 percent; *** significant at 1 percent

Table III (b)— Regression Results for Sample Subgroup: Robust Estimation, 2006–2010

Estimated Variable	All Banks (1)	All Banks (2)	All Banks (3)	Large Banks (4)	Large Banks (5)	Large Banks (6)	Small Banks (7)	Small Banks (8)	Small Banks (9)
Islamic Bank Dummy	-28.73***	-32.37***	-32.37***	-32.98***	-37.95***	-37.95***	-26.69**	-43.56	-43.56
P-value	*(2.43e-05)*	*(0.00777)*	*(0.00777)*	*(3.84e-06)*	*(0.000484)*	*(0.000484)*	*(0.0474)*	*(0.116)*	*(0.116)*
Net Loans / Total Assets (t-1)	0.536***	0.517***	0.517***	0.473***	0.534***	0.534***	0.673***	0.504**	0.504**
P-value	*(0.000322)*	*(0.000532)*	*(0.000532)*	*(0.00384)*	*(0.00431)*	*(0.00431)*	*(0.00247)*	*(0.0190)*	*(0.0190)*
Costs / Net Income (t-1)	-0.0560	-0.0541	-0.0541	-0.174*	-0.163	-0.163	0.132	0.209	0.209
P-value	*(0.513)*	*(0.566)*	*(0.566)*	*(0.0616)*	*(0.116)*	*(0.116)*	*(0.492)*	*(0.396)*	*(0.396)*
Total Assets (t-1)	-0.00320***	-0.00308***	-0.00308***	-0.00391***	-0.00398***	-0.00398***	-0.0382	-0.0166	-0.0166
P-value	*(2.43e-05)*	*(2.45e-05)*	*(2.45e-05)*	*(2.95e-08)*	*(9.20e-08)*	*(9.20e-08)*	*(0.364)*	*(0.682)*	*(0.682)*
Income Diversity (t-1)	-2.086	-2.877	-2.877	0.129	0.398	0.398	-9.645	-24.58	-24.58
P-value	*(0.357)*	*(0.291)*	*(0.291)*	*(0.970)*	*(0.910)*	*(0.910)*	*(0.405)*	*(0.261)*	*(0.261)*
Income Diversity * Islamic Bank Dummy	17.48*	17.58*	17.58*	-0.833	-12.53	-12.53	49.92	49.08	49.08

P-value	(0.0635)	(0.0712)	(0.0712)	(0.930)	(0.255)	(0.255)	(0.153)	(0.232)	(0.232)
Herfindahl Index (t-1)		35.53	35.53		-11.59	-11.59		77.05	77.05
P-value		(0.467)	(0.467)		(0.754)	(0.754)		(0.404)	(0.404)
Share of Islamic Banks (t-1)		175.0	48.35		202.2	34.89		329.4	-368.3
P-value		(0.370)	(0.824)		(0.164)	(0.873)		(0.331)	(0.474)
Share of Islamic Banks * Conventional Bank Dummy (t-1)		-126.7			-167.3			-697.7	
P-value		(0.575)			(0.384)			(0.145)	
Share of Islamic Banks * Islamic Bank Dummy (t-1)			126.7			167.3			697.7
P-value			(0.575)			(0.384)			(0.145)
Constant	18.51***	5.664	5.664	32.90***	32.64*	32.64*	6.475	-10.30	-10.30
P-value	(0.000646)	(0.789)	(0.789)	(1.50e-08)	(0.0563)	(0.0563)	(0.641)	(0.847)	(0.847)
Observations	100	100	100	54	54	54	46	46	46
Adjusted R-squared	0.233	0.220	0.220	0.449	0.426	0.426	0.147	0.195	0.195

ρ values in parentheses
* significant at 10 percent; ** significant at 5 percent; *** significant at 1 percent

Regressions for Bank Sizes at the US$0.75 Billion Cutoff Threshold (Banks with total assets over this threshold are classified as big banks and the rest are considered small banks.)

Table IV (a)—Regression Results for the Full Sample: Robust Estimation, 1996–2010

Estimated Variable	All Banks	All Banks	All Banks	Large Banks	Large Banks	Large Banks	Small Banks	Small Banks	Small Banks
	(1)	(2)	(3)	(4)	(5)	(6)	(7)	(8)	(9)
Islamic Bank Dummy	−19.88***	−16.90***	−16.90***	−32.13***	−29.66***	−29.66***	−8.755	−7.045	−7.045
P-value	*(1.46e-07)*	*(0.00243)*	*(0.00243)*	*(1.62e-06)*	*(2.43e-06)*	*(2.43e-06)*	*(0.131)*	*(0.428)*	*(0.428)*
Net Loans / Total Assets (t-1)	0.335***	0.309***	0.309***	0.0632	0.0222	0.0222	0.538***	0.394***	0.394***
P-value	*(0.00185)*	*(0.00562)*	*(0.00562)*	*(0.673)*	*(0.886)*	*(0.886)*	*(0.000215)*	*(0.00533)*	*(0.00533)*
Costs / Net Income (t-1)	−0.0463**	−0.0723***	−0.0723***	0.0103	0.0451	0.0451	−0.0195	−0.0120	−0.0120
P-value	*(0.0339)*	*(0.00250)*	*(0.00250)*	*(0.905)*	*(0.684)*	*(0.684)*	*(0.291)*	*(0.674)*	*(0.674)*
Total Assets (t-1)	−0.00224***	−0.00225***	−0.00225***	−0.00319***	−0.00327***	−0.00327***	−0.00563	−0.00238	−0.00238
P-value	*(0.000716)*	*(0.00103)*	*(0.00103)*	*(0.00102)*	*(0.000990)*	*(0.000990)*	*(0.135)*	*(0.414)*	*(0.414)*
Income Diversity (t-1)	9.734	8.110	8.110	15.28	15.05	15.05	−1.112	−5.295	−5.295
P-value	*(0.241)*	*(0.314)*	*(0.314)*	*(0.211)*	*(0.238)*	*(0.238)*	*(0.901)*	*(0.633)*	*(0.633)*
Income Diversity * Islamic Bank Dummy	−12.61	−10.51	−10.51	−15.70	−12.81	−12.81	5.079	5.560	5.560

	(1)	(2)	(3)	(4)	(5)	(6)	(7)	(8)	(9)
P-value	(0.131)	(0.202)	(0.202)	(0.164)	(0.258)	(0.258)	(0.643)	(0.645)	(0.645)
Herfindahl Index (t-1)		53.34	53.34		3.317	3.317		97.24	97.24
P-value		(0.148)	(0.148)		(0.911)	(0.911)		(0.137)	(0.137)
Share of Islamic Banks (t-1)		74.56*	101.9		37.98	83.69		95.18	64.53
P-value		(0.0814)	(0.101)		(0.332)	(0.239)		(0.142)	(0.473)
Share of Islamic Banks * Conventional Bank Dummy (t-1)		27.38			45.71			-30.65	
P-value		(0.585)			(0.486)			(0.622)	
Share of Islamic Banks * Islamic Bank Dummy (t-1)			-27.38			-45.71			30.65
P-value			(0.585)			(0.486)			(0.622)
Constant	23.41***	3.136	3.136	39.78***	30.81***	30.81***	9.756**	-19.01	-19.01
P-value	(9.01e-09)	(0.799)	(0.799)	(1.82e-09)	(0.00771)	(0.00771)	(0.0379)	(0.332)	(0.332)
Observations	201	201	201	126	126	126	75	75	75
Adjusted R-squared	0.183	0.192	0.192	0.238	0.252	0.252	0.181	0.230	0.230

ρ values in parentheses

* significant at 10 percent; ** significant at 5 percent; *** significant at 1 percent

Table IV (b)—Regression Results for Sample Subgroup: Robust Estimation, 2006–2010

Estimated Variable	All Banks (1)	All Banks (2)	All Banks (3)	Large Banks (4)	Large Banks (5)	Large Banks (6)	Small Banks (7)	Small Banks (8)	Small Banks (9)
Islamic Bank Dummy	-28.73***	-32.37***	-32.37***	-39.00***	-37.58***	-37.58***	-19.37	-41.99	-41.99
P-value	*(2.43e-05)*	*(0.00777)*	*(0.00777)*	*(6.47e-09)*	*(0.000175)*	*(0.000175)*	*(0.161)*	*(0.137)*	*(0.137)*
Net Loans / Total Assets (t-1)	0.536***	0.517***	0.517***	0.401***	0.404***	0.404***	0.705***	0.566**	0.566**
P-value	*(0.000322)*	*(0.000532)*	*(0.000532)*	*(0.00425)*	*(0.00861)*	*(0.00861)*	*(0.00212)*	*(0.0151)*	*(0.0151)*
Costs / Net Income (t-1)	-0.0560	-0.0541	-0.0541	-0.0995	-0.0813	-0.0813	0.0925	0.186	0.186
P-value	*(0.513)*	*(0.566)*	*(0.566)*	*(0.111)*	*(0.285)*	*(0.285)*	*(0.628)*	*(0.459)*	*(0.459)*
Total Assets (t-1)	-0.00320***	-0.00308***	-0.00308***	-0.00396***	-0.00398***	-0.00398***	-0.0387	-0.0186	-0.0186
P value	*(2.43e-05)*	*(2.45e-05)*	*(2.45e-05)*	*(2.18e-08)*	*(9.00e-08)*	*(9.00e-08)*	*(0.348)*	*(0.649)*	*(0.649)*
Income Diversity (t-1)	-2.086	-2.877	-2.877	0.728	1.316	1.316	-9.593	-22.46	-22.46
P-value	*(0.357)*	*(0.291)*	*(0.291)*	*(0.844)*	*(0.744)*	*(0.744)*	*(0.408)*	*(0.307)*	*(0.307)*
Income Diversity * Islamic Bank Dummy	17.48*	17.58*	17.58*	10.38	9.937	9.937	39.85	42.17	42.17

	(1)	(2)	(3)	(4)	(5)	(6)	(7)	(8)	(9)
P-value	(0.298)	(0.298)	(0.243)	(0.321)	(0.321)	(0.235)	(0.0712)	(0.0712)	(0.0635)
Herfindahl Index (t-1)	74.06	74.06		-15.53	-15.53		35.53	35.53	
P-value	(0.440)	(0.440)		(0.667)	(0.667)		(0.467)	(0.467)	
Share of Islamic Banks (t-1)	-340.7	428.4		15.62	-38.57		48.35	175.0	
P-value	(0.515)	(0.239)		(0.943)	(0.791)		(0.824)	(0.370)	
Share of Islamic Banks * Conventional Bank Dummy (t-1)		-769.1		54.19	54.19			-126.7	
P-value		(0.103)		(0.798)	(0.798)			(0.575)	
Share of Islamic Banks * Islamic Bank Dummy (t-1)	769.1				-54.19		126.7		
P-value	(0.103)				(0.798)		(0.575)		
Constant	-11.28	-11.28	7.265	35.48**	35.48**	32.10***	5.664	5.664	18.51***
P-value	(0.841)	(0.841)	(0.608)	(0.0354)	(0.0354)	(3.27e-08)	(0.789)	(0.789)	(0.000646)
Observations	42	42	42	58	58	58	100	100	100
Adjusted R-squared	0.162	0.162	0.127	0.438	0.438	0.466	0.220	0.220	0.233

ρ values in parentheses
* significant at 10 percent; ** significant at 5 percent; *** significant at 1 percent

Malaysia

Table I (a)— Support Summary Statistics for the Full Sample Period 1996–2010 for the Four Asset Sizes Cutoff Thresholds

Table I (A)—Continued

Cutoff for Bank Asset Size US$750 million	Variables	Conventional Banks	Islamic Banks	Cutoff for Bank Asset Size US$1 billion	Variables	Conventional Banks	Islamic Banks
	ROAA	*1.06*	*-0.09***		*ROAA*	*1.06*	*-0.09***
	Large Banks	1.18	-0.07***		Large Banks	1.18	-0.07***
	Small Banks	0.68	-0.29*		Small Banks	0.69	-0.29*
	Equity / Assets	*10.00*	*15.17***		*Equity / Assets*	*10.00*	*15.17***
	Large Banks	9.63	14.08***		Large Banks	9.45	14.08***
	Small Banks	11.22	22.70***		Small Banks	11.67	22.70***
	Total Nonearning Assets / Assets	*0.23*	*0.32***		*Total Nonearning Assets / Assets*	*0.23*	*0.32***
	Large Banks	0.22	0.30***		Large Banks	0.22	0.30***
	Small Banks	0.24	0.41**		Small Banks	0.24	0.41**
	Cash and Due from Banks / Assets	*0.20*	*0.28***		*Cash and Due from Banks / Assets*	*0.20*	*0.28***
	Large Banks	0.20	0.27***		Large Banks	0.20	0.27***
	Small Banks	0.22	0.39**		Small Banks	0.22	0.39**
	Standard Deviation of ROAA	*0.79*	*1.55***		*Standard Deviation of ROAA*	*0.79*	*1.55***
	Large Banks	0.69	1.71***		Large Banks	0.69	1.71***
	Small Banks	1.13	0.45**		Small Banks	1.09	0.45**

	US$1.5 billion		US$2 billion	
ROAA	**1.06**	**-0.09*****	**1.06**	**-0.09*****
Large Banks	1.09	-0.21***	1.13	0.48***
Small Banks	0.99	0.24*	0.95	-1.27***
Equity / Assets	**10.00**	**15.17*****	**10.00**	**15.32*****
Large Banks	8.52	14.73***	8.45	13.61***
Small Banks	13.03	16.46	12.66	18.43***
Total Nonearning Assets / Assets	**0.23**	**0.32*****	**0.23**	**0.32*****
Large Banks	0.21	0.30***	0.20	0.31***
Small Banks	0.27	0.35*	0.28	0.33
Cash and Due from Banks / Assets	**0.20**	**0.28*****	**0.20**	**0.28*****
Large Banks	0.18	0.27***	0.18	0.27***
Small Banks	0.25	0.33	0.25	0.31
Standard Deviation of ROAA	**0.79**	**2.92*****	**0.79**	**1.55*****
Large Banks	0.64	1.99***	0.63	0.95***
Small Banks	1.11	0.45***	1.07	2.75***

* Significant at 10 percent; ** significant at 5 percent; *** significant at 1 percent

Table I (b)—Support Summary Statistics for the Subsample Period 2006–2010 for the Various Asset Sizes Cutoff Thresholds

Cutoff for Bank Asset Size	Variables	Conventional Banks	Islamic Banks	Cutoff for Bank Asset Size	Variables	Conventional Banks	Islamic Banks
US$750 million				*US$1 billion*			
	ROAA	*1.10*	*-0.07****		*ROAA*	*1.10*	*-0.07****
	Large Banks	1.09	-0.04***		Large Banks	1.11	-0.04***
	Small Banks	1.24	-0.29*		Small Banks	1.07	-0.29*
	Equity / Assets	*10.43*	*14.52****		*Equity / Assets*	*10.43*	*14.52****
	Large Banks	9.24	13.25***		Large Banks	8.72	13.25***
	Small Banks	25.97	22.70***		Small Banks	23.55	22.70***
	Total Nonearning Assets / Assets	*0.28*	*0.30****		*Total Nonearning Assets / Assets*	*0.28*	*0.30****
	Large Banks	0.25	0.29***		Large Banks	0.25	0.29***
	Small Banks	0.68	0.41**		Small Banks	0.51	0.41**
	Cash and Due from Banks / Assets	*0.26*	*0.27****		*Cash and Due from Banks / Assets*	*0.26*	*0.27****
	Large Banks	0.23	0.25***		Large Banks	0.23	0.25***
	Small Banks	0.67	0.39**		Small Banks	0.50	0.39**
	Standard Deviation of ROAA	*0.65*	*1.60****		*Standard Deviation of ROAA*	*0.65*	*1.60****
	Large Banks	0.66	1.78***		Large Banks	0.67	1.78***
	Small Banks	0.44	0.45**		Small Banks	0.46	0.45**

US$1.5 billion

	1.10	-0.07***
ROAA		
Large Banks	1.08	-0.19***
Small Banks	1.18	0.24*
Equity / Assets	**10.43**	**14.52***
Large Banks	7.90	13.81***
Small Banks	20.33	16.46
Total Nonearning Assets / Assets	**0.28**	**0.30***
Large Banks	0.24	0.29***
Small Banks	0.44	0.35*
Cash and Due from Banks / Assets	**0.26**	**0.27***
Large Banks	0.21	0.25***
Small Banks	0.42	0.33
Standard Deviation of ROAA	**0.65**	**1.60***
Large Banks	0.62	2.03***
Small Banks	0.78	0.45***

US$2 billion

	1.10	-0.07***
ROAA		
Large Banks	1.12	0.57***
Small Banks	1.05	-1.27***
Equity / Assets	**10.43**	**14.52***
Large Banks	7.86	12.48***
Small Banks	8.20	18.43***
Total Nonearning Assets / Assets	**0.28**	**0.30***
Large Banks	0.23	0.29***
Small Banks	0.44	0.33
Cash and Due from Banks / Assets	**0.26**	**0.27***
Large Banks	0.20	0.25***
Small Banks	0.43	0.31
Standard Deviation of ROAA	**0.65**	**1.60***
Large Banks	0.61	0.99***
Small Banks	0.76	2.75***

* Significant at 10 percent; ** significant at 5 percent; *** significant at 1 percent

Table I (c)—Support Summary Statistics for the Subsample Period 2008–2009 for the Various Asset Sizes Cutoff Thresholds

Cutoff for Bank Asset Size	Variables	Conventional Banks	Islamic Banks
US$750 million			
	ROAA	*1.13*	*0.54****
	Large Banks	1.13	0.62***
	Small Banks	1.19	-0.03*
	Equity / Assets	*10.39*	*9.71****
	Large Banks	9.38	9.39***
	Small Banks	24.48	11.83***
	Total Nonearning Assets / Assets	*0.28*	*0.32****
	Large Banks	0.25	0.29***
	Small Banks	0.73	0.50**
	Cash and Due from Banks / Assets	*0.26*	*0.29****
	Large Banks	0.22	0.27***
	Small Banks	0.72	0.48**
	Standard Deviation of ROAA	*0.65*	*1.43*
	Large Banks	0.66	1.58***
	Small Banks	0.42	0.42**

Cutoff for Bank Asset Size	Variables	Conventional Banks	Islamic Banks
US$1 billion			
	ROAA	*1.13*	*0.54****
	Large Banks	1.15	0.62***
	Small Banks	0.99	-0.03*
	Equity / Assets	*10.39*	*9.71****
	Large Banks	8.96	9.39***
	Small Banks	21.82	11.83***
	Total Nonearning Assets / Assets	*0.28*	*0.32****
	Large Banks	0.25	0.29***
	Small Banks	0.52	0.50**
	Cash and Due from Banks / Assets	*0.26*	*0.29****
	Large Banks	0.22	0.27***
	Small Banks	0.52	0.48**
	Standard Deviation of ROAA	*0.65*	*1.43****
	Large Banks	0.67	1.58***
	Small Banks	0.45	0.42**

US$1.5 billion

ROAA	*1.13*	*0.54****
Large Banks	1.12	0.64***
Small Banks	1.16	0.32*
Equity / Assets	*10.39*	*9.71****
Large Banks	8.07	8.95***
Small Banks	19.65	11.30
Total Nonearning Assets / Assets	*0.28*	*0.32****
Large Banks	0.24	0.27***
Small Banks	0.46	0.41
Cash and Due from Banks / Assets	*0.26*	*0.29****
Large Banks	0.21	0.26***
Small Banks	0.45	0.37
Standard Deviation of ROAA	*0.65*	*1.43****
Large Banks	0.62	1.91***
Small Banks	0.76	0.44***

US$2 billion

ROAA	*1.13*	*0.54****
Large Banks	1.15	0.78***
Small Banks	1.09	0.15***
Equity / Assets	*10.39*	*9.71****
Large Banks	8.02	8.77***
Small Banks	17.71	11.19**
Total Nonearning Assets / Assets	*0.28*	*0.32****
Large Banks	0.23	0.27***
Small Banks	0.44	0.39
Cash and Due from Banks / Assets	*0.26*	*0.29****
Large Banks	0.20	0.25***
Small Banks	0.43	0.36
Standard Deviation of ROAA	*0.65*	*1.43****
Large Banks	0.61	0.94***
Small Banks	0.75	2.21***

* Significant at 10 percent; ** significant at 5 percent; *** significant at 1 percent

Regressions for Bank Sizes at the US$2 billion Cutoff Threshold (Banks with total assets over this threshold are classified as big banks and the rest are considered small banks.)

Table II (a)—Regression Results for the Full Sample: Robust Estimation, 1996–2010

Estimated Variable	All Banks (1)	All Banks (2)	All Banks (3)	Large Banks (4)	Large Banks (5)	Large Banks (6)	Small Banks (7)	Small Banks (8)	Small Banks (9)
Islamic Bank Dummy	7.252*	20.66**	20.66**	9.171**	21.85***	21.85***	7.407*	26.04**	26.04**
P-value	(0.0523)	(0.0194)	(0.0194)	(0.0423)	(0.0184)	(0.0184)	(0.0950)	(0.0102)	(0.0102)
Net Loans / Total Assets (t-1)	-0.0279	0.0206	0.0206	0.140***	0.187***	0.187***	-0.109*	-0.0109	-0.0109
P-value	(0.574)	(0.697)	(0.697)	(0.00276)	(0.000505)	(0.000505)	(0.0981)	(0.857)	(0.857)
Costs / Net Income (t-1)	-0.0443**	0.0518***	0.0518***	-0.0217**	-0.0313**	-0.0313**	-0.109***	-0.0858**	-0.0858**
P-value	(0.0125)	(0.00354)	(0.00354)	(0.0337)	(0.0208)	(0.0208)	(0.00377)	(0.0283)	(0.0283)
Total Assets (t-1)	5.97e-06	-1.62e-05	-1.62e-05	1.25e-05	6.55e-07	6.55e-07	-0.000232*	0.000264***	0.000264***
P-value	(0.587)	(0.380)	(0.380)	(0.387)	(0.978)	(0.978)	(0.0891)	(0.00570)	(0.00570)
Income Diversity (t-1)	0.517	0.547	0.547	1.804***	1.744**	1.744**	0.164	0.468	0.468
P-value	(0.207)	(0.176)	(0.176)	(0.0227)	(0.0237)	(0.0237)	(0.453)	(0.106)	(0.106)

	(1)	(2)	(3)	(4)	(5)	(6)	(7)	(8)	(9)
Income Diversity * Islamic Bank Dummy	3.089	3.092	3.092	-5.784	-4.331	-4.331	75.31***	58.53***	58.53***
P-value	*(0.800)*	*(0.787)*	*(0.787)*	*(0.585)*	*(0.674)*	*(0.674)*	*(0)*	*(0.00200)*	*(0.00200)*
Herfindahl Index (t-1)		259.4**	259.4**		52.03	52.03		625.8***	625.8***
P-value		*(0.0129)*	*(0.0129)*		*(0.631)*	*(0.631)*		*(0.00730)*	*(0.00730)*
Share of Islamic Banks (t-1)		-120.8	76.15*		-132.2	49.90		-147.2	120.1**
P-value		*(0.221)*	*(0.0591)*		*(0.250)*	*(0.326)*		*(0.161)*	*(0.0257)*
Share of Islamic Banks * Conventional Bank Dummy (t-1)		197.0*			182.1			267.4**	
P-value		*(0.0612)*			*(0.148)*			*(0.0243)*	
Share of Islamic Banks * Islamic Bank Dummy (t-1)			-197.0*			-182.1			-267.4**
P-value			*(0.0612)*			*(0.148)*			*(0.0243)*
Constant	23.85***	-4.664	-4.664	12.23***	4.147	4.147	32.84***	-34.58	-34.58
P-value	*(0)*	*(0.668)*	*(0.668)*	*(8.56e-05)*	*(0.729)*	*(0.729)*	*(0)*	*(0.132)*	*(0.132)*
Observations	327	327	327	216	216	216	111	111	111
Adjusted R-squared	0.014	0.040	0.040	0.021	0.026	0.026	0.108	0.189	0.189

p values in parentheses

* Significant at the 10 percent; ** significant at the 5 percent; *** significant at the 1 percent level for the 95 percent confidence interval.

Table II (b)—Regression Results for the Sample Subgroup: Robust Estimation, 2006–2010

Estimated Variable	All Banks (1)	All Banks (2)	All Banks (3)	Large Banks (4)	Large Banks (5)	Large Banks (6)	Small Banks (7)	Small Banks (8)	Small Banks (9)
Islamic Bank Dummy	-2.078	14.18	14.18	1.705	15.75	15.75	1.834	40.07*	40.07*
P-value	(0.742)	(0.215)	(0.215)	(0.830)	(0.224)	(0.224)	(0.835)	(0.0641)	(0.0641)
Net Loans / Total Assets (t-1)	0.0564	0.0770	0.0770	0.175*	0.235**	0.235**	-0.0292	-0.0980	-0.0980
P-value	(0.586)	(0.467)	(0.467)	(0.0625)	(0.0200)	(0.0200)	(0.862)	(0.597)	(0.597)
Costs / Net Income (t-1)	-0.0267**	-0.0366**	-0.0366**	-0.0118	-0.0156	-0.0156	-0.157	-0.0787	-0.0787
P-value	(0.0298)	(0.0294)	(0.0294)	(0.198)	(0.313)	(0.313)	(0.129)	(0.543)	(0.543)
Total Assets (t-1)	-5.58e-05*	-6.00e-05*	-6.00e-05*	-3.55e-05	-4.04e-05	-4.04e-05	-0.00239	-0.00320	-0.00320
P-value	(0.0977)	(0.0842)	(0.0842)	(0.396)	(0.355)	(0.355)	(0.180)	(0.138)	(0.138)
Income Diversity (t-1)	-16.12	-15.08	-15.08	-13.82	-10.02	-10.02	-15.03	-19.83	-19.83
P-value	(0.150)	(0.169)	(0.169)	(0.354)	(0.471)	(0.471)	(0.298)	(0.252)	(0.252)
Income Diversity * Islamic Bank Dummy	20.50	19.44	19.44	10.63	8.080	8.080	87.71***	93.29**	93.29**

P-value	(0.228)	(0.235)	(0.235)	(0.571)	(0.645)	(0.645)	(0.00885)	(0.0451)	(0.0451)
Herfindahl Index (t-1)		178.0	178.0		437.6	437.6		-301.7	-301.7
P-value		(0.805)	(0.805)		(0.590)	(0.590)		(0.857)	(0.857)
Share of Islamic Banks (t-1)		-119.3	79.72		-59.03	112.0		-352.5	77.37
P-value		(0.407)	(0.338)		(0.720)	(0.214)		(0.323)	(0.741)
Share of Islamic Banks * Conventional Bank Dummy (t-1)		199.0			171.1			429.8*	
P-value		(0.105)			(0.251)			(0.0848)	
Share of Islamic Banks * Islamic Bank Dummy (t-1)			-199.0			-171.1			-429.8*
P-value			(0.105)			(0.251)			(0.0848)
Constant	28.00***	5.418	5.418	17.63**	-34.52	-34.52	48.03***	74.66	74.66
P-value	(0.000476)	(0.941)	(0.941)	(0.0234)	(0.671)	(0.671)	(0.00313)	(0.660)	(0.660)
Observations	109	109	109	84	84	84	25	25	25
Adjusted R-squared	0.007	0.002	0.002	-0.016	-0.034	-0.034	0.194	0.155	0.155

ρ values in parentheses

* Significant at the 10 percent; ** significant at the 5 percent; *** significant at the 1 percent level for the 95 percent confidence interval.

Table II (c)—Regression Results for the Sample Subgroup: Robust Estimation, 2008–2009

Estimated Variable	All Banks	All Banks	All Banks	Large Banks	Large Banks	Large Banks	Small Banks	Small Banks	Small Banks
	(1)	(2)	(3)	(4)	(5)	(6)	(7)	(8)	(9)
Islamic Bank Dummy	-3.144	15.80	15.80	-1.560	26.55	26.55	-2.484	23.55	23.55
P-value	(0.730)	(0.559)	(0.559)	(0.911)	(0.353)	(0.353)	(0.811)	(0.518)	(0.518)
Net Loans / Total Assets (t-1)	0.141	0.137	0.137	0.258*	0.251*	0.251*	-0.0997	-0.129	-0.129
P-value	(0.322)	(0.351)	(0.351)	(0.0509)	(0.0629)	(0.0629)	(0.702)	(0.675)	(0.675)
Costs / Net Income (t-1)	-0.168*	-0.167*	-0.167*	0.0767	0.0754	0.0754	-0.102	-0.0765	-0.0765
P-value	(0.0622)	(0.0688)	(0.0688)	(0.794)	(0.801)	(0.801)	(0.417)	(0.646)	(0.646)
Total Assets (t-1)	-6.54e-05	-6.54e-05	-6.54e-05	-5.58e-05	-5.52e-05	-5.52e-05	-0.00255	-0.00267	-0.00267
P-value	(0.147)	(0.154)	(0.154)	(0.338)	(0.355)	(0.355)	(0.201)	(0.256)	(0.256)
Income Diversity (t-1)	-6.940	-7.558	-7.558	-5.359	-5.874	-5.874	-11.57	-13.80	-13.80
P-value	(0.685)	(0.661)	(0.661)	(0.865)	(0.847)	(0.847)	(0.582)	(0.609)	(0.609)
Income Diversity * Islamic Bank Dummy	12.84	4.799	4.799	5.596	-10.36	-10.36	93.35*	93.48	93.48
P-value	(0.609)	(0.864)	(0.864)	(0.882)	(0.781)	(0.781)	(0.0885)	(0.165)	(0.165)

Herfindahl Index (t-1)	0	0	0		0	0		0	0
P-value									
Share of Islamic Banks (t-1)		-146.1	28.28		-232.5	10.20		-158.2	105.4
P-value		(0.477)	(0.815)		(0.160)	(0.941)		(0.469)	(0.709)
Share of Islamic Banks * Conventional Bank Dummy (t-1)		174.4			242.7			263.6	
P-value		(0.466)			(0.262)			(0.508)	
Share of Islamic Banks * Islamic Bank Dummy (t-1)			-174.4			-242.7			-263.6
P-value			(0.466)			(0.262)			(0.508)
Constant	29.39**	27.11*	27.11*	11.06	10.62	10.62	49.89**	41.42	41.42
P-value	(0.0235)	(0.0849)	(0.0849)	(0.580)	(0.664)	(0.664)	(0.0467)	(0.179)	(0.179)
Observations	61	61	61	46	46	46	15	15	15
Adjusted R-squared	-0.025	-0.057	-0.057	-0.078	-0.122	-0.122	0.142	-0.081	-0.081

ρ values in parentheses

* Significant at the 10 percent; ** significant at the 5 percent; *** significant at the 1 percent level for the 95 percent confidence interval

Regressions for Banks Sizes at the US$1.5 Billion Cutoff Threshold (Banks with total assets over this threshold are classified as big banks and the rest are considered small banks.)

Table III (a)—Regression Results for the Full Sample: Robust Estimation, 1996–2010

Estimated Variable	All Banks (1)	All Banks (2)	All Banks (3)	Large Banks (4)	Large Banks (5)	Large Banks (6)	Small Banks (7)	Small Banks (8)	Small Banks (9)
Islamic Bank Dummy	7.259*	20.66**	20.66**	7.005	22.62**	22.62**	11.99**	27.14***	27.14***
P-value	(0.0523)	(0.0194)	(0.0194)	(0.113)	(0.0114)	(0.0114)	(0.0167)	(0.00633)	(0.00633)
Net Loans / Total Assets (t-1)	-0.0279	0.0206	0.0206	0.108***	0.152***	0.152***	-0.131	-0.0405	-0.0405
P-value	(0.574)	(0.697)	(0.697)	(0.00394)	(0.00255)	(0.00255)	(0.126)	(0.596)	(0.596)
Costs / Net Income (t-1)	0.0443**	0.0518***	0.0518***	-0.0265*	-0.0381**	-0.0381**	-0.0436	-0.00988	-0.00988
P-value	(0.0125)	(0.00354)	(0.00354)	(0.0605)	(0.0147)	(0.0147)	(0.391)	(0.869)	(0.869)
Total Assets (t-1)	5.97e-06	-1.62e-05	-1.62e-05	1.48e-05	2.67e-06	2.67e-06	-0.000280**	0.000295***	0.000295***
P-value	(0.587)	(0.380)	(0.380)	(0.282)	(0.909)	(0.909)	(0.0237)	(0.00173)	(0.00173)
Income Diversity (t-1)	0.517	0.547	0.547	0.264	0.201	0.201	15.33**	13.64**	13.64**
P-value	(0.207)	(0.176)	(0.176)	(0.434)	(0.549)	(0.549)	(0.0220)	(0.0217)	(0.0217)

	(1)	(2)	(3)	(4)	(5)	(6)	(7)	(8)	(9)
Income Diversity * Islamic Bank Dummy	3.089	3.092	3.092	-1.024	-0.0367	-0.0367	53.73***	41.38***	41.38***
P-value	(0.800)	(0.787)	(0.787)	(0.925)	(0.997)	(0.997)	(6.79e-06)	(0.00585)	(0.00585)
Herfindahl Index (t-1)		259.4**	259.4**		77.58	77.58		656.7***	656.7***
P-value		(0.0129)	(0.0129)		(0.464)	(0.464)		(0.00975)	(0.00975)
Share of Islamic Banks (t-1)		-120.8	76.15*		-161.9	48.00		-115.2	147.2**
P-value		(0.221)	(0.0591)		(0.137)	(0.329)		(0.276)	(0.0177)
Share of Islamic Banks * Conventional Bank Dummy (t-1)		197.0*			209.9*			262.4**	
P-value		(0.0612)			(0.0812)			(0.0385)	
Share of Islamic Banks * Islamic Bank Dummy (t-1)			-197.0*			-209.9*			-262.4**
P-value			(0.0612)			(0.0812)			(0.0385)
Constant	23.85***	-4.664	-4.664	14.46***	4.260	4.260	29.15***	-41.15	-41.15
P-value	(0)	(0.668)	(0.668)	(4.28e-09)	(0.718)	(0.718)	(2.76e-06)	(0.104)	(0.104)
Observations	327	327	327	230	230	230	97	97	97
Adjusted R-squared	0.014	0.040	0.040	0.017	0.027	0.027	0.146	0.238	0.238

p values in parentheses

* Significant at the 10 percent; ** significant at the 5 percent; *** significant at the 1 percent level for the 95 percent confidence interval.

Table III (b)—Regression Results for the Sample Subgroup: Robust Estimation, 2006–2010

Estimated Variable	All Banks (1)	All Banks (2)	All Banks (3)	Large Banks (4)	Large Banks (5)	Large Banks (6)	Small Banks (7)	Small Banks (8)	Small Banks (9)
Islamic Bank Dummy	-2.078	14.18	14.18	-0.215	17.16	17.16	7.053	48.74	48.74
P-value	(0.742)	(0.215)	(0.215)	(0.978)	(0.160)	(0.160)	(0.744)	(0.113)	(0.113)
Net Loans / Total Assets (t-1)	0.0564	0.0770	0.0770	0.134	0.196**	0.196**	0.00207	-0.0726	-0.0726
P-value	(0.586)	(0.467)	(0.467)	(0.139)	(0.0447)	(0.0447)	(0.990)	(0.649)	(0.649)
Costs / Net Income (t-1)	-0.0267**	-0.0366**	-0.0366**	-0.0164	-0.0232	-0.0232	0.309	0.379	0.379
P-value	(0.0298)	(0.0294)	(0.0294)	(0.122)	(0.136)	(0.136)	(0.744)	(0.671)	(0.671)
Total Assets (t-1)	-5.58e-05*	-6.00e-05*	-6.00e-05*	-3.42e-05	-3.98e-05	-3.98e-05	-0.00648	-0.00833*	-0.00833*
P-value	(0.0977)	(0.0842)	(0.0842)	(0.409)	(0.358)	(0.358)	(0.119)	(0.0803)	(0.0803)
Income Diversity (t-1)	-16.12	-15.08	-15.08	-13.10	-9.336	-9.336	-8.523	-16.85	-16.85
P-value	(0.150)	(0.169)	(0.169)	(0.290)	(0.410)	(0.410)	(0.638)	(0.518)	(0.518)
Income Diversity * Islamic Bank Dummy	20.50	19.44	19.44	13.37	10.50	10.50	86.50**	98.95*	98.95*

P-value	(0.228)	(0.235)	(0.235)	(0.443)	(0.503)	(0.503)	(0.0214)	(0.0836)	(0.0836)
Herfindahl Index (t-1)		178.0	178.0		353.6	353.6		-258.5	-258.5
P-value		(0.805)	(0.805)		(0.648)	(0.648)		(0.899)	(0.899)
Share of Islamic Banks (t-1)		-119.3	79.72		-107.7	98.59		-309.6	150.1
P-value		(0.407)	(0.338)		(0.485)	(0.250)		(0.468)	(0.625)
Share of Islamic Banks * Conventional Bank Dummy (t-1)		199.0			206.3			459.6	
P-value		(0.105)			(0.144)			(0.101)	
Share of Islamic Banks * Islamic Bank Dummy (t-1)			-199.0			-206.3			-459.6
P-value			(0.105)			(0.144)			(0.101)
Constant	28.00***	5.418	5.418	19.96***	-23.30	-23.30	41.48	63.05	63.05
P-value	(0.000476)	(0.941)	(0.941)	(0.00953)	(0.763)	(0.763)	(0.232)	(0.773)	(0.773)
Observations	109	109	109	89	89	89	20	20	20
Adjusted R-squared	0.007	0.002	0.002	-0.011	-0.021	-0.021	-0.017	-0.068	-0.068

ρ values in parentheses
* Significant at the 10 percent; ** significant at the 5 percent; *** significant at the 1 percent level for the 95 percent confidence interval

Table III (c)—Regression Results for the Sample Subgroup: Robust Estimation, 2008–2009

Estimated Variable	All Banks	All Banks	All Banks	Large Banks	Large Banks	Large Banks	Small Banks	Small Banks	Small Banks
	(1)	(2)	(3)	(4)	(5)	(6)	(7)	(8)	(9)
Islamic Bank Dummy	-3.144	15.80	15.80	-2.851	23.13	23.13	-8.434	47.66	47.66
P-value	(0.780)	(0.559)	(0.559)	(0.824)	(0.452)	(0.452)	(0.741)	(0.257)	(0.257)
Net Loans / Total Assets (t-1)	0.141	0.137	0.137	0.219*	0.212	0.212	-0.122	-0.192	-0.192
P-value	(0.322)	(0.351)	(0.351)	(0.0977)	(0.119)	(0.119)	(0.596)	(0.398)	(0.398)
Costs / Net Income (t-1)	-0.168*	-0.167*	-0.167*	-0.143	-0.152	-0.152	1.236	1.669	1.669
P-value	(0.0622)	(0.0688)	(0.0688)	(0.234)	(0.230)	(0.230)	(0.356)	(0.197)	(0.197)
Total Assets (t-1)	-6.54e-05	-6.54e-05	-6.54e-05	-5.34e-05	-5.27e-05	-5.27e-05	-0.00558	-0.00692	-0.00692
P-value	(0.147)	(0.154)	(0.154)	(0.356)	(0.374)	(0.374)	(0.206)	(0.140)	(0.140)
Income Diversity (t-1)	-6.940	-7.558	-7.558	-7.138	-7.608	-7.608	5.672	8.757	8.757
P-value	(0.685)	(0.661)	(0.661)	(0.763)	(0.735)	(0.735)	(0.770)	(0.771)	(0.771)
Income Diversity * Islamic Bank Dummy	12.84	4.799	4.799	10.77	-4.118	-4.118	83.53*	80.73	80.73
P-value	(0.609)	(0.864)	(0.864)	(0.732)	(0.898)	(0.898)	(0.0625)	(0.124)	(0.124)

Herfindahl Index (t-1)		0	0		0	0		0	0
P-value									
Share of Islamic Banks (t-1)		-146.1	28.28		-219.0	4.471		-283.6	299.2
P-value		(0.477)	(0.815)		(0.290)	(0.972)		(0.185)	(0.266)
Share of Islamic Banks * Conventional Bank Dummy (t-1)		174.4			223.5			582.8	
P-value		(0.466)			(0.364)			(0.107)	
Share of Islamic Banks * Islamic Bank Dummy (t-1)			-174.4			-223.5			-582.8
P-value			(0.466)			(0.364)			(0.107)
Constant	29.39**	27.11*	27.11*	22.40	22.79	22.79	12.58	-22.81	-22.81
P-value	(0.0235)	(0.0849)	(0.0849)	(0.154)	(0.259)	(0.259)	(0.744)	(0.499)	(0.499)
Observations	61	61	61	49	49	49	12	12	12
Adjusted R-squared	-0.025	-0.057	-0.057	-0.051	-0.091	-0.091	-0.011	0.036	0.036

ρ values in parentheses

* Significant at the 10 percent; ** significant at the 5 percent; *** significant at the 1 percent level for the 95 percent confidence interval

Regressions for Bank Sizes at the US$0.75 Billion Cutoff Threshold (Banks with total assets over this threshold are classified as big banks and the rest are considered small banks.)

Table IV (a)—Regression Results for the Full Sample: Robust Estimation, 1996–2010

Estimated Variable	All Banks	All Banks	All Banks	Large Banks	Large Banks	Large Banks	Small Banks	Small Banks	Small Banks
	(1)	(2)	(3)	(4)	(5)	(6)	(7)	(8)	(9)
Islamic Bank Dummy	7.252*	20.66**	20.66**	5.639	22.72***	22.72***	44.48***	22.35***	22.35***
P-value	(0.0523)	(0.0194)	(0.0194)	(0.140)	(0.00889)	(0.00889)	(0)	(0.00558)	(0.00558)
Net Loans / Total Assets (t-1)	-0.0279	0.0206	0.0206	0.121***	0.156***	0.156***	-0.571***	-0.389***	-0.389***
P-value	(0.574)	(0.697)	(0.697)	(2.49e-05)	(2.63e-05)	(2.63e-05)	(2.16e-08)	(0.000102)	(0.000102)
Costs / Net Income (t-1)	-0.0443**	0.0518***	0.0518***	-0.0260*	-0.0400**	-0.0400**	-0.0456	-0.0462	-0.0462
P-value	(0.0125)	(0.00354)	(0.00354)	(0.0733)	(0.0138)	(0.0138)	(0.302)	(0.314)	(0.314)
Total Assets (t-1)	5.97e-06	-1.62e-05	-1.62e-05	6.93e-06	-6.14e-06	-6.14e-06	-0.000174	0.000290***	0.000290***
P-value	(0.587)	(0.380)	(0.380)	(0.566)	(0.746)	(0.746)	(0.329)	(0.00958)	(0.00958)
Income Diversity (t-1)	0.517	0.547	0.547	0.320	0.248	0.248	21.97***	18.23***	18.23***
P-value	(0.207)	(0.176)	(0.176)	(0.369)	(0.475)	(0.475)	(0.00564)	(0.00438)	(0.00438)
Income Diversity * Islamic Bank Dummy	3.089	3.092	3.092	0.585	0.0889	0.0889	-53.76***	-93.43***	-93.43***

P-value	(0.800)	(0.787)	(0.787)	(0.954)	(0.992)	(0.992)	(0.000104)	(0)	(0)
Herfindahl Index (t-1)		259.4**	259.4**		95.72	95.72		824.1**	824.1**
P-value		(0.0129)	(0.0129)		(0.307)	(0.307)		(0.0246)	(0.0246)
Share of Islamic Banks (t-1)		-120.8	76.15*		-166.9*	56.06		362.5***	201.1***
P-value		(0.221)	(0.0591)		(0.0829)	(0.162)		(2.42e-05)	(0.00612)
Share of Islamic Banks * Conventional Bank Dummy (t-1)		197.0*			223.0**			-161.4*	
P-value		(0.0612)			(0.0320)			(0.0522)	
Share of Islamic Banks * Islamic Bank Dummy (t-1)			-197.0*			-223.0**			161.4*
P-value			(0.0612)			(0.0320)			(0.0522)
Constant	23.85***	-4.664	-4.664	14.45***	2.846	2.846	53.02***	-34.45	-34.45
P-value	(0)	(0.668)	(0.668)	(0)	(0.779)	(0.779)	(0)	(0.332)	(0.332)
Observations	327	327	327	261	261	261	66	66	66
Adjusted R-squared	0.014	0.040	0.040	0.029	0.049	0.049	0.498	0.567	0.567

ρ values in parentheses

* Significant at the 10 percent; ** significant at the 5 percent; *** significant at the 1 percent level for the 95 percent confidence interval

Table IV (b)—Regression Results for the *Sample Subgroup*: Robust Estimation, 2006–2010

Estimated Variable	All Banks (1)	All Banks (2)	All Banks (3)	Large Banks (4)	Large Banks (5)	Large Banks (6)	Small Banks (7)	Small Banks (8)	Small Banks (9)
Islamic Bank Dummy	-2.078	14.18	14.18	0.236	19.18*	19.18*			
P-value	(0.742)	(0.215)	(0.215)	(0.969)	(0.0802)	(0.0802)			
Net Loans / Total Assets (t-1)	0.0564	0.0770	0.0770	0.188**	0.228***	0.228***			
P-value	(0.586)	(0.467)	(0.467)	(0.0100)	(0.00222)	(0.00222)			
Costs / Net Income (t-1)	-0.0267**	-0.0366**	-0.0366**	-0.0123	-0.0227	-0.0227			
P-value	(0.0298)	(0.0294)	(0.0294)	(0.196)	(0.123)	(0.123)			
Total Assets (t-1)	-5.58e-05*	-6.00e-05*	-6.00e-05*	-3.88e-05	-4.37e-05	-4.37e-05			
P-value	(0.0977)	(0.0842)	(0.0842)	(0.241)	(0.201)	(0.201)			
Income Diversity (t-1)	-16.12	-15.08	-15.08	-6.028	-3.736	-3.736			
P-value	(0.150)	(0.169)	(0.169)	(0.541)	(0.684)	(0.684)			
Income Diversity * Islamic Bank Dummy	20.50	19.44	19.44	7.641	4.742	4.742			

P-value	(0.228)	(0.235)	(0.235)	(0.607)	(0.720)	(0.720)
Herfindahl Index (t-1)		178.0	178.0	364.1	364.1	364.1
P-value		(0.805)	(0.805)	(0.594)	(0.594)	(0.594)
Share of Islamic Banks (t-1)		-119.3	79.72	-117.9	102.1	102.1
P-value		(0.407)	(0.338)	(0.394)	(0.172)	(0.172)
Share of Islamic Banks * Conventional Bank Dummy (t-1)		199.0		220.0*		
P-value		(0.105)		(0.0705)		
Share of Islamic Banks * Islamic Bank Dummy (t-1)			-199.0		-220.0*	-220.0*
P-value			(0.105)		(0.0705)	(0.0705)
Constant	28.00***	5.418	5.418	15.89***	-26.98	-26.98
P-value	(0.000476)	(0.941)	(0.941)	(0.00314)	(0.693)	(0.693)
Observations	109	109	109	102	102	102
Adjusted R-squared	0.007	0.002	0.002	0.008	0.011	0.011

ρ values in parentheses

* Significant at the 10 percent; ** significant at the 5 percent; *** significant at the 1 percent level for the 95 percent confidence interval.

Table IV (c)—Regression Results for the Sample Subgroup: Robust Estimation, 2008–2009

Estimated Variable	All Banks	All Banks	All Banks	Large Banks	Large Banks	Large Banks	Small Banks	Small Banks	Small Banks
	(1)	(2)	(3)	(4)	(5)	(6)	(7)	(8)	(9)
Islamic Bank Dummy	-3.144	15.80	15.80	-1.365	23.39	23.39			
P-value	(0.730)	(0.559)	(0.559)	(0.883)	(0.358)	(0.358)			
Net Loans / Total Assets (t-1)	0.141	0.137	0.137	0.274***	0.282***	0.282***			
P-value	(0.322)	(0.351)	(0.351)	(0.00173)	(0.00137)	(0.00137)			
Costs / Net Income (t-1)	-0.168*	-0.167*	-0.167*	-0.132	-0.138	-0.138			
P-value	(0.0622)	(0.0688)	(0.0688)	(0.171)	(0.163)	(0.163)			
Total Assets (t-1)	-6.54e-05	-6.54e-05	-6.54e-05	-4.94e-05	-4.88e-05	-4.88e-05			
P-value	(0.147)	(0.154)	(0.154)	(0.269)	(0.281)	(0.281)			
Income Diversity (t-1)	-6.940	-7.558	-7.558	4.152	4.740	4.740			
P-value	(0.685)	(0.661)	(0.661)	(0.786)	(0.741)	(0.741)			
Income Diversity * Islamic Bank Dummy	12.84	4.799	4.799	2.104	-11.98	-11.98			
P-value	(0.609)	(0.864)	(0.864)	(0.927)	(0.593)	(0.593)			

Herfindahl Index (t-1)		0	0		0	0
P-value						
Share of Islamic Banks (t-1)		-146.1	28.28		-220.4	-6.672
P-value		(0.477)	(0.815)		(0.240)	(0.953)
Share of Islamic Banks * Conventional Bank Dummy (t-1)		174.4			213.7	
P-value		(0.466)			(0.331)	
Share of Islamic Banks * Islamic Bank Dummy (t-1)			-174.4			-213.7
P-value			(0.466)			(0.331)
Constant	29.39**	27.11*	27.11*	16.41*	16.67	16.67
P-value	(0.0235)	(0.0849)	(0.0849)	(0.0814)	(0.246)	(0.246)
Observations	61	61	61	57	57	57
Adjusted R-squared	-0.025	-0.057	-0.057	-0.012	-0.042	-0.042

p values in parentheses

* Significant at the 10 percent; ** significant at the 5 percent; *** significant at the 1 percent level for the 95 percent confidence interval

List of Banks in Samples

Bahrain

Retail Islamic Banks:
Al Amin Bank*
Al Baraka Islamic Bank B.S.C.
Al-Salam Bank-Bahrain B.S.C.
Bahrain Islamic Bank
Ithmaar Bank B.S.C.
Kaleeji Commercial Bank
Kuwait Finance House (Bahrain)
Shamil Bank of Bahrain B.S.C.*

Wholesale Islamic Banks:
ABC Islamic Bank (E.C.)
Arab Islamic Bank (E.C.)*
Arcapita Bank
Capivest
Citi Islamic Investment Bank
Elaf Bank
First Energy Bank
Global Banking Corporation BSC
Gulf Finance House BSC
International Investment Bank B.S.C.

Investors Bank
Seera Investment Bank
Unicorn Investment
Venture Capital Bank

Retail Conventional Banks:
Alhi United Bank (Bahrain) B.S.C.*
Ahli United Bank BSC
Bahraini Saudi Bank
BBK
BMI Bank
Future Bank
National Bank of Bahrain

Wholesale Conventional Banks:
Alubaf Arab International Bank
Arab Banking Corporation
Awal Bank
Commercial Bank of Bahrain B.S.C.
Gulf International Bank BSC
Gulf One Investment Bank BSC
Investcorp Bank BSC
TAIB Bank B.S.C.
United Gulf Bank (BSC) EC
* Bank no longer in existence at the end of 2010. It merged with another bank, was acquired by another bank or discontinued operations.

Malaysia

Islamic Banks: Locally Owned
Affin Islamic Bank Berhad

Alliance Islamic Bank Berhad
AmIslamic Bank Berhad
Bank Islam Malaysia Berhad (BIMB)
Bank Muamalat Malaysia Berhad
CIMB Islamic Bank Berhad
EONCAP Islamic Bank Berhad
Hong Leong Islamic Berhad
Maybank Islamic Berhad
OCBC Al-Amin Bank Berhad
Public Islamic Bank Berhad
RHB Islamic Bank Berhad

Islamic Banks: Foreign Owned
Al Rajihi Banking & Investment Corporation (Malaysia) Berhad
Asian Finance Bank Berhad
HSBC Amanah Malaysia Berhad
Kuwait Finance House (Malaysia) Berhad
Standard Chartered Saadiq Berhad

Conventional Banks: Locally Owned
Affin Bank Berhad
Affin Discount Berhad*
Alliance Bank Malaysia Berhad
AmBank (M) Berhad
Ban Hin Lee Bank Berhad – BHL Bank*
Bank Bumiputra Malaysia Berhad*
Bank Utama (Malaysia) Berhad*
BSN Commercial Bank (Malaysia) Berhad*
Chung Khiaw Bank (Malaysia) Berhad*
CIMB Bank Berhad
EON Bank Berhad
Hock Hua Bank Berhad*

Hong Leong Bank Berhad
Malayan Banking Berhad
OCBC Bank (Malaysia) Berhad
Oriental Bank Berhad*
Pacific Bank Berhad*
PhilleoAllied Bank (Malaysia) Berhad*
Public Bank Berhad
RHB Bank Berhad
Sabah Bank Berhad*
Sime Bank Berhad*
Southern Bank Berhad*
Wah Tat Bank Berhad*

Conventional Banks: Foreign Owned
Bangkok Bank Berhad
Bank of America Malaysia Berhad
Bank of China (Malaysia) Berhad
Bank of Nova Scotia Berhad
Bank of Tokyo-Mitsubishi UFJ (Malaysia) Berhad
Citibank Berhad
Deutsche Bank (Malaysia) Berhad
HSBC Bank Malaysia Berhad
Industrial and Commercial Bank of China (Malaysia)
International Bank Malaysia Berhad*
J.P. Morgan Chase Bank Berhad
Overseas Union Bank (Malaysia) Berhad*
Royal Bank of Scotland Berhad
Standard Chartered Bank Malaysia Berhad
United Overseas Bank (Malaysia) Bhd.
* Bank no longer in existence at the end of 2010. It merged with another bank, was acquired by another bank or discontinued operations.

References

Acemoglu, D., S. Johnson, and J. Robinson. 2004. Institutions as the Fundamental Cause of Long-Run Growth. In P. Aghion, and S. Durlauf, *Handbook of Economic Growth*. New York: North-Holland.

Aggarwal, R., and T. Youef. 2000. Islamic Banks and Investment Financing. *Journal of Money, Credit and Banking*, 32, 93–120.

Ahmed, H. 2002. Incentive-compatible Profit-Sharing Contracts: a Theoretical Treatment. In M. Iqbal, and D. Llewellyn, *Islamic Banking and Finance—New Perspectives on Profit-Sharing and Risk*, 40–56. Cheltenham: Edward Elgar.

Ahmed, H., and T. Khan. 2001. Risk Management—An Analysis of Issues in Islamic Financial Industry. *Islamic Research and Training*, *Occassional Paper* 5:22–191.

Akerlof, G. A., and R. J. Shiller. 2009. *Animal Spirits*. Princeton, NJ: Princeton University Press.

Al-Deehani, T., R. A. A. Karim, and V. Murinde. 1999. The Capital Structure of Islamic Banks under the Contractual Obligations of Profit Sharing. *International Journal of Theoretical and Applied Finance* 2 no. 3:243–283.

Al-Omar, Fouad A. 2003. *Introduction to the History of Islamic Economy and its Develpoment*. Jeddah: Islamic Research and Training Institute.

Al-Qaradawi, Y. 2006. *The Lawful and The Prohibited in Islam*. New Delhi: Kitab Bhavan (Indian Edition).

Algaoud, L. M., and M. Lewis. 2001. *Islamic Banking.* Northampton, MA: Edward Elgar.

Allen, F., and D. Gale. 2000. Bubbles and Crises. *Economic Journal* 110:236–255.

———. 1998. Optimal Financial Crises. *Journal of Finance* 53:1245–1284.

Allen, F., and A. M. Santomero. 1996. *The Theory of Financial Intermediation.* Philadelphia: The Wharton Financial Institutions Center, University of Pennsylvania.

Al-Tabari, A. 1987. *Jami' al-bayan 'an ta 'wil ay al-Quran.* New York: Oxford University Press.

Altman, E. I., and A. M. Saunders. 1998. Credit Risk Measurement: Development over the Last 20 Years. *Journal of Banking and Finance* 21:505–529.

Altunbas, Y., L. Evans, and P. Molyneux. 2001. Bank Ownership and Efficiency. *Journal of Money, Credit and Banking*: 926–954.

Ang, J. B. 2008. A Survey of Recent Developments in the Literature of Finance and Growth. *Journal of Economic Survey Surveys* 22 no. 3:536–76.

Aoki, M. 2005. Monitoring Characteristics of the Main Banking System: An Analytical and Development View. In M. A. Patrick, *Japanese Main System,* 16–28. New York: The Oxford Press.

Aoki, M. 1994. Monitoring Characteristics of the Main Banking System: An Analytical and Development View. In M. Aoki, and H. Patrick, *Japanese Main Bank System.* New York: Oxford University Press.

Arberry, A. 1964. *The Koran Interpreted.* London: Oxford University Press.

Asian Strategy and Leadership Institute. 2005. *Malaysia's Economic Growth Moderating but Improvement in Second Half Expected.* Asian Strategy and Leadership Institute.

Auda, Jasser. 2008. *Maqasid Al-Shariah as Philosophy of Islamic Law.* London: The International Institute of Islamic Thought.

Ayub, M. 2007. *Understanding Islamic Finance.* West Sussex: John Wiley & Sons, Ltd.

Bader, M. K., T. Hassan, and S. Mohamad. 2008. Efficiency of Conventional Versus Islamic Banks: International Evidence Using the Stochastic Frontier Approach (SFA). Journal of Islamic Economics, Banking and Finance 4 (2), 107-130.

Bagehot, W. 1873. *Lombard Street: A Description of the Money Market.* London: H. S. King.

Bahrain, C. B. 2010 (February 5). *Central Bank of Bahrain,* www. cbb.gov.bh/cmsrule/index.jsp?action=article&ID=18: http://www.cbb.gov.bh (retrieved 2010).

Bank Negara Malaysia. 2010 (July 15). *Bank Negara Malaysia.* Bank Negara Malaysia, http://www.bnm. gov.my/microsites/financial/0204_ib_takaful.htm (retrieved July 15, 2010).

Benaissa, N. E., X. Jopart, M. Maddux, O. Tanrikulu, and F. Whelan. 2007. *Impact of Regulation on the Future of Islamic Finance.* Harvard University, Harvard Law School. Cambridge: Islamic Finance Project.

Berglof, E., and S. Claessens. 2004. *Enforcement and Corporate Governance.* The World Bank. Washington: World Bank.

BIS. 1996. *Supervisory Lessons to be Drawn from the Asian Crisis.* Bank for International Settlements, Working Paper No. 2.

Bisignano, J. 1998. Precarious Credit Equilibria: Reflections on the Asian Financial Crisis. *Asia: An Analysis of Financial Crisis.* Federal Reserve Bank of Chicago.

Blinder, A. S. 1998. *Asking about Prices: A New Approach to Understanding Price Stickiness.* New York: Russell Sage Foundation.

Boatright, J. 2002. Contractors as Shareholders: Reconciling Stakeholders Theory with Nexus-of-Contractor Firms. *Journal of Banking and Finance* 26:1837–52.

Bordo, M. 1986. Financial Crises, Banking Crises, Stock Market Crashes and the Money Supply: Some International Evidence, 1870–1933. In F. Capie, & G.E. Woods (eds.), *Financial Crises and the World Banking System,* 190–248. New York: St. Martin Press.

———. 1985. Some Historical Evidence 1870–1933 on the Impact and Transmission of Financial Crises. NBER Working Paper No. 1606.

Bordo, M., D. Eichengreen, D. Klingebiel, and M Martinez-Peria. 2001 (April). Is the Crisis Problem Growing More Severe? *Economic Policy* 53–82.

Boyd, J. H., and D. E. Runkle. 1993. Size and Performance of Banking Firms. *Journal of Monetary Economics* 31:47–67.

Branson, W. H. 1989. *Macroeconomic: Theory and Policy.* New York: Harper & Row.

Brown, K., and M. Skully. 2004. Islamic Banks: A Cross-Country Study of Cost Efficiency Performance. *Accounting, Commerce and Finance: The Islamic Perspective Journal* 8 no. 1 and 2:43–79.

Brown, K., K. M. Hassan, and M. Skully. 2007. Operational Efficiency and Performance of Islamic Banks. In K. M. Hassan, and M. K. Lewis, *Handbook of Islamic Banking.* Northampton, MA: Edward Elgar.

Bryant, J. 1980. A Model of Reserves, Bank Runs, and Deposit Insurance. *Journal of Banking and Finance* 4:335–344.

Calomiris, C. W. 2000. Universal Banking and the Financing of Industrial Development. In G. Caprio, and D. Vittas, *Reforming Finance: Some Lessons from History*. Cambridge and New York: Cambridge University Press.

Caplin, A. S., and D. F. Spulber. 1987. Menu Costs and the Neutrality of Money. *Quarterly Journal of Economics* 102:703–725.

CBB. 2010. *Licensing & Policy Directorate*. Al Manama: Central Bank of Bahrain.

———. 2010 (February 5). *Overview*. Central Bank of Bahrain, www.cbb.gov.bh/cmsrule/index.jsp?action=&ID=16 (retrieved February 5, 2010).

Chang, R., and A. Velasco 1998. The Asian Liquidity Crisis. NBER Working Paper No. 6796.

Chapra, M. U. 2000. Why Has Islam Prohibited Interest? Rationale behind the Prohibition of Interest in Islam. *Review of Islamic Economics* 9:5–20.

———. 1992. *Islam and Economic Challange*. Leicester, UK: The Islamic Foundation.

———. 1985. *Towards a Just Monetary System*. Leicester, UK: The Islamic Foundation.

Chapra, M., and H. Ahmed. 2002. Corporate Governance in Islamic Financial Institutions. *Islamic Research and Training Institute, Jeddah, Saudi Arabia*, Occassional Paper No. 6.

Chapra, U. M. 2002. Alternative Visions of International Monetary Reform. In M. I. (eds)., *Islamic Banking and Finance: New Perspectives on Profit Sharing and Risk*, 219–38. Cheltenham, UK, and Northampton, MA: Edward Elgar.

Chari, V., and R. Jagannathan. 1988. Banking Panics, Information, and Rational Expectation Equilibrium. *Journal of Finance* 43:749–61.

Cibils, V., V. Garcia, and R. Maino. 2004 (March). Remedy for Banking Crisis: What Chicago and Islam Have in Common. *Islamic Economic Studies, 11 (2), 1-22.*

Cihak, M., and H. Hesse. 2008. *Islamic Banks and Financial Stability: An Empirical Analysis.* Washington: International Monetary Fund.

Clark, B. 1998. *Principles of Political Economy: A Comparative Approach.* Westport, CT: Praeger.

Coase, R. H. (1960). The Problem of the Social Cost. *The Journal of Law and Economics , 3,* 1-44.

Cole, H. L., and N. Kocherlakota. 1998. Zero Nominal Interest Rates: Why They're Good and How to Get Them. *Federal Reserve Bank of Minneapolis Quarterly Review* 22, no. 2:2–10.

Cubb-Othone, A., and M. Murgia. 2000. Mergers and Shareholder Wealth in European Banking. *Journal of Banking and Finance* 24 no. 6:831–859.

Da Rin, M., and T. Hellmann. 2002. Banks as Catalysts for Industrialization. *Journal of Financial Intermediation* 11 no. 4:366–97.

Damjanovic, T., and G. Pastor. 2001. *The Russian Financial Crisis and Its Consequences for Central Asia.* Washington: IMF.

Daniel, K., D. Hirsheleifer, and A. Subrahmanyam. 2001. Overconfidence, Arbitrage, and Equilibrium Asset Pricing. *Journal of Finance* 56:921–965.

Davies, G. 2002. *A History of Money: From Ancient Times to the Present Day.* 2nd ed. Cardiff: University of Wales Press.

Davies, R. 2002 (June). Malaysia Capsule. *Orient Pacific Century.*

Davis, K., and M. Lewis. 1982. *Economies of Scale in Financial Institutions.* Commissioned Studies and Selected Papers. Canberra: Australian Government Publishing Service.

DeLong, J., A. Shleifer, L Summers, and R. J. Waldman. 1990. Noise Trader Risk in Financial Markets. *Journal of Political Economy* 98:703–738.

Dhalia, E. H., W. Grais, and Z. Iqbal. 2003. Regulating Islamic Financial Institutions: The Nature of the Regulated. *Worldbank Paper.*

Diamond, D., and P. Dybvig. 1983. Bank Runs, Deposit Insurance, and Liquidity. *Journal of Political Economy* 91:401–419.

Doi, A. R. 1989. *Shari'a: The Islamic Law.* Kuala Lumpur: AS Noordeen.

Donaldson, T., and L. Peterson. 1995. The Stakeholder Theory of the Corporation: Concepts, Evidence and Implications. *Academy of Management Review* 20, no. 1:65–91.

Eagleton, C., and J. Williams. 1997. *Money: A History.* New York: Firefly Books.

Edwards, W. 2003 (December). Lack of Liquid Assets Ups Demand for Instruments. *Islamic Banker:* 94, 95.

Economist, (The). 2000. Financial Regulation: Basle Bust. *The Economist.* April 15, 1993–4.

Eichengreen, B. 1995. *Golden Fetters.* New York: Oxford University Press.

El-Gamal, M. A. 2000. A Basic Guide to Contemporary Islamic Banking and Finance, Indiana: Islamic Banking and Finance America.

El-Hawary, D.; Grais, W.; Iqbal, Z. 2004. Regulating Islamic Financial Institutions: The Nature of the Regulated. *World Bank Policy Research Paper # 3227.*

El Qorchi, M. 2005. Islamic Finance Gears Up. *Finance and Development.* Washington: IMF.

Elton, E., and M. Gruber. 1998. *Modern Portfolio Theory and Investment Analysis.* 6th ed. New York: John Wiley & Sons.

Engle, R., and W. Granger. 1987. Co-integration and Error Correction: Representation, Estimation and Testing. *Econometrica* 55:251–76.

Englund, P., and V. Vihriala. 2006. Financial Crisis in Developed Economies: The Cases of Finland and Sweden. In L. Jonung, J. Kiander, P. Vartia, L. Jonung, J. Kiander, & P. Vartia (Eds.), Macroeconomic Performance and Economic Policies in Finland and Sweden in the 1990s: A Comparative Approach. (pp. 71-130). Northampton, Massachusset.

Errico, L., and J. Sundarajan. 1997. Islamic Financial Institutions and Products in the Global Financial Systems: Key Issues in Risk Management and Challenges Ahead. IMF Working Paper.

Ferguson, N. 2008. *The Ascent of Money*. New York: The Penguin Press.

Fischer, D. 1996. *The Great Wave, Price Revolution and the Rhythm of History*. New York, NY: Oxford University Press.

Fisher, I. 1933. The Debt-Deflation Theory of the Great Depression. *Econometrica*: 337–357.

Fisher, I. 1911. *The Purchasing Power of Money; Its Determinants and Relation to Credit, Interest, and Crises*. 2nd ed. New York: Macmillan.

Fischer, S. 1977 (February). Long-Term Contracts, Rational Expectations, and the Optimal Money Supply Rule. *Journal of Political Economy, 85* (1), 191-205.

Folin, C. 1998. Banking Systems and Economic Growth: Lessons from Britain and Germany in the Pre-World War Era. *Review, Federal Reserve Bank of St. Louis* 80 no. 3:27–54.

Friedman, M. 1969. *The Optimum Quantity of Money and Other Essays*. Transaction Pub.

Friedman, M., and A. Schwartz. 1963. *A Monetary History of the United States, 1867–1960.* Princeton: Princeton University Press.

Galbraith, J. K. 1990. *A Short History of Financial Euphoria.* New York: A Penguin Book.

Gallarotti, G. 1995. *The Anatomy of an International Monetary Regime: The Classical Gold Standard, 1880–1914.* Oxford: Oxford University Press.

Glick, R. 1998. Thoughts on the Origins of the Asian Crisis: Impulses and Propagation. *Asia: An Analysis of Financial Crisis.* Federal Reserve Bank of Chicago.

Goitein, S. 1967. *A Mediterranean Society.* Berkeley and Los Angeles: University of California Press.

———. 1966. *Studies in Islamic History and Institutions.* Leiden: Brill.

Gorton, G. 1988. Banking Panics and Business Cycles. *Oxford Economics Papers* 40:751–81.

Grais, W., and M. Pellegrini. 2006. *Corporate Governance and Shareholders' Financial Interests in Institutions Offering Islamic Financial Services.* Working paper, World Bank, Research Department, Washington.

Greenwald, B., and J. Stiglitz. 1993. New and Old Keynesians. *Journal of Economic Perspectives* 4:23–44.

———. 1988. *Imperfected Information, Finance Constraints and Business Fluctuations.* Cambridge: NBER.

Greenwalt, M., and J. F. Sinkey. 1988. Bank Loan-loss Provisions and the Income Smoothing Hypothesis: An Empirical Analysis, 1976–84. *Journal of Financial Services Research* 1:301–318.

Greenwood, J., and B. D. Smith. 1997 (January). Financial Markets in Development, and the Development of Financial Markets. *Journal of Economic Dynamics and Control,* 145–81.

Greuning, H. V., & Iqbal, Z. (2008). Risk Analysis for Islamic Banks. Washtingon, DC: The World Bank.

Hallaq, W. B. 1997. *Islamic Legal Theories*. New York: Cambridge University Press.

Hallwood, C., and R. MacDonald. 2000. *International Money and Finance*. 3rd ed. Malden, MA: Blackwell Publishing.

Hallwood, C., R. MacDonald, and I. Marsh. 1996. Credibility and Fundamentals: Were the Classical and Inter-war Gold Standards Well-Behaved Target Zones? In B. E. T. Bayoumi, *Modern Perspectives on the Gold Standard*. Cambridge: Cambridge University Press.

Hamilton, L. C. 2002. *Statistics with Stata*. Belmon, CA: Duxbury.

Hassan, A. Y. 2001. *Factors behind the Decline of Islamic Science after the Sixteenth Century*. UNESCO, Science and Technology in Islam. Paris: UNESCO.

Hassan, K. M., and M. Choudhury. 2004. *Islamic Banking Regulations in Light of Basel II*. Harvard University, Harvard Law School. Cambridge: Islamic Legal Studies Program.

Hassan, K. M., and T. Zaher. 2001. A Comparative Literature Survey of Islamic Finance and Banking. *Financial Markets, Institutions and Instruments* 10 no. 4:155–99.

Hassan, K. M., and Mervyn Lewis. 2007. *Handbook of Islamic Banking*. Northhampton, MA: Edward Elgar Publishing Inc.

Hassan, M. 2005. The X Efficiency of Islamic Banks. 12th ERF Conference Cairo, 19–21 August. Cairo, Egypt.

Hassan, M., and K. Hussien. 2003. Static and Dynamic Efficiency in the Sudanese Banking System. *Review of Islamic Studies* 14:5–48.

Hayek, F. A. 1976. *Denationalizaion of Money: An Analysis of the Theory of Practice of Concurrent Currencies.* London: Institute of Economic Affairs.

———. 1967 (1935). *Prices and Production.* 2nd ed. New York: Augustus M. Kelly.

Hegazy, W. 2005. Fatwas and the Fate of Islamic Finance: A Critique of the Practice of Fatwa in Contemporary Islamic Financial Markets. In *Islamic Finance—Current Legal and Regulatory Issues,* 133–49. Cambridge, MA: ISLP Harvard University.

Heiskanen, R. 1993. The Banking Crisis in the Nordic Countries. *Kansallis Economic Review* 2:13–19.

Hermes, N., and R. Lensink. 2000. Financial System Development in Transition Economies. *Journal of Banking and Finance* 24:507–24.

Hillegeist, S. A., E. K. Keeting, D. P. Cram, and K. G. Lundstedt. 2002. *Assessing the Probability of Bankruptcy.* Northconventional University.

Hirshleifer, D. 2001. Investor Pyschology and Asset Pricing. *Journal of Finance* 64:1533–1597.

Hirshleifer, D., and S. H. Teoh. 2003. Herd Behavior and Cascading in Capital Markets: A Review and Synthesis. *European Financial Management* 9:25–66.

Hussain, J. 1999. *Islamic Law and Society.* Sydney, Australia: The Federation Press.

IMF. 2009. *Malaysia—Staff Report for the 2009 Article IV Consultation.* IMF. Washington: IMF.

IMF. 2009. *Regional Economic Outlook: Middle East and Central Asia.* International Monetary Fund. Washington: IMF.

IMF. 2006. *Financial System Stability Assessment.* International Monetary Fund, Monetary and Financial Sytems and Middle East and Central Asia. Washington: IMF.

IMF. 2004. *Compilation Guide on Financial Soundness Indicators.* Washington DC: International Monetary Fund.

IMF. 2003. *Lessons from the Crisis in Argentina.* Washington DC: IMF.

IMF. 1999. *World Economic Outlook.*

Iqbal, M., and Ausaf Ahmad. 2005. *Islamic Finance and Economic Development.* New York, NY: Palgrave MacMillan.

Iqbal, M., and D. T. Llewellyn. 2002. *Islamic Banking and Finance: New Perspective on Profit-Sharing and Risk.* Cheltenham, UK: Edward Elgar Publishing.

Iqbal, Z., and A. Mirakhor. 2007. *Introduction to Islamic Finance.* Singapore: John Wiley & Sons (Asia) Pte Ltd.

Iqbql, Z., and H. Van Greuning. 2008. *Risk Analysis for Islamic Banks.* Washington DC: The World Bank.

Islam, M. 1999. Al-Mal: The Concept of Property in Islamic Legal Thought. *Arab Law Quarterly,* 361–68.

Jackson-Moore, E. 2009. *The International Handbook of Islamic Banking and Finance.* Kent: Global Professional Publishing.

Jang, J. H. 2005. *Taming Political Islamist by Islamic Capital: The Passions and Interests in Turkish Islamic Society.* Austin: University of Texas at Austin.

Jensen, M., and W. Meckling. 1976. Theory of the Firm: Managerial Behavior, Agency Cost and Ownership Structure. *Journal of Financial Economics* 3:305–360.

Jobst, A. A. 2007. *The Economics of Islamic Finance and Securitization.* Money and Capital Markets. Washington: IMF.

John, K., T. John, and A. Saunders. 1994. Universal Banking and Firm Risk-Sharing. *Journal of Banking and Finance* 18:307–323.

Johnson, S., K Kochhar, T. Milton, and N. Tamirisa. 2006. *Malaysian Capital Controls: Macroeconomic and Institutions.* IMF, Reseach Department.

Kashap, A. K. 1995. Sticky Prices: New Evidence from Retail Catalogs. *Quarterly Journal of Economics* 110:245–274.

Kazarian, E. 1993. *Islamic versus Traditional Banking: Financial Innovation in Egypt.* Boulder, CO: Westview Press.

Keeley, M. C. 1990. Deposit Insurance, Risk, and Market Power in Banking. *American Economic Review* 80:1183–1200.

Keen, S. 1997. From Prohibition to Depression: the Conventional Attitude to Usury. *Accounting, Commerce and Finance: The Islamic Perspective Journal* 1 no. 1: 26–55.

Kennedy, H. 2007. *The Great Arab Conquests.* Philadelphia: Perseus Books Group.

Keynes, J. M. 1997 (1936). *The General Theory of Employment, Interest and Money.* New York: Prometheus Books.

Khan, M. 1987. Islamic Interest-Free Banking: A Theoretical Analysis. In K. A. Mirakhor, and K. A. Mirakhor (Ed.), *Theoretical Studies in Islamic Banking and Finance.* Houston, Texas: IRIS Books.

Khan, M. S., and A. S. Senhadji. 2000. Financial Development and Economic Growth: An Overview. IMF Working Paper WP/00/209.

Kindleberger, C. 1993. *A Financial History of Conventional Europe.* New York: Oxford University Press.

———. 1978. *Manias, Panics, and Crashes: A History of Financial Crises.* New York: Basic Books.

King, R., & Levine, R. (1993a). Finance and Entrepreneurship and Growth: Theory and Evidence. *Journal of Monetary Economics* , 32, 513-42.

———. 1993b. *Finance and Growth: Schumpter Might be Right*. *Quarterly Journal of Economics* 108:707–37.

Krichene, N., and A. Mirakhor. 2009 (April 01). *NEWHORIZON*. Institute of Islamic Banking and Finance, http://www.newhorizon-islamicbanking.com/index.cfm?section=academicarticles&id=10775 &action=view&return=home (retrieved May 03, 2009).

Krugman, P. 2009. *The Return of Depression Economics and the Crisis of 2008*. New York: W. W. Norton & Company Inc.

———. 1998. What Happened to Asia, http://web.mit.edu/krugman/www/disinter.html.

Kuran, T. 2004. *Islam and Mammon*. Princeton: Princeton University Press.

———. 1995. Islamic Economics and the Islamic Subeconomy. *Journal of Economic Perspectives* 9 no. 4:155–173.

Laeven, L., & R. Levine. 2005. Is There a Diversfication Discount in Financial Conglomerates? *Journal of Financial Economics, 85* (2), 331-367.

Levine, R. 2004. Finance and Growth: Theory and Evidence. *NBER Working Paper Series*, Working Paper No. 10766.

———. 1997. Financial Development and Economic Growth. *Journal of Economic Literature* 53 no. 2:31–67.

Levine, R., N. Loayza, and T. Beck. 1999. *Financial Intermediation and Growth: Causality and Causes*. Washington, DC: The World Bank.

Lewis, B. 1982. *The Muslim Discovery of Europe*. New York: W. W. Norton.

Lewis, D. L. 2008. *God's Crucibile: Islam and the Making of Europe, 570–1215*. New York: W. W. Norton.

Lewis, M. 2007. Comparing Islamic and Christian Attitudes to Usury. In K. Hassan, and M. Lewis, *The Handbook of Islamic Banking*, 64–81. Northampton, MA: Edward Elgar Publishing, Inc.

Lewis, M., and K. Davis. 1987. *Domestic and International Banking.* Oxford: Philip Allan.

Lindert, P. H. 1969. Key Currencies and Gold, 1900–1913. *Princeton Studies in International Finance* 24.

Lucas, R. E. 1972. Expectations and the Neutraility of Money. *Journal of Economic Theory* 4:103–124.

Maechler, A., S. Mitra, and D. Worrell. 2005. Exploring Financial Risks and Vulnerabilities in New and Potential EU Member States. *Second Annual DG ECFIN Research Conference: Financial Stability and the Convergence Process in Europe* (October 6–7).

Malaysia, B. N. 2009. *Financial Stability Report—2008.* Bank Negara Malaysia. Kuala Lumpur, Bank Negara Malaysia.

Malaysa, B. N. 1998 (September 1). *Measures to Regain Monetary Independence.* Retrieved from www.bnm.gov. my.

Mankiw, G. 2007. *Macroeconomics.* 6th ed. New York, NY: Worth Publishers.

Mankiw, G. N. 1985. Small Menu Costs and Large Business Cycles: A Macroeconomic Model of Monopoly. *Quarterly Journal of Economics* 100:529–37.

Marshall, A. 1965 (1923). *Money, Credit and Commerce.* Rev. ed. New York: Augustus M. Kelly.

McKinnon, R. I. 1973. *Money and Capital in Economic Development.* Washington DC: Brookings Institute.

Meltzer, A. 1998. Asian Problems and the IMF. *The Cato Journal* 17 no. 3.

Mercieca, S., K. Schaaeck, and S. Wolfe. 2007. Small European Banks: Benefits from Diversification? *Journal of Banking and Finance* 31:1975–1998.

Merton, R. 1974. The Pricing of Corporate Debt: The Risk Structure of Interest Rates. *Journal of Finance* 29 no. 2:449–470.

Merton, R. C., and Z. Bodie. 1995. A Conceptual Framework for Analyzing the Financial Environment. In *The Global Financial System: A Finanicial Perspective.* Boston, MA: Harvard Business School Press.

Merton, R., and Z. Bodie. 1993. Deposit Insurance Reform: a Functional Approach. *Carnegie-Rochester Conference Series on Public Policy* 38 no. 13.

Mill, J. 1929 (1848). *Principles of Political Economy, with some of Their Applications to Social Philosophy.* 7th reprinted ed. London: Longmans, Green.

Mills, P. S., and J. Presley. 1999. *Islamic Finance: Theory and Practice.* London: Macmillan.

Minksy, H. 2008 (1986). *Stabilizing an Unstable Economy.* New York: McGraw Hill.

Mirakhor, A. 1988. *Equilibrium in a Non-Interest Open Economy.* Washington: International Monetary Fund.

Mirakhor, A., and I. Zaidi. 2007. Profit-and-Loss Sharing Contracts in Islamic Finance. In M. Hassan, and M. Lewis, *Handbook of Islamic Banking,* 49–63. Northamption, MA: Edward Elgar Publishing Limited.

Mises, L. V. 1953 (1912). *The Theory of Money and Credit.* New Haven, CT: Yale University Press.

Mishkin, F. S. 1995. *The Economics of Money, Banking, and Financial Markets.* New York: Harper Collins Colllege Publications.

Mishkin, F., and S. G. Eakins. 2008. *Financial Markets and Institutions.* Boston: Addison-Wesley.

Mitchel, W. 1941. *Business Cycles and Their Causes.* Berkeley, CA: University of California.

Moktar, H., and S. Al Habshi. 2006. Efficiency of Islamic Banks in Malaysia: A Stochastic Frontier Approach. *Journal of Economic Cooperation Among Islamic Countries* 27 no. 2:37–70.

Morgan-Webb, C. 1934. *The Rise and Fall of the Gold Standard.* New York: Macmillan.

Movassaghi, H., and R. M. Zaman. 2002. Interest-Free Islamic Banking: Ideal and Reality. *The International Journal of Finance* 14 no. 4:2428–2443.

Pango, M. 1993. Financial Markets and Growth: An Overview. *European Economic Review* 28 no. 2:613–22.

Parkman, F. 1909. *The Jesuits of North America.* Vol. 1. Boston: Little, Brown, & Co.

Phelps, E., and J. Taylor. 1977 (February). Stabilizing Powers of Monetary Policy under Rational Expectations. *Journal of Political Economy, 85* (1), 163-90.

Postlewaite, A., and X. Vives. 1987. Bank Runs as an Equilibrium Phenomenon. *Journal of Political economy* 95:485–91.

Radelet, S., and J. Sachs. 1998. *The East Asian Financial Crisis: Diagnosis, Remedies, Prospects.* New York: Brookings Institution.

Ramadan, T. 2004. *Conventional Muslims and the Future of Islam.* New York: Oxford University Press.

Ready, R. C., and D. Hu. 1995. Statistical Approaches to the Fat Tail Problem for Dichotomous Choice Contingent Valuation. *Land Economics* (77), 491-99.

Rochet, J. C. 2008. *Why Are There so Many Banking Crises?* Princeton, NJ: University of Princeton.

Romer, D. 1993. The New Keynesian Synthesis. *Journal of Economic Perspectives* 7:5–22.

Rosly, S. A., and M. A. Abu Bakar. 2003. Performance of Islamic and Mainstream Banks in Malaysia. *International Journal of Social Economics* 30 no. 12.

Rowley, C., and N. Smith. 2009. *Economic Contractions in the United States: A Failure of Government.* Fairfax, VA: The Lock Institute in association with the Institute of Economic Affairs.

Runciman, S. 1965. *The Fall of Constantinpole 1453.* Cambridge, UK: Cambridge University Press.

Saleh, N. A. 1986. *Unlawful Gain and Legitimate Profit in Islamic Law.* Cambridge: Cambridge University Press.

Samad, A. 1999. Comparative Efficiency of the Islamic Bank vis-à-vis Conventional Banks in Malaysia. *Journal of Economics and Management:* 1–25.

Saunders, A., and M. M. Cornett. 2003. *Financial Institutions Management.* 4th ed. McGraw-Hill Irwin.

Schacht, J. 1964. *An Introduction to Islamic Law.* Oxford: Oxford University Press.

Schatzmiller, M. 1994. *Labour in the Medieval Islamic World.* Leiden: Brill.

Scheepens, M. 1996. *Prospects of an International Islamic Financial Market and Islamic Approved Derivatives.* Amsterdam: VU University.

Schmidt-Hebbel, K., L. Serven, and A. Solimano. 1996. Saving and Investment: Paradigms, Puzzles, and Policies. *The World Bank Research Observer,* 1/11 (February): 87–117.

Schultz, G., W. Simon, and W. Wriston. 1998. Who Needs the IMF. *Wall Street Journal,* February 3.

Shaw, E. S. 1973. *Financial Deepening in Economic Development.* New York: Oxford University Press.

Shiller, R. J. 2000. Conversation, Information and Herd Behavior. *American Economic Review* 85:181–185.

Shiller, R. J. 1981. Do Stock Prices Move too Much to be Justified by Subsequent Changes in Dividends? *American Economic Review* (June): 421–36.

Shleifer, A., and R. Vishny. 1997. The Limits to Arbitrage. *Journal of Finance* 52:35–55.

Siddiqi, M. 1988. *Banking without Interest.* Leicester, UK: The Islamic Foundation.

———. 1981. *Muslim Economic Thinking: A Survey of Contemporary Literature.* Leicester, UK: The Islamic Foundation.

———. 2007. Shari'a, Economics, and the Progress of Islamic Finance: The Role of Shari'a Experts. In E. S. Nazim Ali, *Integrating Islamic Finance into the Mainstream: Regulation, Standardization and Transparency.* 99–107. Cambridge, MA: Islamic Finance Project, ILSP, Harvard University.

Simon, H. 1948. *Economic Policy for a Free Society.* Chicago: University of Chicago.

Sinkey, J., and R. Nash. 1993. Assessing the Riskiness and Profitability of Credit-Card Banks. *Journal of Financial Services Research* 7:127–150.

Sjaastad, L. 1997. Deposit Insurance: Do We Really Need It? In *Preventing Banking Sector Distress and Crises in Latin America.* Washington, DC: World Bank.

Smith, A. 1937 (1776). *An Inquiry into the Nature and Causes of the Wealth of Nations.* New York: Modern Library.

Snowdon, B., and H. R. Vane. 2005. *Modern Macroeconomic.* Northampton, MA: Edward Elgar Publishing, Inc.

Stiglitz, J., and A. Weiss. 1981. Credit Rationing in Markets with Imperfect Information. *American Economic Review* 71:393–410.

Sufian, F. 2007. Financial Crisis and Banks' Performance: A Comparative Analysis of Domestic and Foreign

Banks in Malaysia. *MFA 9th Conference—12th & 13th, June 2007.* The Malaysian Finance Association.

Sundarajan, V., and L. Errico. 2002. Islamic Financial Institutions and Products in the Global Financial System: Key Issues in Risk Management and Challenges Ahead. IMF Working Paper, No. 02/192. Washington: IMF.

Taleb, N. N. 2007. *The Black Swan.* New York: Random House.

Taylor, J. 1980. Aggregate Dynamics and Staggered Contracts. *Journal of Political Economy* 88:1–23.

———. 1979. Staggered Wage Setting in a Macro Model. *American Economic Review* 69:108–113.

The Banker. (2010). *Top 500 Islamic Financial Institutions.* London: Financial Times.

Thorton, H. 1802. *An Enquiry into the Nature and Effects of the Paper Credit of Great Britain.* London: Hatchard.

Tobin, J. 1965. Commercial Banks as Creators of Money. In S. Teigen, *Readings in Money, National Income and Stabilization Policy.* Homewood, IL: Richard D. Irwin.

Udovitch, A. L. 1981. Bankers without Banks: Commerce, Banking and Society in the Islamic World of the Middle Ages. *Princeton Near East Paper no. 30.*

———. 1970. *Partnership and Profit in Medieval Islam.* Princeton, NJ: Princeton University Press.

Van Horne, J. C. 2000. *Financial Market Rates and Flows.* 6th ed. Upper Saddle River, NJ: Prentice Hall.

Visser, H. 2009. *Islamic Finance—Principles and Practice.* Northampton, MA: Edward Elger.

Vogel, E. F., and S. L. Hayes. 1998. *Islamic Law and Finance: Religion, Risk, and Return.* The Hague: Kluwer Law International.

Warde, I. 2007. Introduction. In N. S. Ali, *Integrating Islamic Finance into the Mainstream: Regulation, Standarization and Transparency.* Cambridge, MA: Harvard Legal Islamic Program.

———. 2005. Introduction. In N. S. Ali, *Islamic Finance: Current and Regulatory Issues.* Cambridge, MA: Islamic Legal Studies Program, Harvard University.

Whelan, K. 2009. *International Monetary Economics: Banks and Financial Intermediaries.* Dublin: University College Dublin, School of Economics.

White, E., ed. 1990. *Crashes and Panics: The Lessons from History.* Homewood, IL: Dow-Jones Irwin.

Wicksell, K. 1936 (1898). *Interest and Prices.* London: Macmillan.

Wilson, J., R. Sylla, and C. Jones. 1990. Financial Market Panics and Volatility in the Long Run, 1830–1988. In E. White. (ed.), *Crashes and Panics*, 85–125. Illinois: Dow-Jones Irwin.

Yaquby, N. 2002. What Can Islamic Banks Do Besides Eliminating Riba? Cambridge: Fifth Harvard University Forum on Islamic Finance.

Yudsitira, D. 2004. Efficiency in Islamic Banking: An Empirical Analysis of Eighteen Banks. *Islamic Economic Studies*, 12, no. 1:119.

Zingales, L. 1997. Corporate Governance. *NBER Working paper 6309.*

Index

Bold refers to definition

A

AAOIFI. *See* Accounting and Auditing Organization for Islamic Financial Institutions (AAOIFI)

ABN AMRO, 12

Abu Dhabi Islamic Bank, 9n3

Accounting and Auditing Organization for Islamic Financial Institutions (AAOIFI), 13, 20t1.2, 167

ACRCIFI. *See* Arbitration and Reconciliation Center for Islamic Financial Institutions (ACRCIFI)

adverse selection, 62, 117–18, 123, 255. *See also* moral hazard

aggregate demand, 26–28, 30–32, 109

aggregate demand disturbances, 31

aggregate output changes, 30

ahadith (hadith) (sayings), **xxiii,** 137, 137t7.1, 141–42

Ahmad-al-Najjar (social activist), 145

Akerlof, George (American economist), 40–41, 47

Algeria, 15

allocation of resources, optimal, 42

ALM. *See* asset-liability management (ALM)

al-Shafii, Imam, 138

AMAGX. *See* Amana Growth Fund (AMAGX)

amana (safekeeping purposes), 73

amana (trust), **xxiii,** 69–70, 73, 75

Amana Growth Fund (AMAGX), 8

Amana Trust Income (AMANX), 8

arbitrage forces, 42

Arbitration and Reconciliation Center for Islamic Financial Institutions (ACRCIFI), xix

arbun (non-refundable deposit), **xxiii**

Argentinean crisis (2001–2002), 54, 57

ariya (lending for gratuitous use), **xxiii**

The Ascent of Money (Ferguson), 119–20

Asian crisis (1997–1998). *See* East Asian financial crisis

asset boom-bust business cycles, 46

asset bubbles, 46

asset-liability management (ALM), xix

Austrian business cycle theory of financial crises, 46–47

Austrian economists, 38–39

Austrian theory of financial crisis, 37–39